ANTIQUE TRADER BOOKS

American & European Furniture
Price Guide

Edited by
Michael Regan

Antique Trader Books
Dubuque, IA 52004

STAFF

Managing Editor - Books/Price Guides . . . . .Kyle Husfloen

Art Director . . . . .Jaro Sebek

Design Associate . . . . .Aaron Roeth

Design Assistant . . . . .Louise Paradis

Assistant Editor . . . . .Elizabeth Stephan

Editorial Assistant . . . . .Ruth Willis

Customer Service/Order Fulfillment . . . . .Bonnie Rojemann

ISBN: 0-930625-50-1
Library of Congress Catalog Card No. 94-79664

Other books and magazines published by Antique Trader Publications:

Antiques & Collectibles Annual Price Guide
American Pressed Glass & Bottles Price Guide
American & European Decorative & Art Glass Price Guide
Ceramics Price Guide
The Antique Trader Weekly
Collector Magazine & Price Guide
Toy Trader Magazine
Postcard Collector Magazine
Discoveries Magazine
Big Reel Magazine
Military Trader Magazine
Baby Boomer Collectibles Magazine

To order additional copies of this book or other publications listed above, contact:

**Antique Trader Publications
P.O. Box 1050
Dubuque, Iowa 52004
1-800-334-7165**

Table of Contents

ABOUT THE AUTHOR:

Michael Regan is an antiques dealer living in Greensboro, North Carolina. A graduate of Cornell and Brown Universities, he has been a teacher, newspaper editor, editor of *The Antiques Journal*, long-time collector and, since 1981, a dealer with a special love for American furniture.

ON The Cover: Upper left: a turn-of-the-century side-by-side secretary-china cabinet, $1,600, courtesy of L.F.K. Art & Antiques, Kansas City, Kansas. Center right: a turn-of-the-century carved oak dining table, 60" d., part of a 14 piece set, $4,250, courtesy, of Gene Harris Antique Auction Center, Marshalltown, Iowa. Bottom: American Classical carved and stenciled recamier, ca. 1826-30, $18,400, courtesy of Sotheby's, New York, New York.

   Back cover: a turn-of-the-century oak hall rack, $1,295, courtesy of A Touch of Banowetz, Galena, Illinois.

   Cover design: Jaro Sebek.

CREDITS: For photographs, artwork, data or permission to photograph in their shops, we sincerely express appreciation to the following auctioneers, galleries, museums, individuals and shops: A Touch of Banowetz, Galena, Illinois; Christie's, New York, New York; DeFina Auctions, Austenburg, Ohio; William Doyle Galleries, New York, New York; Dunnings Auction Service, Elgin, Illinois; Garth's Auctions, Inc., Delaware, Ohio; Morton M. Goldberg Auction Galleries, New Orleans, Louisiana.

   Also to the Gene Harris Antique Auction Center, Marshalltown, Iowa; James Julia, Fairfield, Maine; Neal Auction Company, New Orleans, Louisiana; Dave Rago Arts & Crafts, Trenton, New Jersey; Vito Sico, Liberty, North Carolina; Skinner, Inc., Bolton, Massachusetts; Sotheby's, New York, New York; and Don Treadway Gallery, Cincinnati, Ohio.

Introduction

In the following pages, the reader will find a wide range of antique and collectible furniture and a listing of prices at which they sold. All are items sold in the United States in 1994. For each piece cited, I have included a detailed description noting condition, alterations or repairs which might affect the value.

The book is intended as a guide. Most of the values cited are those realized at auction. As most collectors know, a piece of furniture at auction may sell at "retail" price, the highest amount collectors are willing to pay. On the other hand, the piece may wind up in the hands of a dealer paying what he feels is wholesale. The object will then be subject to a mark-up when he resells it later.

Other factors, such as the desirability of certain forms, styles, or periods in certain parts of the country, need to be taken into consideration when pricing any piece of furniture. Auction prices listed in this book do include the buyer's premium when this has been added to the final bid, and I have excluded pieces for which the price seemed unrealistically high or low. The prices cited are intended as a report, an indication of transactions currently taking place in the American antiques market; they are not intended to establish values.

In addition to listing a wide variety of furniture forms and styles, I have standardized the terminology as much as possible and presented it in a consistent order to make it easier for readers to navigate the sometimes confusing verbal waters of technical description. The reader will find an accompanying series of drawings illustrating specific styles and elements of furniture with the terminology used in this guide.

All listings are arranged alphabetically by the type of furniture (such as beds, chairs, desks) and then alphabetically within the category by the style or type, such as Chippendale, Federal, Queen Anne. Names and dates of various styles of American, English and other furniture are charted for the reader's convenience. Keep in mind that all pieces listed are American unless otherwise indicated in the listing. Further, the reader should note that furniture described as "country-style" was often constructed later than other pieces within the same style. Consequently a "country-style Chippendale chair" may actually have been made well into the Federal period. Also, when a piece of furniture has the word "Style" (note the capital "S") included with the stylistic definition (i.e. Chippendale-Style), this indicates that the piece is a *reproduction* of the original style and dates from a later period.

This book has been designed to cover the full gamut of American and foreign furniture from the 17th century through the mid-20th century. Although it reflects market activity in 1994, it serves as a benchmark and offers comparisons that readers should find useful for years to come.

Michael Regan

A Few Words on Collecting:

For collectors, the world of antique furniture can be a complex one. What should you collect, and where can you find it? What do you look for in a particular piece, and what should you look *out* for? Last, but never least, how much should you pay? This book provides general pricing guidelines to help you answer the last question. The others I'll address here.

As most dealers do, I started out as a collector. In my first year out of college working as a secondary school teacher, I found myself making the occasional foray into small antiques shops that dot the villages along the Hudson River Valley north of New York. The impulse was largely curiosity. I didn't buy, partly because of the restraints of an academic salary but also because I realized that this was a brave new world of which I knew little.

That summer and the following year I found myself getting acquainted with some of the shops and dealers in southeastern Pennsylvania. It was there I got hooked. In two of the shops, I found myself drawn to one of the local fads — a barrel-shaped butter churn turned on end, mounted with short legs and converted into a stubby floor lamp. I could envision the aesthetic improvement to my sparsely furnished bachelor apartment. The country look was not nearly as intimidating as a Philadelphia rococo highboy. But the price was a whopping $40, and I dithered.

Finally, in one of the shops where I had spent an inordinate amount of time without making a single purchase (the dealer was still helpful and courteous), I discovered an identical butter churn out in the barn where pieces "in the rough" were kept. It had not yet been modified or improved, and the price was right — $5.

More than three decades later, it still sits in an enclosed porch, refinished (but sans legs and not electrified) and upended to serve as a small table. Of course, today I would not do this simple utilitarian country piece the indignity of sanding it mercilessly, staining it and putting a glossy finish on it as we all did back then. But then, even Henry Ford had to start somewhere.

The first criterion for any collector should be enthusiasm. If you don't like antique furniture, in fact if you can't get passionate about it, find something else to collect that does stir your emotions. Consider collecting china, glass, old typewriters, old typewriter ribbon tins, anything else at all.

Without enthusiasm, collecting is either a manifestation of the pack rat syndrome or just work. Enthusiasm does require some brakes, however. I have known collectors who have filled houses and barns to the ceiling, bought other structures and continued the process. Common sense and the limits of the pocketbook usually dictate here.

The more important factor tempering enthusiasm should be knowledge. Not assumptions, not second-hand popular wisdom, but *expertise* — learning your field. For the serious collector, becoming an expert in his field is an ongoing process — the more you learn, the more you discover there is to know.

The first thing the collector needs to know is, very simply, *what's out there.* What can he or she expect to find within the constraints of time and pocketbook? (A well-known collector and now a museum curator once observed that collecting takes either time *or* money. Even though it may seem to take more of the latter these days, the observation still holds.) If you want to collect Windsor chairs, for example, you need to know what the standard forms are — such as bow-back, fan-back, comb-back, or continuous arm. Then it's a question of knowing what constitutes the *best of the form* — strength and delicacy of turnings, drama in the rake of the legs or playing off one element against another while still managing harmony overall. The aesthetic effect of original paint or the presence of several successive layers of paint touched only by honest wear can also contribute to quality. Eventually, you can even learn the nuances of regional styles. For example, a New England bow-back differs from one crafted in Pennsylvania.

The single greatest source of information about what's out there is your neighborhood dealer, the dealer several miles out in the country, the dealer in the nearest big city, or wherever you can find an experienced dealer. It is in the dealer's shop where you can truly get hands-on experience. You can pick things up, turn them upside down, check marks, and pull out drawers.

What are you looking for? Inside drawers you can see if dovetails match. You can compare oxidation or darkening of color and see if it one drawer is consistent with another. Inconsistencies reveal repairs and replacements. Are drawer bottoms properly beveled into the slots at the sides, or are they of dangerously modern uniform thickness? If so, part of the piece may be new.

Examine nails and hardware to determine age. Learn what tools were used in each period of craftsmanship and how to identify the marks they leave. Drag out a magnifying lens and one of these marvelous new miniature flashlights with both broad spectrum and concentrated beam to examine areas hidden from view. Check with a small magnet to see if a darkened protrusion is a rose head nail or a hand-whittled peg or if the hardware is solid brass or modern brassplate. Take a tape measure to a round table top. Wood shrinks more across the grain than with it; the top on an antique table should actually be oval rather than round.

Run your hands around the turned members of a Windsor chair looking for the lack of lateral shrinkage that indicates a replaced element. (Practice, with your eyes closed, on a new piece of 1" hardwood dowel from your local hardware store until you are familiar with the feel.)

Of course, as you explore you must use common sense about things you might accidentally damage; it's usually best to ask permission before handling a dealer's inventory.

In the course of your examinations, don't forget to ask questions. Most dealers are eager to share the information they have acquired, in many cases, over a long period of time. The late John Walton, legendary New England dealer, was famous for the time he spent with young or beginning collectors. If they couldn't afford or appreciate the nuances of some of the masterpieces he carried, they might be able to find one of the more affordable but still good pieces in his shop. And they were on their way to becoming more knowledgeable collectors after the purchase. Perhaps they would become repeat customers. Many dealers maintain this philosophy. Yes, making a sale is nice, but making a customer who comes to trust you and rely on your guidance can be more important. So, definitely, ask questions. Don't worry about whether your question will reveal that you are a beginner. But *never* ask questions that are hostile in tone, that imply the dealer is the biggest crook since Al Capone, or demean what he is selling.

In addition to the single-dealer shop, you can get more hands-on experience in an increasing phenomenon of the last several years — the multiple-dealer or group shop. These are the shops where, for any variety of reasons, a number of dealers, from a few to more than a hundred, have banded together in one location. The major advantage for the collector is convenience — one-stop shopping, as it were. One disadvantage is that dealers seldom manage their own booths or display areas. The collector's questions are frequently limited to the information on the tag.

A second and perhaps more serious disadvantage for the furniture collector is that, for many dealers, a group shop is a secondary outlet. A dealer often has his own shop elsewhere or spends most of his time on the road exhibiting at shows. Consequently, the furniture in the group shop may not represent the best he has to offer. This observation is not engraved in stone. I have found many fine, even superb pieces of furniture in shops like this.

The third best place for learning about antiques is the antiques show. For a show, a number of dealers gather to exhibit for a single day or up to a week. There are indoor and outdoor shows, local shows, regional shows, and even some in major cities that can only be considered national shows. As he does at a single-dealer shop, the collector at a show has the advantage of being able to ask specific questions of dealers. It is also possible to make comparisons between the offerings of a number of dealers. Check local newspapers and trade papers for listings of shows in your area. Most of the medium-size and larger shows also have mailing lists for notice of future shows. Ask to receive their flyers.

Museums are also great places to learn about antique furniture. While this is a hands-off experience, it gives the collector a chance to study some of the finest examples, the best forms, often with the help of an experienced curator or staff member. There are a number of major museums, some with breathtaking furniture and collections, such as The Metropolitan Museum of Art in New York; The Henry Francis du Pont Winterthur Museum in Delaware; The Henry Ford Museum in Dearborn, Michigan; The Wadsworth Atheneum in Hartford, Connecticut; the Museum of Early Southern Decorative Arts in Winston-Salem, North Carolina; and The Bayou Bend Collection in Houston. Collectors should also visit their local museums. Many small museums, while not known far out of the area, have excellent collections. They may also reflect regional styles and preferences. Similarly, local historic houses sometimes have collections which can aid in the pursuit of knowledge.

The serious collector also takes advantage of the wealth of books about antiques. I used to advise beginning collectors to start with three works: Wallace Nutting's *Furniture Treasury* (Vols. I, II), Moreton Marsh's *The Easy Expert in American Antiques*, and *The Impecunious Collector's Guide To American Antiques* by John T. Kirk. The Nutting volumes are still readily available. And, although modern research has found they contain several errors such as English pieces represented as American, they remain a valuable source of photos of early American furniture. *The Easy Expert* provides good help in identifying and dating furniture, and *The Impecunious Collector* is marvelous in developing an "eye" for furniture. Unfortunately both of the latter volumes are out of print, a fate that has also befallen some of the works in the bibliography provided at the back of this book. The collector may be able to find some of them in a local library, but other good places to search are the larger antiques shows which frequently feature a booth devoted to reference books on antiques.

As much as a collector needs to know what to look for, sadly, he also needs to know what to *look out* for. The antiques world seems awash in fakes, frauds and every variation of ignorance or misrepresentation. A fake is something deliberately made from scratch that purports to be an antique. A fraud is a deliberate misrepresentation of age, origin, condition or anything that may affect the value.

Less sinister but perhaps of more concern to the collector is determining just what has been done to a piece since it left the hands of its maker. For the col-lector armed ahead of time with knowledge of what a particular piece should look like, it's a detective game. Check the most exposed, most vulnerable elements — legs, feet, stretchers, spindles, finials, brasses — for repairs or replacements. Look for differences in finish or coloration, differences in wood grain or continuation of grain. Gain a reasonable familiarity with early tools, the ways in which they were used and the marks they left. For example, early chairmakers usually left scribe marks to indicate where they intended to place stretchers and slats. Be suspicious if they fail to line up with what you see. Or, if you find the unmistakable marks of a rotary saw that did not come into general use until the mid-19th century, you know you are not looking at an unaltered 18th century piece. Check tables carefully. Tops are often replaced; look for screw holes in places for which there is no logical reason. Search for a pattern of paint or oxidation that does not conform to the apron and legs.

When examining a case piece made in two or more parts, such as a highboy or chest-on-chest, look out for "married" pieces — tops and bottoms that did not start out in life together. Check drawer dovetails; those in the top section should match those in the lower. Check the mid-molding; an unusually wide molding is a warning sign. If there is carving on both sections, see if it appears to be by the same hand. With the dealer's assistance, pull the piece away from the wall and see if the back boards match up. Don't overlook the obvious: Once, in a dealer's shop, I was asked for my opinion on the authenticity of a chest-on-chest. After pulling out only a few drawers I somewhat reluctantly, out of consideration for the dealer's feelings and apparent honesty, pointed out that the grain of the drawer bottoms in the top ran front to back while the grain of those in the lower section ran side to side. The heart-breaker was when the dealer next asked the significance of this obvious clue. The two parts were not made at the same time.

The collector also needs to be on the lookout for "embellishments." This is when someone takes a simple and perhaps even ordinary piece and "improves" it to enhance the value. Most notorious here are added carvings or inlay. Added inlay, particularly if done fifty or eighty years ago, can be extremely difficult to detect. Frequently, however, it will be either stylistically incorrect or so skimpy and tentative as to reveal a lack of familiarity with the idiom. It won't appear "natural." The same characteristics apply to later carving. Since the carver did not have the full thickness needed to start with, the carved detail will appear on an element too thin to support it.

The collector also needs to keep an eye out for reproductions. New or even recent reproductions are easy enough to spot. Older reproductions can cause serious problems as they age. They may have sold as honest copies or replicas of earlier pieces a hundred years ago, but now they cause confusion. With the U.S. Centennial of 1876 and the several decades that followed, many craftsmen copied Colonial and Pilgrim Century American furniture. Similarly, in England, 19th century craftsmen copied 18th century pieces. These pieces, many now bearing a century of wear, can pose a serious problem for the collector. They require more serious detective work. One of the best books to come out in recent years to help the collector over the problem areas of antique sleuthing is Myrna Kaye's *Fake, Fraud, or Genuine? Identifying Authentic American Antique Furniture* (Boston: Little, Brown, 1987). It has since been reprinted in paperback, and it's a guide I highly recommend.

Finally, when it comes to buying, the collector faces a dilemma. Is it best to buy from a dealer or buy at auction? The answer, of course, is that both can be great sources; each has a positive side and each has potential drawbacks. A *reputable* dealer will stand behind what he sells. If you have thoroughly examined a piece of furniture, asked whatever questions you thought were necessary or appropriate and are ready to buy, make sure you get a *written* receipt with the age of the piece, origin, condition including any repairs or restorations, and anything else (such as provenance, which means history of ownership) that might affect the value. Get a clear statement of your rights to return an item that does not meet the written description.

When buying at auction, you may be able to pay less than a dealer would charge for the same piece. However, at an auction there are *no guarantees*. Here you are absolutely on your own. The major auction houses include in their catalogs a preliminary statement that no matter how detailed their descriptions or what the auctioneer may say about a piece on the floor, they guarantee nothing. Even local auctioneers at estate sales make similar disclaimers.

What protections are there? Other than being well-informed beforehand, the collector needs to inspect whatever he's interested in as carefully as possible. Unlike examining something in a dealer's shop, this must frequently be done under considerable time pressure and often under atrocious lighting conditions. Whenever possible, take advantage of any opportunity to "preview" the merchandise. If this can be done a day or two before the sale, all the better; for smaller sales, however, any previews take place just a few hours before the sale. After you make your inspection, you might even have time to do a little research (some collectors will even carry a few basic volumes in their car or van).

Do antiques make good investments? It's up to the collector. Some antiques have gone up in value. A collector who bought a Philadelphia tea table in 1986 for $1,045,000 sold it in January 1995 for $2,242,500. But values for some antiques have gone down. The same collector paid $264,000 for a desk in 1988 to have it sell in 1995 for $96,000. My advice to collectors is to buy what you *like,* buy what you're passionate about. If at some point in the future you decide to sell and you get more than you paid, you're money ahead. If not, you still didn't pay more than it was worth to you. Meanwhile, you've had the pleasure of owning it all that time.

Soon after I began collecting I fell under the tutelage of a sometimes gruff but totally dedicated engineer-turned-antiques dealer named Frank Pierce. He ran a shop out of his home near Collegeville, Pennsylvania. He told me to buy the best you can afford, and always buy one great piece rather than two or three lesser ones. It was good advice then, and it still holds for today's collector.

FURNITURE DATING CHART

AMERICAN FURNITURE

Pilgrim Century - 1620-1700

William & Mary - 1685-1720

Queen Anne - 1720-50

Chippendale - 1750-85

Federal - 1785-1820

    Hepplewhite - 1785-1800
    Sheraton - 1800-20

Classical (American Empire) - 1815-40

Victorian - 1840-1900

    Early Victorian - 1840-50
    Gothic Revival - 1840-90
    Rococo (Louis XV) - 1845-70
    Renaissance Revival - 1860-85
    Louis XVI - 1865-75
    Eastlake - 1870-95
    Jacobean & Turkish Revival - 1870-90
    Aesthetic Movement - 1880-1900

Art Nouveau - 1895-1918

Turn-of-the-Century - 1895-1910

Mission-style (Arts & Crafts movement) 1900-15

Art Deco - 1925-40

ENGLISH FURNITURE

Jacobean - Mid-17th century

William & Mary - 1689-1702

Queen Anne - 1702-14

George I - 1714-27

George II - 1727-60

George III - 1760-1820

Regency - 1811-20

George IV - 1820-30

William IV - 1830-37

Victorian - 1837-1901

Edwardian - 1901-10

FRENCH FURNITURE

Louis XV - 1715-74

Louis XVI - 1774-93

Empire - 1804-15

Louis Philippe - 1830-48

Napoleon III (Second Empire) - 1848-70

Art Nouveau - 1895-1910

Art Deco - 1925-35

Germanic Furniture

Since the country of Germany did not exist before 1870, furniture from the various Germanic states and the Austro-Hungarian Empire is generally termed simply "Germanic." From the 17th century onward furniture from these regions tended to follow the stylistic trends established in France and England. General terms are used for such early furniture usually classifying it as "Baroque," "Rococo" or a similar broad stylistic term. Germanic furniture dating from the first half of the 19th century is today usually referred to as *Biedermeier*, a style closely related to French Empire and English Regency.

AMERICAN FURNITURE TERMS

CASE PIECES

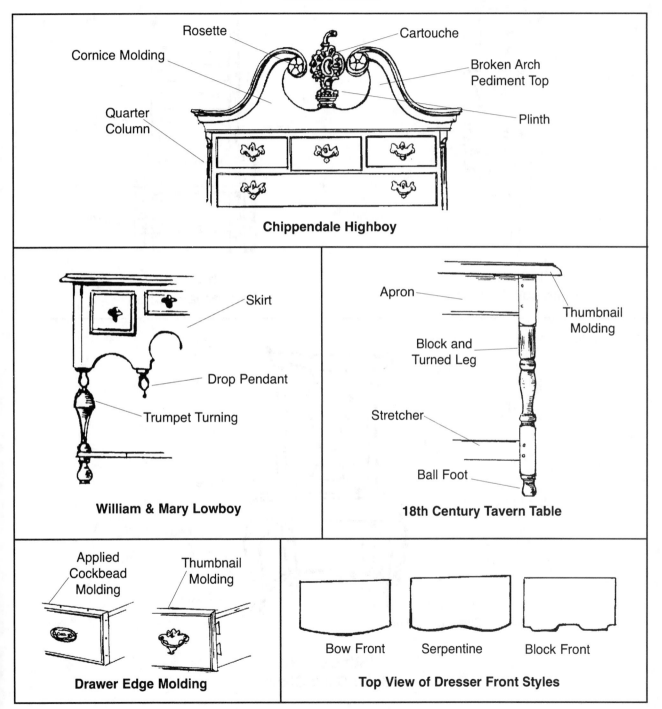

Rosette

Cartouche

Cornice Molding

Broken Arch
Pediment Top

Quarter
Column

Plinth

Chippendale Highboy

Skirt

Drop Pendant

Trumpet Turning

William & Mary Lowboy

Apron

Thumbnail
Molding

Block and
Turned Leg

Stretcher

Ball Foot

18th Century Tavern Table

Applied
Cockbead
Molding

Thumbnail
Molding

Drawer Edge Molding

Bow Front

Serpentine

Block Front

Top View of Dresser Front Styles

SEATING FURNITURE

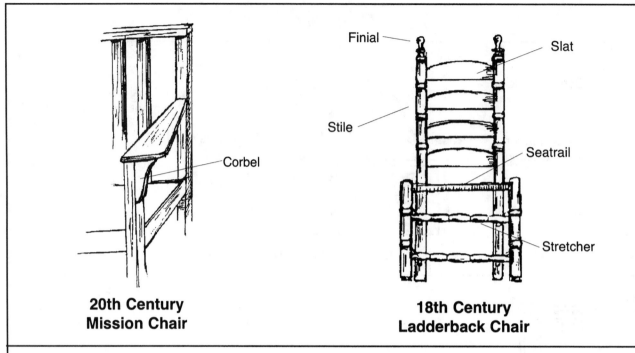

**20th Century
Mission Chair**

Corbel

**18th Century
Ladderback Chair**

Finial
Slat
Stile
Seatrail
Stretcher

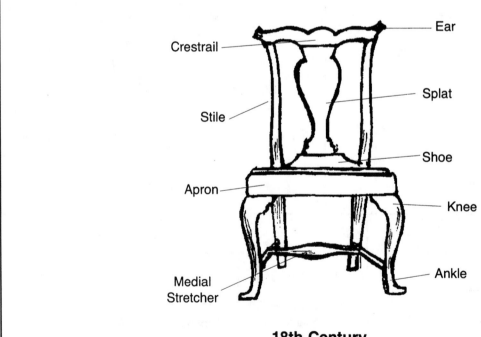

Ear
Crestrail
Splat
Stile
Shoe
Apron
Knee
Medial
Stretcher
Ankle

**18th Century
Splat Back Chair**

LEGS & FEET

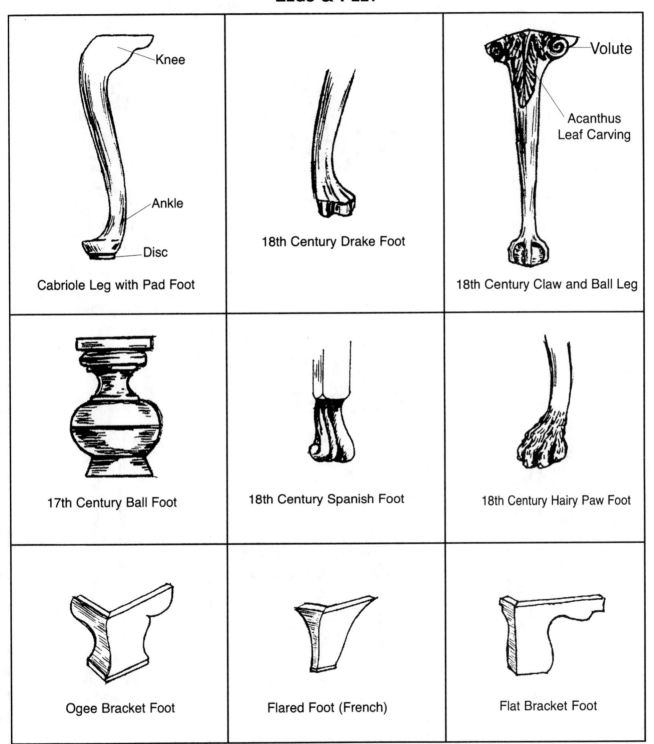

Cabriole Leg with Pad Foot

Knee
Ankle
Disc

18th Century Drake Foot

18th Century Claw and Ball Leg

Volute
Acanthus Leaf Carving

17th Century Ball Foot

18th Century Spanish Foot

18th Century Hairy Paw Foot

Ogee Bracket Foot

Flared Foot (French)

Flat Bracket Foot

FINIALS AND CARVING DETAILS

Flame and Urn Finial

Shell Carving

18th Century Ball and Ring
Chair Finial

Anthemion Carving

Stop Flute
Column

Gadroon Carving

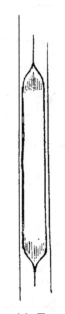

Lamb's Tongue
Carving

BEDS

Art Nouveau bed, bentwood, the arched head- and footboards w/tightly scrolled bentwood designs above oval panels, the scrolled siderails w/similar oval panels, on scrolled feet on casters, Continental, late 19th century 2,420.00
(Illustration: Beds 1)

Art Nouveau bed, carved mahogany, the rectangular headboard & footboard w/rounded corners carved w/leafing vines framing wide burl panels, France, late 19th - early 20th c., 60 x 80", 5' 2" h. 1,150.00
(Illustration: Beds 2)

Beds 2: Art Nouveau Mahogany Bed

**Beds 1:
Art Nouveau
Bentwood Bed**

Classical low poster bed,
maple, the ring- and
baluster-turned headposts
w/turned finials centering a
shaped headboard, on
tapering ring-turned cylindrical legs, the similarly
turned footposts centering
a ring-turned cylindrical
stretcher, probably
Pennsylvania, ca. 1830,
51¼" w., 82¼" l.,
42¾" h............................460.00

Classical low poster bed,
walnut, head- and foot
crestrails w/boldly turned
acorn finials above head- &
footboards each w/two
crotch walnut panels, the
posts w/acorn finials above
block- and column-turned
legs on ball feet, original
siderails extended, early
19th century, interior
42" w., 75" l., 4' 6" h. (age
crack in one post) 550.00

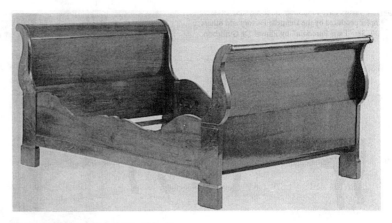

Beds 3: Classical Sleigh Bed

Classical sleigh bed,
mahogany, serpentine
scrolling head- and
footboards above scalloped
deep siderails w/carved
beading, on straight legs
ending in molded block
feet, mid-19th century,
interior 55¾" w., 40" h. .1,210.00
(Illustration: Beds 3)

Classical tester bed,
mahogany, the posts
w/turned vase-form capitals
above faceted posts on
capsule-shaped feet
enclosing an arched
headboard w/down-swept
voluted crestrail &
serpentine footboard &
rails, probably lower
Mississippi Valley, ca.
1830-1840, 56" w.,
7" 1" h..........................2,530.00
(Illustration: Beds 4)

**Country-style low poster
bed**, painted red, the block-
and baluster-turned
headposts w/ball finials &
ball feet centering a
triangular shaped head-
board, the similarly turned
footposts centering a
rectangular footboard,
Pennsylvania, ca. 1810,
49 ½" w., 82" l., 33" h. 748.00

Federal tall poster bed,
carved mahogany, the
headboard w/a spiral-
carved crestrail scrolling
down to acanthus-carved
rosettes above a raised
panel flanked by reeded
acanthus-carved posts

Beds 4: Classical Tester Bed

w/acanthus-carved urn
finials & ending in tapering
reeded feet, simple
siderails & footrails flanked
by similarly carved
footposts, early 19th
century, 52" w., 78" l.,
7' 11" h..........................4,125.00
(Illustration: Beds 5)

Federal tall poster bed,
cherry & pine, the baluster-
and urn-turned headposts
centering a scalloped &
shaped headboard, on
ring-turned cylindrical legs,
the similarly turned
footposts centering a
shaped footboard,
surmounted by a flat tester,
Pennsylvania, ca. 1820,
56" w., 84 ¼" l., 7' 7 ¼" h.
(tester replaced) 1,840.00

Federal tester bed,
mahogany, the reeded
footposts waterleaf- and
bead-carved ending in flattened-ball feet, the
headposts chamfered &
centering a shaped
headboard, surmounted by
a molded tester, Mass-
achusetts, ca. 1810, 63" w.,
82 ½" l., 7' 4" h. (tester
replaced) 8,625.00

George III tester bed,
mahogany, the molded
tester on foliate-carved
fluted posts w/festoons, on
block feet, England, last
quarter 18th century,
8' 1 ½" h. 2,300.00
(Illustration: Beds 6)

Beds 5: Federal Tall Poster Bed

Beds 6: George III Tester Bed

Beds 7: Mission Single Bed

Beds 9: Victorian Half-tester Bed

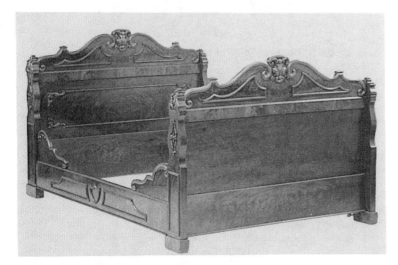

Beds 8: Victorian Rococo Bed

Mission-style (Art & Crafts movement) single bed, oak, tapered posts & four wide vertical slats across the head- and footboard, original medium finish, branded mark of Gustav Stickley, ca. 1912, 46¾" w., 79" l., 46¼" h. 1,725.00
(Illustration: Beds 7)

Victorian bed, Rococo substyle, mahogany, the scrolled molded head- and footboards w/foliate-carved crest above scalloped molded siderails w/vase-form molded end posts w/acanthus-carved finials, on block feet, mid-19th century, 55 ½" w., 70" l., 46" h. 1,540.00
(Illustration: Beds 8)

Victorian half-tester bed, Renaissance Revival substyle, walnut, the half-tester w/a bowed front raised atop tall square posts w/pierced scroll-cut brackets, the tall head-board w/an arched scroll-carved & paneled crest above raised shaped burl panels flanking a molded roundel above two large recessed oval burl panels, the low footboard w/a plain arched crestrail over raised shaped panels & a center roundel flanked by scroll-carved curved corner posts, ca. 1860 ....2,695.00

Victorian half-tester bed, Rococo substyle, carved rosewood, the shaped half-tester w/oval cabochon flanked by pierced scrolls & urn finials on cluster-columned posts enclosing

a scroll-crested shaped-panel headboard, the shaped side-rails w/carved shell & scrolls continuing to low cluster-columned footposts headed by scroll & urn mosquito pole finials, enclosing a footboard carved like the siderails, attributed to Prudent Mallard, New Orleans, mid-19th century, 63 ½" w., 8' 9 ½" h. 6,325.00
(Illustration: Beds 9)

Victorian tester bed, Rococo substyle, mahogany, the wide cove-molded rectangular tester raised on four heavy slightly tapering clustered column posts w/square bases w/chamfered corners, the high arched headboard w/a carved fruit & leaf cluster cartouche flanked by large leafy scrolls above a pair of arched recessed panels, serpentine side- and endrails each centered by a shell carving, attributed to Prudent Mallard, New Orleans, from the Pinckney Family, ca. 1850, 72 x 82", 8' 8" h. 13,200.00
(Illustration: Beds 10)

Beds 10: Rococo Tester Bed

Turn of the century: tall-back bed & chest of drawers; oak, the tall bed headboard w/a flat bead-trimmed crestrail w/curved corners over a panel w/long carved scrolls above two plain horizontal panels, the lower footboard w/a flat crestrail, the matching chest of drawers w/a tall superstructure w/swiveling mirror above a case w/three long drawers, ca. 1890-1910, bed 57" w., 6' 2 ½" h., chest of drawers 48" w., 6' 10" h., 2 pcs. 3,600.00
(Illustration: Bedroom Suites 1, bed)

Victorian Eastlake substyle: tall-back bed, chest of drawers & commode; walnut & burl walnut, the tall bed headboard w/a low carved center crest on the flat crestrail above a band of line-incised diamonds over cut-out sawtooth bands & burl panels, the chest of drawers & commode w/a matching crestrail above large rectangular beveled mirrors, the chest w/a rectangular red marble top over a case of three long drawers, the commode w/a red marble splashback & rectangular top over a case w/a long drawer over two short drawers & a small door, all w/rectangular brass pulls, on white porcelain casters, ca. 1880, bed 56" w., 6' h., the chest of drawers 40" w., 6' 6" h., commode 31 ½" h., 6' 6" h., 3 pcs. 5,400.00
(Illustration: Bedroom Suites 2, commode)

Bedroom Suites 2:
Eastlake Commode

Victorian Renaissance Revival substyle: highback bed & dresser; walnut, the dresser w/upper section w/carved palmetto crest above a rectangular mirror plate flanked by foliate-carved candlestands, the lower section w/white marble-topped drop-well flanked by two pairs of marble-topped short drawers over two carved long drawers, on a bracket base, 53 ½" w.,

Bedroom Suites 1:Turn of the Century Oak bed

**Bedroom Suites 3:
Renaissance Revival Dresser**

22" d., 8' 9" h., 2 pcs. ...4,400.00
(Illustration: Bedroom Suites 3, dresser)

Victorian Renaissance Revival substyle:
highback bed & dresser; rosewood, the high arched bed headboard w/a scroll-carved cartouche at the top center above a pair of curved tapering panels framing small roundels & raised panels, the lower slightly arched footboard w/a roundel-carved bar panel; the dresser w/a tall superstructure w/a

cartouche-carved & paneled arched crest above a conforming tall mirror flanked by candle shelves above small hanky drawers atop the rectangular white marble top w/molded edge & rounded corners, the conforming case w/three long drawers w/raised oval band panels & fruit- and leaf-carved pulls, molded base w/disc front feet on white porcelain casters, bed w/original siderails, dresser 21 ¼ x 47", 7' 3 ½ h., bed headboard 7' 5¼" h., 2 pcs. 3,080.00
(Illustration: Bedroom Suites 4, bed)

**Bedroom Suites 4:
Renaissance Revival Bed**

Victorian Renaissance Revival substyle: bed, dresser & wardrobe; carved faux rosewood, each piece w/a very high crest composed of a palmette above a paneled crown crest flanked by scrolls & arched panels w/carved acanthus at the outer corners, an upper frieze band w/carved scallops above arched panels fitted w/long mirrors on the dresser & wardrobe doors, the dresser w/shaped framing around the mirror w/candle shelves above two small hanky drawers on the rectangular white marble top over three long drawers, the wardrobe w/two drawers at the base, signed "P. Dejan(?)," New Orleans, Louisiana, ca. 1870s, bed 65 x 84", 7' 11" h., wardrobe 21 x 55", 9' 8" h., dresser 21 x 46", 8' 8" h., the set................................7,150.00
(Illustration: Bedroom Suites 5, dresser & wardrobe)

Victorian Renaissance Revival substyle: bed, dresser & armoire; bronze-mounted carved walnut, each piece w/a high arched & step-carved crestrail centered by a rounded palmette above a wide burl panel-framed inset panel centered by a round bronze plaque w/a classical bust portrait of a lady framed by scrolls & flanked by quarter-round knob-trimmed panels w/pointed fleur-de-lis-carved finials, all above a wide burl panel, the lower footboard w/a plain arched crestrail over another recessed panel w/an inset bronze plaque & flanked by small burl panels & scroll-carved corners, late 19th century, the set.........................37,400.00
(Illustration: Bedroom Suites 6, bed)

**Bedroom Suites 5:
Renaissance Revival Bedroom Suite**

**Bedroom Suites 6:
Ornate Renaissance Revival Bed**

BENCHES

Bucket (or water) bench, painted pine, simple rectangular top over three shelves & one-board down-scrolled sides w/cyma curve cut-out feet, old worn greyish ivory paint over darker grey, 36" w., 17½" d., 4' 10 ½" h. 1,650.00
(Illustration: Benches 1)

Bucket (or water) bench, pine w/old brown finish, wide one-board ends, dovetailed top & one shelf, cut-out feet, 39 ½" w., 13 ¼" d., 30" h. 385.00
(Illustration: Benches 2)

Bucket (or water) bench, red-painted pine, three shelves w/front rails & back braces mortised into scrolled-top beaded-edge sides, above a base w/two cupboard doors on shoe feet, repairs to feet, one

Benches 2: Early Water Bench

front shelf rail & one back brace replaced, 32" w., 11" d., 5' 4" h. 1,705.00

Child's bench, painted & decorated poplar, a wide back slat w/a gently arched & notched crest flanked by

turned stiles w/knob finials & raised above a slatted seat flanked by flat, shaped arms raised on arm supports, turned legs on casters, original green paint & striping & decoration in bronze, black & pale blue, 26" l. 495.00

Mission-style (Arts & Crafts movement) bench, oak, the canted wide ends pierced w/four squares, the ends w/slender tapering triangles flanking the rectangular seat, Charles Limbert Company branded mark, Model No. 243 ½, 17 ½ x 24" h. 2,750.00
(Illustration: Benches 3)

Benches 1: Painted Pine Bucket Bench

Benches 3: Mission-style Bench

Piano bench, Arts & Crafts style, oak, rectangular lift seat above a deep apron & shaped flat through-tenoned & keyed legs, new dark brown finish, Miller company mark, early 20th century, 18 ¼ x 38", 20 ¾" h. 1,760.00

Victorian bench, Renaissance Revival substyle, satinwood, marquetry & gilt-incised, rectangular upholstered seat above an apron inlaid w/a band of small leaves & arches, cross-carved corner blocks over reeded panels & curved corner blocks, reeded knob-turned legs joined by box stretchers & turned spindles, late 19th century...... ....6,900.00
(Illustration: Benches 4)

Window bench, George III, mahogany, the upholstered outswept ends carved w/flowerheads above an upholstered serpentine seat, on paterae-carved

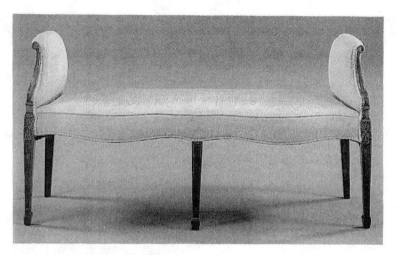

Benches 5: George III Window Bench

legs ending in square tapering feet, England, late 18th century, restorations to legs, 51" l..................3,450.00
(Illustration: Benches 5)

Window bench, Mission-style (Arts & Crafts movement) oak, the raised ends w/square posts w/through-tenoned rails above an upholstered rectangular seat over a

through-tenoned medial stretcher, red decal mark of Gustav Stickley, Model No. 178, ca. 1902, painted green, 36" w., 18" d., 27" h. 2,415.00
(Illustration: Benches 6)

Benches 4: Victorian Window Bench

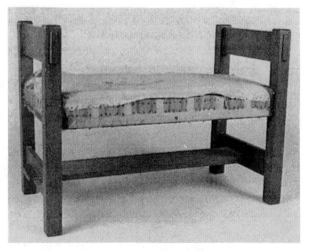

Benches 6: Mission Window Bench

Bookcases

Art Deco bookcases, walnut, an upright rectangular stepped case w/stepped open shelves, the front edges painted black, in the style of Paul Frankl, ca. 1935, 9 ¼ x 23 ⅝" 5'4" h., pr. 5,290.00
(Illustration: Bookcases 1)

Classical bookcase on chest, mahogany, the canted cornice projecting over an arched frieze on round tapered columns w/foliate capitals flanking a pair of glazed doors w/Gothic arch panes opening to shelves, over a lower section w/projecting banded deep drawer over three graduated molded drawers flanked by turned, carved & baluster-shaped columns, on turned feet on casters, ca. 1840, 44" w., 23" d., 8' 1" h. 2,200.00
(Illustration: Bookcases 2)

Federal 'extension' bookcase, mahogany, the bookcase comprised of seven separate graduated shelves, each w/two hinged glazed doors, above a base w/two cupboard doors, on vase-turned

Bookcases 2: Classical Mahogany Bookcase

Bookcases 1: Art Deco Bookcases

Bookcases 3: Federal Bookcase

Bookcases 4: George III Bookcase

feet, ca. 1830, 66 ¼" w., 15 ¾" d., 7' 9 ½" h. 5,175.00
(Illustration: Bookcases 3)

George III bookcase, mahogany, two-part construction: the upper section w/molded swan's-neck pediment terminating in rosettes above a pair of glazed mullioned doors opening to shelves, on a molded base; the lower section w/pair of paneled doors on a plinth, England, third quarter 18th century, 52" w., 18" d., 7' 11 ½" h. 10,350.00
(Illustration: Bookcases 4)

George III breakfront bookcase, mahogany, the molded cornice w/swan's-neck pediment above a plain frieze & glazed doors opening to shelves fitted w/arched astragal mold-ings, the outset lower part w/four molded doors, raised on a plinth, England, late 18th century, 18" x 128", 7' 11" h. (cornice later) 17,250.00

George III stepback bookcase, mahogany, two-part construction: the top section w/canted molded cornice above a plain frieze over a pair of doors w/diamond-shaped glazed panels centered by rosettes, flanked by half-round columns; the projecting lower section w/two cockbeaded short drawers over a pair of molded cabinet drawers, on a molded platform base on turned ball feet, England, early 19th century, 45 ½" w., 23 ¼" d., 7' 2" h. 2,200.00
(Illustration: Bookcases 5)

Bookcases 6: Georgian-Style Bookcase

Bookcases 7: Stickley Mission Bookcase

**Bookcases 5:
George III Stepback Bookcase**

Georgian-Style breakfront bookcase, painted pine, two-part construction: the upper section w/projecting-center molded cornice over a conforming frieze above four glazed mullioned doors opening to shelves; the lower section w/four molded paneled cupboard doors on a molded plinth base, England, 19th century, 98" w., 16" d., 8' h. 5,060.00
(Illustation: Bookcases 6)

Mission-style (Arts & Crafts movement) bookcase, oak, the galleried rectangular top tenoned through the sides & keyed, above a pair of 6-pane glazed cabinet doors, over a keyed tenon base on cut-out feet, original medium finish & black finished hardware, red decal mark of Gustav Stickley, Model No. 525, ca. 1901, two panes replaced, interior mold-ing strip repair, 39" w., 11 ¾" d., 45" h. 6,900.00
(Illustration: Bookcases 7)

Mission-style (Arts & Crafts movement) bookcase, oak, the rectangular top w/pro-truding corner posts above three short drawers w/hammered copper pulls, over three glazed doors w/geometric gridwork, on square feet, original dark brown finish, Lifetime Fur-niture Company, Grand Rapids, Michigan, 65" w., 14 ¾" d., 4' 6" h. 3,520.00
(Illustration: Bookcases 8)

Mission-style (Arts & Crafts movement) bookcase, oak, 'ebonoak' line, a gently arched backsplash w/a narrow oblong caned panel above the rectangular top overhanging corbels & a pair of tall glazed cupboard doors opening to three shelves, dark wood inlaid bands down the front stiles, gently ached apron & square legs, original reddish brown finish, branded mark of the Charles Limbert Furniture Company, Grand Rapids, Michigan, Model No. 801-22, 14 x 48", 5' h...........3,740.00

Regency breakfront bookcase, mahogany, the molded arcaded cornice above four glazed mullioned doors opening to shelves over a projecting lower section, the break-fronted center section w/secretary drawer & three graduated drawers, flanked by false-fronted doors opening to shelves, on bracket feet, England, first quarter 19th century, 21 ½" x 7' 2", 7' 6" h....10,350.00

Victorian bookcase, Classical substyle, rosewood, the slightly arched molded cornice above a pair of glazed doors w/carved quarter fan corners opening to shelves, above an outset base w/two short drawers & scal-loped skirt on short bracket feet, mid-19th century, 58 ¼" w., 24" d. 2,090.00
(Illustration: Bookcases 9)

Bookcases 8: Lifetime Furniture Bookcase

**Bookcases 9:
Victorian Classical Bookcase**

Bookcases 10: Victorian Oak Bookcase

Bookcases 11: Victorian Renaissance-Style Bookcase

Victorian bookcase, oak, the molded cornice w/dentil-carved frieze above two glazed doors & paneled sides, interior fitted w/five adjustable shelves, on a molded plinth base, late 19th century, 65" w., 16 ½" d., 8' 3 ½" h. ....935.00 (Illustration: Bookcases 10)

Victorian bookcase, Renaissance-Style, carved mahogany, the molded rectangular cornice w/outthrust corners above an acanthus-carved frieze over three molded glazed doors opening to shelves, flanked by columns headed by carved caryatids and terminating in carved phoenixes on a plinth base, the front feet carved w/the face of a muse between scrolls, late 19th century, 88" w., 18" d., 5' 7 ½" h. ....3,740.00 (Illustration: Bookcases 11)

Victorian bookcase, Renaissance Revival substyle, carved walnut, rectangular top w/a gallery, the front w/a raised templeform pediment centered above panels of pierced roundels flanked by corner blocks w/urn finials, tall glazed cupboard doors w/double-arched tops & raised panels below carved w/griffins, the doors flanked by chamfered corners

Bookcases 12: Renaissance Revival Bookcase

w/reeded bands above ropetwist-carved bands, a long drawer w/paneled veneer at the bottom, on turned bun front feet & block back feet, ca. 1885, 19 ½ x 50", 8' 6" h. 1,540.00
(Illustration: Bookcases 12)

Victorian breakfront bookcase, Renaissance Revival substyle, mahogany, the molded

cornice above a projecting central section w/glazed arched-panel door opening to shelves, flanked by two similar smaller doors, on a plinth base, 78" w., 7' 1" h. 1,870.00
(Illustration: Bookcases 13)

William IV bookcase, mahogany, a molded cornice above three open-shelved sections, the base

w/two central doors flanked by open shelves, on a plinth, England, second quarter 19th century, 17 x 89", 11' 7" h. 7,475.00
(Illustration: Bookcases 14)

Bookcases 13: Victorian Breakfront Bookcase

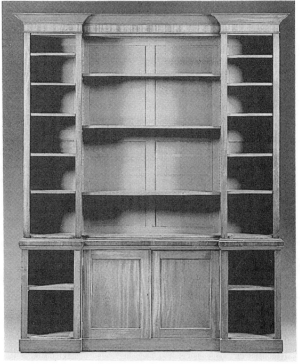

Bookcases 14: William IV Bookcase

Cabinets

Cellaret, George III, mahogany, the rectangular hinged top opening to a bottle well, the case w/oval & line inlay above a line-inlaid frieze drawer, the sides mounted w/carrying handles, on a stand w/square tapering legs w/brass feet on casters, England, third quarter 18th century, 14 ½" w., 14 ½" d., 30" h. 2,070.00
(Illustration: Cabinets 1)

China cabinet, Mission-style (Arts & Crafts movement) oak, rectangular top above a pair of glazed doors & glazed sides, each w/a central organic design dividing geometric designs at the top & bottom, the doors w/copper butterfly hinges & latches & door-knobs, on square tapering legs ending in Mackmurdo feet & joined by a medial shelf, original reddish brown finish, script Roycroft signature, Model No. 05, Roycroft Shop, East Aurora, New York, two side panels of glass replaced, 23 x 51", 5' h. 20,900.00
(Illustration: Cabinets 2)

Cabinets 1: George III Mahogany Cellaret

**Cabinets 2:
Roycroft China Cabinet**

Cabinets 3:
Turn of the Century China Cabinet-Secretary

Cabinets 4:
Aesthetic China Cabinet

China cabinet-secretary, turn of the century, oak, rectangular top w/an ogee molded edge above a deep open shelf backed by a rectangular mirror, one side of shelf bowed above a conforming curved glass china cabinet door opening to three shelves beside a short geometrically-glazed cupboard door over a slant-front opening to a fitted interior above a stack of three drawers, tall columns down the sides, on C-scroll front feet, ca. 1910, 14 x 42 ½", 5' 7" h. 2,300.00
(Illustration: Cabinets 3)

China cabinet, Victorian, Aesthetic Movement substyle, rosewood & marquetry, two part construction: the upper section w/galleried top over a paneled frieze over a pair of glazed doors opening to shelves; the stepped out lower section w/floral-carved panels over a pair of glazed cupboard doors above an apron w/short spindles, on turned feet, fourth quarter 19th century, 54 ½" w., 20 ½" d., 9' 1" h. 2,415.00
(Illustration: Cabinets 4)

Corner cabinet on stand, Chippendale-Style, carved mahogany, two-part construction: the top section w/a broken arch molded cornice w/pierced fretwork panels above a geometrically glazed door opening to shelves within a carved fretwork frame; the outset lower section w/fretwork frieze, raised on three tapering square legs joined by a scalloped shelf w/fretwork gallery, on spade front feet, labeled "H. Blackmore & Co., Exmouth," England, early 20th century, 29" w., 14 ½" d., 5' 10 ¾" h. 522.00
(Illustration: Cabinets 5)

Display cabinet, Art Deco 'sky-scraper' style, two-part construction: the super-structure w/tall stepped boxed shelves; the lower section w/a wide rectangular top w/boxed end sections w/shelves, painted black & red, in the manner of Paul Frankl, ca. 1930s, 18 ½ x 79", 7' 8" h. 1,870.00
(Illustration: Cabinets 6)

Display cabinet, George III-Style, satinwood & inlaid rosewood, two-part construction: the upper section w/a rectangular top w/a broken scroll pediment above a molded cornice & frieze band over a pair of long geometrically-glazed cupboard doors opening to

Cabinets 5:
Chippendale-Style Corner Cabinet

Cabinets 6: Art Deco Display Cabinet

shelves; the lower slightly stepped-out section w/a pair of geometrically-glazed cupboard doors, on simple bracket feet, England, late 19th century, 18 x 48", 7' 11 ½" h.......9,775.00
(Illustration: Cabinets 7)

Display cabinet, Victorian, Rococo Revival substyle, mahogany, the shaped & carved broken scroll pediment above a kidney-shaped mirror plate w/a scroll-carved conforming surround & candle shelves, the projecting lower section w/a pair of scroll-decorated

glazed doors opening to shelves, flanked by scroll-decorated glazed panels, on carved cabriole legs, ca. 1850 ....660.00
(Illustration: Cabinets 8)

Liquor cabinet, Arts & Crafts style, oak, a rectangular top opening to a deep well lined in red suede w/compartments for gaming devices & silver accessories including juicer, bottle holders marked "Sterling Tiffany & Co.," the exterior of the case fitted w/brass corner straps & bail end handles,

a long drawer at the base, raised on heavy slightly tapering legs joined by stretchers, retailed by Tiffany & Company, New York, cabinet stamped in gold "Tiffany & Co., New York," decanters & glassware missing, early 20th century, 14 ¾ x 18 ¼", 30" h. 1,265.00
(Illustration: Cabinets 9)

Liquor cabinet, Arts & Crafts style, 'Jamestown' type, oak, a rectangular top overhanging an apron curving inward to a single drawer over a case w/a

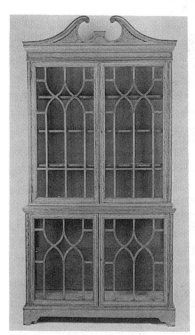

Cabinets 7:
George III-Style Cabinet

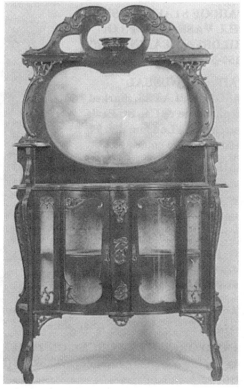

Cabinets 8:
Victorian Rococo Display Cabinet

Cabinets 9: Arts & Crafts
Liquor Cabinet

Cabinets 10: Jamestown Liquor Cabinet

**Cabinets 11:
Louis XV-Style Music Cabinet**

pair of flat doors w/over-
sized wooden hinges &
large latch opening to a
revolving bottle rack, on a
platform base on short
shaped feet, in the style of
Charles Rohlfs, original
dark finish, unmarked,
early 20th century,
25 ¾ x 40", 29 ½" h. 1,870.00
(Illustration: Cabinets 10)

Music cabinet, Louis XV-
Style, gilt-bronze mounted
kingwood & parquetry, the
rectangular top w/ser-
pentine edges above a
bombé case w/a pair of
shaped doors, raised on
slender tapering gently
outswept legs ending in
brass *sabots* & joined by a
shaped medial shelf, the
top, sides & front w/an
overall diamond parquetry
design & fitted w/leafy
scroll ormolu mounts,
France, late 19th century,

18 x 29", 37" h. 4,600.00
(Illustration: Cabinets 11)

Music cabinet, turn of the
century, mahogany veneer,
a low crestrail w/curved
sides & a conforming
beveled mirror above the
rectangular top w/a molded
edge above a long ogee
drawer w/two brass knobs
above a tall door w/a
decoupage musical trophy
reserve & a brass knob,
on simple cabriole front
legs, ca. 1910, 13 ¾ x 20",
37 ¼" h. 340.00
(Illustration: Cabinets 12)

Music cabinet, Victorian
Rococo substyle,
rosewood, the variegated
rouge marble rectangular
top w/outset corners above
molded oval glazed panels
& two glazed panel doors,
raised on four carved
double-tiered reverse-

**Cabinets 12:
Turn of the Century Music
Cabinet**

scrolled legs & central turned shaft w/carved drop finial, on casters, mid-19th century, 25" w., 17" d., 39 ½" h. 1,100.00
(Illustration: Cabinets 13)

Side cabinet, Classical, mahogany, molded cornice above round tapered columns w/gilt acanthus-carved capitals flanking glazed cabinet doors opening to shelves, glazed sides, on gilt paw front & turned ball rear feet on casters, mid-19th century, 50 ½" w., 20" d., 6'1" h. 1,815.00
(Illustration: Cabinets 14)

Cabinets 13: Victorian Rococo Music Cabinet

Side cabinet, Victorian Aesthetic Movement substyle, ebonized & marquetry, the super-structure w/a high rectangular top panel w/a leaf-carved frieze band over panels of delicate leafy vine & bird marquetry over the half-round mirror above an open shelf supported on four reeded posts above the rectangular top above a flower & vine inlaid cabinet door flanked by beveled glass panels & ends, cut-out bracket feet on a base molding, late 19th c., 16 ½ x 40 ¼", 5' 2 ¼" h. 1,840.00
(Illustration: Cabinets 15)

Cabinets 14: Classical Side Cabinet

Cabinets 15: Victorian Aesthetic Movement Cabinet

Spool cabinet, Victorian, walnut & burl walnut, a rectangular top w/molded edge above two stacks of four narrow graduated drawers, each w/a raised burl walnut panel & two white porcelain knobs, molded base, ca. 1870-90, 17 ¾ x 28 ½", 13 ½" h...995.00 *(Illustration: Cabinets 16)*

Cabinets 16: Victorian Spool Cabinet

Vitrine cabinet, Louis XV-Style, ormolu-mounted *Vernis Martin*-type, the shaped *bombé* cornice w/rocaille-embellished crest above a hand-painted scene of Eros & cherubs, over a *bombé* glazed central door w/cartouche of bucolic courting scenario flanked by *bombé* side doors w/hand-painted cartouches of the underworld, the sides displaying hand-painted landscapes, raised on out-curved tapering legs, late 19th century..........................2,640.00 *(Illustration: Cabinets 17)*

**Cabinets 17:
Louis XV-Style Vitrine Cabinet**

Chairs

Art Nouveau armchair, oak, pierced concave back over bowed seat w/floral design velvet upholstery, flanked by shaped & bowed arms over pierced floral design side panels, on scrolled feet joined by flat stretchers, stenciled Model No. 381, ca. 1900, 27 ¼" w., 39 ¾" h. $805.00
(Illustration: Chairs 1)

Art Nouveau armchairs, mahogany, each arched & molded back enclosing a backrest flanked by carved & scrolling foliage, the framework continuing forward to form arms, enclosing a D-form seat raised on foliate carved legs, upholstered in blue-green patterned silk,

**Chairs 2:
Art Nouveau Armchair**

France, ca. 1900, pr. ...2,760.00
(Illustration: Chairs 2)

Art Nouveau rocking chair w/arms, gilt-bronze mounted fruitwood, the narrow crestrail w/a central cartouche set w/a gilt-bronze mount cast as stylized leafage & buds above the leather-upholstered back & seat flanked by molded curved open arms, on curved scroll-molded rockers, designed by Louis Majorelle, France, ca. 1900 ....10,350.00
(Illustration: Chairs 3)

Art Nouveau side chair, carved & painted pine, the tall slender back carved w/the head of a maiden amid a stylized iris blossom

Chairs 1: Art Nouveau Armchair

Chairs 3: Art Nouveau Rocking Chair

& leafage above the rounded seat carved w/various leaves & clusters of organic pods, raised on an irregular root-like base, Continental, ca. 1900 ...1,150.00 (Illustration: Chairs 4)

Arts & Crafts side chair, woven wicker, the squared back w/a diamond lattice woven design above low sides flanking the cushioned seat, tightly woven seatrail w/arched apron, on short wrapped legs, unmarked Gustav Stickley, early 20th century, 20 x 21", 33" h. ....247.50 (Illustration: Chairs 5)

Bannister-back armchair, maple, the shaped crest flanked by turned finials above four split-baluster uprights & down-swept arms ending in scrolled hand-holds, the rush seat on turned legs joined by stretchers, painted dark

Chairs 4: Art Nouveau Carved Side Chair

green over blue-green over red, attributed to New Hampshire, 1710-60.....4,600.00 (Illustration: Chairs 6)

Bannister-back side chair, painted, the arched crest-rail w/pierced scrolls above three split bannisters flanked by ring- and rod-turned stiles w/oblong knob finials, woven rush seat, ring-turned front legs w/button feet joined by knob-turned double stretchers, double knob-turned side stretchers & single turned back stretcher, old brown grain painting, 18th century, 43" h. ....2,530.00 (Illustration: Chairs 7)

Bentwood armchairs, the shield-shaped back w/molded ogee crestrail flanked by shaped arms centering a seat w/serpentine front raised on square cabriole legs

Chairs 5: Art & Crafts Wicker Chair

Chairs 6: Bannister-back Armchair

Chairs 7: Bannister-back Side Chair

Chairs 8: Bentwood Armchair

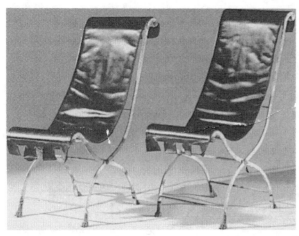

ending in brass sabot, attributed to Gustav Siegal, branded "J, & J. KOHN - AUSTRIA," Model 326/F, ca. 1900, pr. 1,610.00
(Illustration: Chairs 8, one of two)

Campaign chairs, folding type, painted steel & leather, the folding curule frames terminating in rosettes & covered w/black leather upholstery ending in fringed panels, the legs joined by circular rod stretchers on acanthus-decorated lion's paw feet, France, early 19th century, 35 ¼" h., pr. 2,200.00
(Illustration: Chairs 9)

Child's highchair, Early American country-style, old red repaint, three slats flanked by stiles w/turned finials, turned arm supports over a splint seat, turned legs joined by three sets of box stretchers, 19th century, 39" h..................605.00

Child's ladder-back side chair, country-style, wood & paper rush, the back w/three arched slats between simple turned

Chairs 9: French Campaign Chairs

stiles w/turned finials above a worn paper rush seat, w/simple turned legs joined by box stretchers, old dark brown finish over earlier red, 19th century, 30 ½" h., seat 13" h. 121.00

Child's Windsor highchair, painted red, the slightly bowed bamboo-turned crestrail above five bamboo-turned spindles flanked by bamboo-turned

Chairs 10: Windsor Child's Highchair

stiles over a shaped seat, on splayed bamboo-turned legs joined by a shaped footrest & bamboo-turned stretchers, 1800-1830, 34 ¾" h. 1,265.00
(Illustration: Chairs 10)

Child's Windsor highchair, the simple curved crestrail over three tapering spindles flanked by bamboo-turned stiles w/bamboo-turned arms & arm supports enclosing a shaped seat on tall raking bamboo-turned legs joined by box stretchers, old worn green repaint w/red & black striping & floral-decorated crestrail, ca. 1815, 34 ¾" h. (repaired box edge split in seat) 220.00

Chippendale armchair, carved cherry, the arched serpentine-carved crest w/carved scrolled ears above a pierced Gothic splat flanked by shaped

Chairs 11: Chippendale Carved Armchair

Chairs 12: Chippendale Wing Armchair

arms w/carved scrolled hand-holds over serpentine arm supports, w/a trapezoidal slip-seat & molded rails w/beaded lower edge, on cabriole legs w/ball-and-claw feet, Philadelphia, 1760-80, 18¼ x 21¼", 38" h. 3,220.00
(Illustration: Chairs 11)

Chippendale wing armchair, mahogany, the arched crest flanked by downswept shaped wings ending in vertical scrolls above an upholstered seat, on square stop-fluted legs joined by stretchers, Rhode Island, 1760-1790.......11,500.00
(Illustration: Chairs 12)

Chippendale wing armchair, mahogany, the arched upholstered back flanked by ogival wings & outscrolled arms, the trapezoidal seat above square molded legs joined by stretchers, New England, ca. 1775 ....2,300.00

Chippendale wing armchair, mahogany, the arched crest flanked by ogival wings w/outscrolled arms, on square molded legs joined by stretchers, appears to retain an old & possibly original finish, New England, ca. 1785, thin patch to beaded molding on left front leg........5,462.00
(Illustration: Chairs 13)

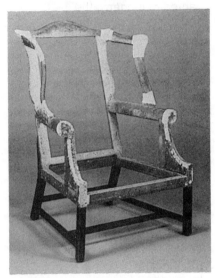

Chairs 13: Chippendale Wing Armchair

Chippendale country-style corner chair, cherry, the U-shaped crest & back rail continuing to form outscrolled handholds above volute-carved vase-form splats & turned supports, above a seatrail enclosing a slip seat & deep apron to conceal a chamber pot, on beaded square legs, 18th century, glued repairs to one support & crest, 33" h...1,540.00

Chippendale "lolling" armchair, mahogany, the wide leather-upholstered back w/a gently arched crest, padded open arms w/curved arm supports, leather-upholstered seat w/tack trim, square legs joined by flat stretchers, probably Massachusetts, ca. 1780, 36" h. 2,760.00
(Illustration: Chairs 14)

Chippendale "lolling" armchair, mahogany, the arched back above shaped arms & molded down-curving arm supports, the over-upholstered seat on square legs joined by stretchers, New England, ca. 1795 (rear leg spliced) 4,312.00

Chippendale "lolling" armchair, mahogany, the rectangular upholstered back above upholstered shaped arms & down-curving arm supports, the over-upholstered saddle

Chairs 14: Chippendale "Lolling" Armchair

**Chairs 15:
Chippendale
Country-Style Chair**

seat on square legs joined
by stretchers, retains old
finish, probably Phila-
delphia, ca. 1765 (repairs
to one stretcher) 13,800.00

**Chairs 17: Chippendale
Mahogany Side Chair**

**Chippendale country-style
side chair**, maple & other
hard-woods, oxbow-
shaped crest w/molded
ears above a vase-shaped
splat over a splint seat, on
square legs w/molded cor-
ner joined by box
stretchers, ca. 1800,
replaced seat, minor
repairs, 37 ¼" h., 16 ½" h.
seat................................418.00
(Illustration: Chairs 15)

Chippendale side chair,
carved mahogany, the
shaped crest continuing to
flared terminals above a
pierced volute-carved
strapwork splat, the
balloon-seat below
enclosing a slip seat on
cabriole legs joined by
stretchers, ending in claw-
and-ball feet, Boston, ca.
1760 ....4,600.00
(Illustration: Chairs 16)

Chippendale side chair,
carved mahogany, the
oxbow crestrail w/a carved
shell crest above a pierced
scroll-cut splat, upholstered
drop-in seat, cabriole front
legs ending in cushioned
pad feet, joined by turned
stretchers, Essex County,
Massachusetts, ca. 1770,
old finish, 38" h. 5,462.00
(Illustration: Chairs 17)

Chippendale side chair,
carved walnut, the shaped
crest centering a carved
shell flanked by volute-
carved terminals above a
pierced vase-form splat
w/egg- and-dart-carved
shoe, the molded shell-
carved seat frame
enclosing a slip seat &
continuing to shell-carved

**Chairs 16: Boston
Chippendale Side Chair**

cabriole legs ending in
claw-and-ball feet,
Philadelphia, ca. 1765
(patches to crest & some
repair to front left feet) ..2,875.00

**Chairs 18: Chippendale
Cherry Side Chair**

Chairs 19: Pennsylvania Chippendale Side Chair

Chippendale side chair, cherry, the serpentine crest w/carved arch above a pierced splat & over-upholstered seat, on Marlboro legs w/outer bead joined by H-stretchers, Connecticut, 1760-80, patches to splat,

Chairs 20: Upholstered Chippendale Side Chair

18 x 21½", 39½"...........1,265.00
(Illustration: Chairs 18)

Chippendale side chair, mahogany, the shaped crest centering a carved shell above a pierced &

volute-carved vase-form splat & shaped seat frame enclosing a slip seat, the shell- and volute- carved cabriole legs ending in claw-and-ball feet, Philadelphia, ca. 1770 (upper section of splat repaired) 6,325.00

Chippendale side chair, walnut, the eared oxyoke crest centered by a carved shell above a lattice pierce-carved splat, trapezoidal upholstered seat, cabriole front legs w/shell-carved knees & ending in claw-and-ball feet, Pennsylvania, ca. 1780, old refinish, 38" h. 4,887.50
(Illustration: Chairs 19)

Chippendale side chair, upholstered, the tall upholstered back w/an arched crest, wide upholstered seat on square legs joined by flat stretchers, possibly New York, ca. 1770, 39" h. 747.50
(Illustration: Chairs 20)

Chippendale side chairs, curly maple, each w/serpentine crest continuing to scrolled ears above a pierced strapwork splat, the rectangular slip seat on square molded legs joined by an H-stretcher, New England, ca. 1780, pr. 3,450.00
(Illustration: Chairs 21)

Chippendale side chairs, mahogany, the bow-shaped crestrail centering a carved shell flanked by molded & scrolled ears above a pierced scrolled splat flanked by plain stiles

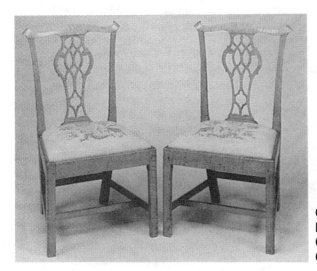

Chairs 21: Curly Maple Chippendale Chairs

Chairs 22: Philadelphia Chippendale Chair

Chairs 23: Carved Mahogany Chippendale Side Chairs

over a trapezoidal slip seat, the flattened-arch front seatrail centering a carved shell, on cabriole legs w/shell-carved knees ending in ball-and-claw feet, Philadelphia, ca. 1765, pr. 27,600.00
(Illustration: Chairs 22, one of two)

Chippendale side chairs, carved mahogany, each having a shaped C-scrolled-carved crest above a pierced Gothic splat, the molded seatrail below enclosing a slip seat, the shaped skirt continuing to cabriole legs, ending in

claw-and-ball feet, one chair marked "V," the other "IV," Philadelphia, ca. 1770, one chair w/repair to stile at juncture w/seatrail, pr. 6,990.00
(Illustration: Chairs 23)

Chippendale side chairs, walnut, each w/shaped crest centering a carved shell above a pierced baluster-form splat, the slip seat above a shaped apron on shell-carved cabriole legs ending in claw-and-ball feet, Philadelphia, ca. 1770, two similar but not a pair, one w/some restoration to splat & crest, each w/patches & repairs to one rear foot, 2 pcs. 5,462.00
(Illustration: Chairs 24)

Chippendale side chairs, carved walnut, each having a shaped crest w/flared terminals above a pierced vase-form splat, the molded trapezoidal seat

Chairs 24: Walnut Chippendale Chairs

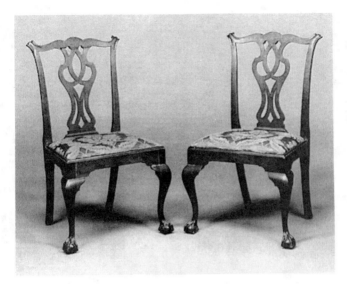

Chairs 25: Philadelphia Chippendale Side Chairs

Chairs 26: Chippendale Side Chair

below continuing to cabriole legs ending in claw-and-ball feet, Philadelphia, ca. 1770, each w/numerous repairs & one chair w/leg returns replaced, pr. 4,312.00
(Illustration: Chairs 25)

Chippendale side chairs, carved mahogany, each having a shaped crest ending in scrolled terminals above a pierced breaker-form splat, the molded & gadrooned seat frame enclosing a slip seat, on cabriole legs ending in claw-and-ball feet, each appears to retain its original finish, New York, ca. 1775, set of three 16,100.00
(Illustration: Chairs 26, one of three)

Classical "sabre-leg" armchair, carved mahogany, the arched crotch-figured crest above shaped arms w/swan-carved arm

supports, the upholstered seat on sabre legs, retains old finish, probably New York state, ca. 1820, repair to one arm & stile at juncture w/backrail........2,300.00
(Illustration: Chairs 27)

Classical country-style rocking chair w/arms, painted, the shaped & bowed crestrail above a baluster-shaped splat &

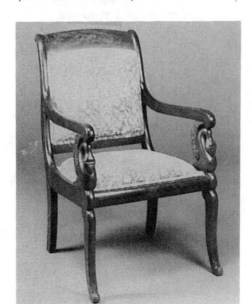

Chairs 27: Classical "Sabre-leg" Armchair

Chairs 28: Country-style Rocking Chair

**Chairs 29: Classical
Country-Style Side Chair**

**Chairs 30: Classical
Country-Style Chair**

Chairs 31: New York Classical Side Chairs

down-scrolled arms on swelled cylindrical supports over a plank seat on tapering cylindrical legs w/turned front & rear stretchers, worn original red & black flame graining w/white striping, 19th century, 41" h..................159.00
(*Illustration: Chairs 28*)

Classical country-style side chairs, painted & decorated, the shaped crestrail above a vase-shaped splat flanked by flattened turned stiles over a cane seat, on turned legs joined by box stretchers, back seatrails stenciled "W. Corey, Portland, Md.," 19th century, original graining to imitate rosewood, new caning, 33 ¾" h., set of 4..............................242.00
(*Illustration: Chairs 29, one of four*)

Classical country-style side chairs, painted & decorated, each w/balloon back w/arched & pierced crestrail above a baluster-shaped splat over a balloon-shaped plank seat, on ball- and cylinder-turned legs tapering at both ends, joined by turned box stretchers, original red &

black grain painting w/yellow striping & roses in pink, green, yellow & white on splats & crests, Pennsylvania, ca. 1830, some wear & one w/repaired split in crest, 34 ½" h., 17 ½" seat h., set of 6............................825.00
(*Illustration: Chairs 30, one of six*)

Chairs 32: Classical Side Chairs

Classical side chairs, carved & figured mahogany, each having a crotch-figured paneled crest above a cornucopia-carved backrail & slip seat on molded sabre legs, New York City, ca. 1820, repairs, set of four 3,162.00
(Illustration: Chairs 31)

Classical side chairs, mahogany & mahogany veneer, each curved w/veneered crestrail on curved stiles flanking a curved slat, upholstered seat, sabre legs, early 19th century, set of 6 ....2,750.00
(Illustration: Chairs 32, three of six)

Country-style ladder-back armchair, painted, turned stiles enclosing five graduated arched slats, scrolled arms on baluster-turned arm supports continuing to turned legs & stretchers on ball-turned feet, dark repaint over earlier red, possibly Pennsylvania, late 18th century, 41" h. (replaced paper rush seat) 660.00

Danish Modern armchairs, hardwood, a flat U-form crestrail forming arms raised above five central spindles & canted stiles continuing to form the rear legs, woven rush seat on slender turned legs joined by high stretchers, original medium finish, stamped "Made in Denmark," loose, 22" w., 29 ½" h., set of 4 ....172.50
(Illustration: Chairs 33, two of four)

Federal country-style "fancy" armchair, painted & decorated, plain stenciled crestrail over turned stiles & downscrolled arms centering turned spindles w/medallions above a plank seat on turned legs & box stretchers, old black paint over red w/yellow & gold striping, bottom of seat branded "B.W.W.," ca. 1820, 34" h. 412.00
(Illustration: Chairs 34)

Federal country-style "thumb-back" side chairs, painted & decorated, plain crestrail over medial stayrail & four turned spindles flanked by thumb-back stiles, above plank seat on turned legs & box stretchers, worn original red & black graining w/blue & yellow striping & polychrome floral decoration, Pennsylvania, ca. 1810, one seat w/age crack, pr..........................187.00
(Illustration: Chairs 35, one of two)

Federal "lolling" armchair, inlaid mahogany, the upholstered arched back above upholstered shaped arms & line- and- dot inlaid

Chairs 33: Danish Modern Armchairs

Chairs 34: Federal "Fancy" Armchair

Chairs 35: "Thumb-Back" Side Chair

incurvate arm supports, the trapezoidal over-upholstered seat on line- and dot-inlaid square tapering legs joined by stretchers, New England, ca.. 1800 ....11,500.00

Federal "lolling" armchair, mahogany, the arched upholstered back above shaped arms & over-upholstered seat, on square tapering legs joined by molded stretchers, probably Rhode Island, ca. 1810, feet slightly reduced in height.......................4,312.00
(Illustration: Chairs 36)

Federal "lolling" armchair, mahogany, the serpentine crest above shaped open arms, the trapezoidal seat on square molded tapering legs joined by stretchers, Massachusetts, ca. 1800 ....3,737.00
(Illustration: Chairs 37)

Federal "lolling" armchair, inlaid mahogany & maple, the serpentine crest above an upholstered back w/shaped arms w/ser-pentine line-inlaid arm supports, the rectangular seat flanked by rectangular inlaid dies, on ring-turned tapering legs, deep brown patina, back appears to retain original straw stuff-ing, Massachusetts, early 19th century, small repair to front left leg.............16,100.00
(Illustration: Chairs 38, left)

Federal "lolling" armchair, inlaid mahogany, the serpentine crest above an unusually tall upholstered back w/shaped arms, the

Chairs 36: Rhode Island "Lolling" Armchair

Chairs 37: Massachusetts "Lolling" Armchair

trapezoidal upholstered seat on square tapering legs joined by stretchers, warm brown patina, Massachusetts, ca. 1800 ....13,800.00
(Illustration: Chairs 38, right)

Federal wing armchair, mahogany, the arched crest flanked by ogival wings & scrolled arms, the seat w/loose cushion on ring-turned & reeded tapering legs ending in

Chairs 38: Fine Federal "Lolling" Armchairs

Chairs 39: Federal Wing Armchair

brass casters, retains old finish, Boston, Massachusetts, ca. 1810 ....4,600.00
(Illustration: Chairs 39)

Federal side chair, carved & figured mahogany, the

Chairs 41: Federal Shield-Back Side Chair

Chairs 40: Federal Sabre-Leg Side Chair

paneled & figured flat crestrail above a foliate-carved back rail, the molded seatrail enclosing a slip seat on molded sabre legs, New York, ca. 1820 ....1,150.00
(Illustration: Chairs 40)

Federal side chair, satinwood-inlaid mahogany, the molded shield back w/serpentine crest centering vine & floral inlay above five molded ribs over an inlaid fan, above a trapezoidal over-upholstered seat w/serpentine front seatrail, on molded tapering legs joined by H-stretchers, New England, ca. 1800, 37 ½" h. 690.00
(Illustration: Chairs 41)

Federal side chair, mahogany, the rectangular back w/a stepped crestrail w/center fluted panel &

flowerhead-carved corners above four slender spindles w/fan-carved tops above the over-upholstered seat w/tack trim, on square tapering reeded legs ending in spade feet, appears to retain original finish, School of Slover & Taylor, New York, New York, ca. 1810 ....1,380.00

Federal side chairs, carved mahogany, shield-shaped back w/beaded edges, pierced splats terminating in leaf-carved lunettes, above serpentine seatrails on molded tapering legs joined by box stretchers, upholstered seat, Charlestown or Boston, Massachusetts, 37" h., pr. 2,970.00

Federal side chairs, mahogany, each w/shield-shaped back, the racquet-form splat carved w/leafage & a stylized pineapple above a slip seat, one w/square seat frame, the other serpentine, each w/molded square tapering legs joined by stretchers, Baltimore, ca. 1800, two similar built not a pair, 2 pcs............................1,840.00

Federal "ladder-back" side chairs, mahogany, the shaped, pierced crestrail w/scrolled leaf-carved ears centering a carved crowned anthemion above three identically carved slats, flanked by molded & reeded stiles above an over-upholstered seat on molded & reeded square legs joined by stretchers,

Chairs 42: Federal "Ladder-Back" Side Chairs

Chairs 43: French Provincial Side Chairs

Massachusetts, ca. 1800, 37 ½" h., set of 4 ....8,625.00
(Illustration: Chairs 42, two of four)

French Provincial side chairs, ladder-back style,

Chairs 44: George II Armchair

the scalloped crestrail carved w/a floral reserve above two scalloped slats flanked by flat serpentine stiles, woven rush seat, simple cabriole front legs ending in scroll feet, square canted back legs, late 19th century, set of 8 ....1,870.00
(Illustration: Chairs 43, two of eight)

George II armchair, walnut, the back w/undulating drapery-carved crestrail above a pierced foliate-carved splat, scrolled arms above over-upholstered seat, on foliate-carved cabriole legs ending in scrolled feet, England, mid-18th century.........17,250.00
(Illustration: Chairs 44)

George II corner armchair, mahogany, the rounded back w/pierced splats & columnar uprights, above drop-in upholstered seat,

on foliate-carved cabriole legs, the central leg ending in claw-and-ball foot, the others in pad feet, England, mid-18th century, restorations to seatrails 5,750.00
(Illustration: Chairs 45)

Chairs 45: George II Corner Chair

Chairs 47: George III Beechwood Armchair

Chairs 46: George III "Barrel-Back" Armchair

George II side chairs, walnut, each w/serpentine crest carved w/acanthus foliage above a pierced backsplat, the drop-in seat w/gadrooned apron, raised on foliate-carved cabriole

legs ending in scrolled feet, England, mid-18th century, set of 6......................10,350.00

George III "barrel-back" armchair, mahogany, upholstered barrel-back

w/bowed loose-cushioned seat raised on straight tapering front & back-swept rear legs, England, ca. 1800 ....1,265.00
(Illustration: Chairs 46)

George III armchair, beechwood, the oval padded back rest above a serpentine seat flanked by padded open arms w/curved supports, raised on fluted legs, England, ca. 1775 ....1,725.00
(Illustration: Chairs 47)

George III armchairs, mahogany, each w/molded serpentine back centering a husk-swagged anthemion- and urn-carved pierced splat, molded out-curved arms on molded serpentine supports, above a padded upholstered seat on straight tapering legs w/beaded corners joined by stretchers, England, ca. 1770, pr. (partly re-railed) 4,370.00

George III dining chairs, satinwood-inlaid mahogany, set comprising two armchairs & six side chairs, each armchair w/concave cresting & pierced backrest, the seat flanked by downswept arms, raised on circular legs, England, ca. 1800, set of 8..........................6,900.00
(Illustration: Chairs 48, two of eight)

George III hall chairs, mahogany, each w/oval radiating back w/central armorial above bowed plank seat on square

Chairs 48: George III Dining Chairs

Chairs 49:
George III Hall Chair

tapering legs w/cuffs,
England, late 18th century,
pr. 2,300.00
(Illustration: Chairs 49, one of two)

Louis XVI armchair, giltwood, the arched, beaded & foliate-carved crest w/acanthus-carved ears above an upholstered back, the beaded & foliate-carved stiles continuing to upholstered armrests & scrolled acanthus-carved handholds over upholstered sides & acanthus-carved arm supports, centering a loose cushion over a fluted, beaded seatrail, on tapering spiral-turned legs on turned feet, France, early 19th century, 26" w., 21" d., 38" h. 2,475.00
(Illustration: Chairs 50)

Mission-style (Arts & Crafts movement) Morris armchair, oak, rectangular back w/four horizontal slats, flat rectangular arms above a drop-in seat, on square legs, medium finish, branded mark of Limbert

Chairs 50:
Louis XVI Armchair

Furniture Company, Grand Rapids, Michigan, ca. 1907, back hinge damage, staining to arms, 28 ½" w., 37 ½" h. 2,990.00
(Illustration: Chairs 51)

Chairs 51: Mission Morris Chair

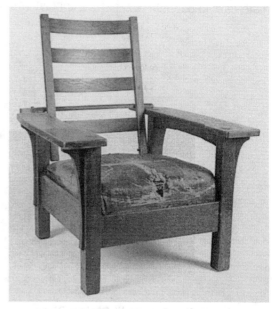

Chairs 52: "Paddle Arm" Morris Chair

Chairs 53: Mission Dining Chairs

Mission-style (Arts & Crafts movement) "paddle arm" Morris armchair, oak, rectangular back w/four horizontal slats flanked by square stiles, flat slightly curved arms w/corbels, on square legs,

**Chairs 54:
L. & J.G. Stickley Rocker**

original medium finish & upholstery, L. & J.G. Stickley, Model No. 412, ca. 1910, 35" w., 41" h. 5,462.00
(Illustration: Chairs 52)

Mission-style (Arts & Crafts movement) dining chairs, oak, flat crestrail above three straight splats flanked by square stiles, above a rush seat w/arched rail, on square legs joined by box stretchers, branded mark of Gustav Stickley, Model No. 353, ca. 1912, restoration, some refinishing, 14 ¼" w., 39" h., set of four 1,495.00
(Illustration: Chairs 53)

Mission-style (Arts & Crafts movement) rocking chair w/arms, oak, flat crestrail above ten slender spindles flanked by square stiles, flat corbelled arms above original leather seat, square legs joined by an H-stretcher, original finish, red mark of L. & J.G.

Stickley, 24" w., 34" h. 825.00
(Illustration: Chairs 54)

Mission-style (Arts & Crafts movement) rocking chair w/arms, oak, wide crestrail above five wide vertical splats

**Chairs 55:
Charles Stickley Rocker**

flanked by square stiles, flat corbelled arms above wide vertical slats, on square legs, original finish, reupholstered, unsigned Charles Stickley, 28 ¼" w., 36 ½" h. 489.00
(Illustration: Chairs 55)

Mission-style (Arts & Crafts movement) rocking chair without arms, oak, crestrail above nine spindles flanked by square stiles above a seat w/spindles from seatrails to side stretchers, on square legs, refinished, new leather seat, unmarked Gustav Stickley, Model No. 377, 16 ¾" w., 36 ½" h. ...440.00

Mission-style (Arts & Crafts movement) side chairs, oak, flat crestrail & bottom rails enclosing an H-shaped splat flanked by square stiles over an upholstered drop-in seat, on tapering square legs

Chairs 56: Mission Oak Side Chairs

joined by box stretchers, some wear to original medium finish, red decal mark of Gustav Stickley, 32 ¼" h., set of 4 ....1,760.00
(Illustration: Chairs 56)

Modern style armchair, bent beechwood, the oblong back panel w/seven

flat curved slats, high curved arms above five-slat sides flanking the red leather seat, straight legs, stained dark brown, designed by Adolf Lorenz, metal tag impressed "SYSTEM - PROF. DR. ADOLF LORENZ," produced by Thonet, Austria, ca. 1910 ....2,300.00
(Illustration: Chairs 57)

Modern style armchair, upholstered, the canted upholstered back w/a large cushion flanked by long low upholstered flat arms over the thick upholstered seat w/inwardly canted & ribbed upholstered seatrail, designed by Gilbert Rohde, ca. 1930s.....................3,850.00
(Illustration: Chairs 58)

Modern style side chair, oak, the slant plank back ending between block-footed legs, a drop-in leatherette seat, designed

Chairs 57: Modern Style Bentwood Armchair

Chairs 58: Modern Style Armchair

Chairs 59: Frank Lloyd Wright Side Chair

**Chairs 60:
Neo-Classical Armchair**

**Chairs 61: Pilgrim
Century "Great Chair"**

**Chairs 62:
Early Slat-Back Armchair**

by Frank Lloyd Wright for
the Unity Temple, Oak
Park, Illinois, some wear to
original finish, unmarked,
14 ½ x 18", 40" h. 9,900.00
(Illustration: Chairs 59)

Neo-Classical armchair,
carved fruitwood, the
curved crestrail w/ebonized
molding above a curved
rectangular splat flanked by
downswept stiles & lotus
leaf-carved armrests over
an upholstered seat
w/swan-carved arm
supports continuing to
curved tapering legs, front
legs ending in carved
stylized paw feet, Con-
tinental, 19th century 1,430.00
(Illustration: Chairs 60)

**Pilgrim Century turned
"great chair,"** Carver-type,
ash, the back w/the rails,
the lower two w/three
baluster-turned spindles,
flanked by stiles w/acorn &

ball finials, turned armrests
joining front posts
w/flattened-ball handholds,
the legs joined by double
turned stretchers on the
front & sides, single rear
stretcher, Scituate or

**Chairs 63: Pilgrim
Century Side Chair**

Plymouth, Massachusetts,
1670-1700, refinished,
45 ½" h., seat 18 h. 3,737.00
(Illustration: Chairs 61)

**Pilgrim Century slat-back
armchair,** maple & ash,
the tall back w/three arched
wide slats between turned
stiles w/oblong knob finials,
angled rod arms to balus-
ter-turned arm supports
w/knob grips, woven rush
seat, double stretchers join
the legs, Norwich-Lebanon,
Connecticut area, 1680-
1760, old finish, restora-
tion, 45½" h. 3,737.50
(Illustration: Chairs 62)

Pilgrim Century side chair,
black cherry, the back
comprising two turned
finials above flattened ball
turned stiles centering five
turned uprights & two
sausage-turned back rails,
the rush seat below on
turned legs joined by

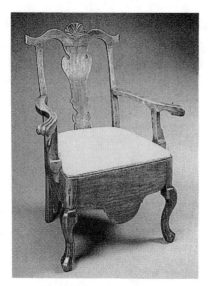

Chairs 64: Queen Anne Armchair

stretchers, New York or northern New Jersey, 1690-1740, feet reduced in height........................5,750.00
(Illustration: Chairs 63)

Queen Anne armchair, carved walnut, the incised serpentine crest centering an arched foliate reserve flanked by shaped ears above a vase-shaped splat flanked by incised S-scrolled stiles over serpentine arms w/carved handholds above shaped supports, over a trapezoidal slip seat above a deep shaped apron, on cabriole legs w/chamfered knees ending in stockinged trifid feet, Lancaster County, Pennsylvania, ca. 1760, 42" h. 9,775.00
(Illustration: Chairs 64)

Queen Anne wing armchair, walnut, the arched crest flanked downswept shaped wings w/vertically scrolled arms above an upholstered seat, on cabriole legs joined by stretchers & ending in pad feet, Massachusetts, ca. 1745, 33 ¼" w., 4' 1 ⅝" h. 17,250.00
(Illustration: Chairs 65)

Queen Anne country-style armchair, stained maple, the shaped crest above a vase-form splat & scrolled arms, the rush seat on vase- and block-turned legs ending in elongated ball feet, joined by robustly turned stretchers, probably original finish, New England, probably Connecticut, 18th century........................6,325.00
(Illustration: Chairs 66)

Queen Anne armchair, tiger maple, the yoked crestrail above a solid vasi-form splat & a rushed seat

Chairs 65: Queen Anne Wing Chair

flanked by baluster-turned stiles & shaped armrests w/baluster turned legs joined by a bulbous frontal stretcher, New England, 1740-60, 33" h. 920.00
(Illustration: Chairs 67)

Chairs 66: Queen Anne Country-Style Armchair

Chairs 67: Queen Anne Tiger Maple Armchair

Chairs 68: Queen Anne "Bannister-back" Armchair

Queen Anne "bannister-back" armchair, turned & painted maple & pine, the pierced volute-carved crest flanked by turned finials above five split-baluster uprights, the rush seat flanked by scrolled arms on turned legs joined by

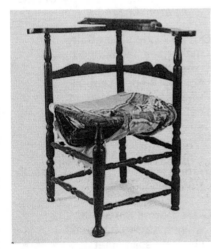

Chairs 70: Queen Anne Country Corner Chair

turned stretchers, painted black 9,200.00
(Illustration: Chairs 68)

Queen Anne corner chair, walnut, the continuous arm supports & pierced splats w/volutes over a slip seat & arched skirt, on cabriole legs w/articulated pad feet, the front leg embellished w/a carved shell, appears to retain original slip seat, Pennsylvania, 1740-60, 18" w., 30" h. 4,600.00
(Illustration: Chairs 69)

Queen Anne corner chair, walnut, the continuous arms w/shaped crest & outscrolled handholds over pierced vase-form splats & serpentine arm supports over a slip seat & arched skirt, on cabriole legs ending in pad feet, the front leg w/carved shell, Pennsylvania, ca.1750, 30" h. 4,600.00

Queen Anne corner chair, old red paint, the continuous arms w/shaped crest & outscrolled handholds over scrolled slats & baluster-turned arm supports over a rush seat on turned legs joined by baluster-turned double stretchers, the front leg w/pad foot, New England, late 18th century, repairs, 30" h., seat 17" h. 1,840.00
(Illustration: Chairs 70)

Queen Anne country-style side chair, maple, the yolked crestrail above a solid vase-shaped splat flanked by tapering stiles, over a trapezoidal rush seat w/corner blocks above

Chairs 69: Queen Anne Corner Chair

block & baluster legs ending in ball feet, joined by baluster- and ring-turned frontal stretcher & double side stretchers, the lower ones similarly turned, Connecticut, ca. 1749, 40" h. 1,265.00
(Illustration: Chairs 71)

Chairs 71: Queen Anne Country-Style Side Chair

Chairs 72: Queen Anne Side Chair

Chairs 73: Rhode Island Queen Anne Chair

Chairs 74: Boston Queen Anne Chair

Queen Anne side chair,
maple, the shaped shell-carved crest w/exaggerated terminals above a volute-carved vase-form splat, the shaped seatrail enclosing a slip seat on shell-carved cabriole legs ending in stockinged trifid feet, Pennsylvania, ca.1750..........................4,600.00
(Illustration: Chairs 72)

Queen Anne side chair,
walnut, the shaped crestrail centering a carved shell above a vase-form splat over a compass slip seat, on cabriole legs ending in claw-and-ball feet, joined by block-turned stretchers, Rhode Island, ca. 1750, 38 ⅛" h. 14,375.00
(Illustration: Chairs 73)

Queen Anne side chair,
mahogany, the shaped crest above a vase-form splat & shaped seatrail enclosing a slip seat on cabriole legs joined by stretchers ending in pad feet, Boston, Massachusetts, 1750-70, three leg returns replaced 2,587.00
(Illustration: Chairs 74)

Queen Anne side chair,
walnut, having a shaped crestrail, solid splat & rectangular seat on

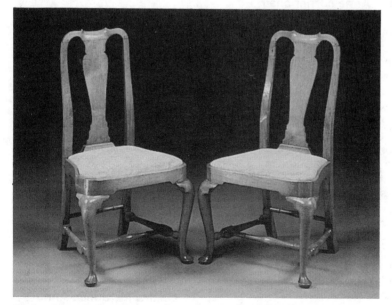

Chairs 75: Queen Anne "Balloon-Seat" Side Chairs

Chairs 76: Queen Anne Mahogany Side Chairs

Chairs 77: Queen Anne Walnut Side Chair

cabriole legs ending in pad feet, Philadelphia area, ca. 1760 ....1,495.00

Queen Anne "balloon-seat" side chairs, the shaped crest above a vase-form splat, the serpentine seat below continuing to cabriole legs ending in pad feet, Boston, Massachusetts, 1740-60, one w/small patch to inside seatrail, pr...................21,850.00
(Illustration: Chairs 75)

Queen Anne side chairs, mahogany, simple shaped & arched crestrail above a vase-form splat over the upholstered balloon-seat, cabriole front legs ending in pad feet, square canted back legs, legs joined by turned stretchers, Massachusetts, ca. 1760, 40" h., pr. 31,050.00
(Illustration: Chairs 76)

Queen Anne side chairs, carved walnut, each having

a shaped crest w/exaggerated projecting volute-carved terminals above vase-form splat & shaped seatrail enclosing a slip seat, each appears to retain an old & possibly original finish & original pine front glue-blocks, Philadelphia, ca. 1750, pr. 16,100.00
(Illustration: Chairs 77)

Queen Anne side chairs, walnut, each having a shaped crest above a vase-form splat, the shaped skirt below enclosing a slip seat on angular cabriole legs joined by stretchers ending in pad feet, marked "III" & "IIII" on frames, Boston, Massachusetts, 1750-70, pr. 8,050.00

Queen Anne side chairs, walnut, each having a shaped vase-form splat, the balloon-shaped seatrail enclosing a slip seat continuing to cabriole legs

ending in paneled pointed snake feet, Philadelphia, 1730-50, various repairs, set of four 51,750.00
(Illustration: Chairs 78, one of four)

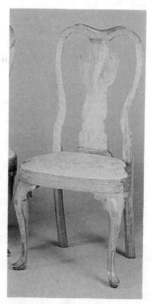

Chairs 78: Philadelphia Queen Anne Side Chair

Chairs 79: English Queen Anne Chair

Chairs 80: Queen Anne Walnut Side Chairs

Queen Anne side chairs, mahogany, each w/arched back & solid vase-form splat above an upholstered drop-in seat, on cabriole legs joined by stretchers, the front legs ending in pad feet, England, early 18th century, set of four........4,140.00
(Illustration: Chairs 79, one of four)

Queen Anne side chairs, walnut, each having a shaped crest above a vase-form splat & trapezoidal-shaped seat enclosing a slip seat, on cabriole legs joined by turned stretchers, ending in pad feet, Boston area, 1750-70, each w/some replaced leg returns & each w/old repairs to crest at juncture w/stiles & repairs to feet, set of four 8,050.00
(Illustration: Chairs 80, three of four)

Queen Anne side chairs, walnut, each w/shaped crest above a vase-form elongated splat, the molded seat frame below enclosing a slip seat, on cabriole legs joined by turned stretchers ending in pad feet, Massachusetts, ca. 1750, one chair w/crest replaced, set of six 40,250.00

Queen Anne Revival rocking chair w/arms, walnut, the arched crestrail w/flaring ears above a three-panel caned back, slender shaped open arms on incurved arm supports, wide trapezoidal caned seat, cabriole front legs ending in pad feet & canted square back legs on

Chairs 81: Queen Anne Revival Rocking Chair

Chairs 82:
Queen Anne Revival Chair

rockers, ca. 1920s,
34 ½" h. 325.00
(Illustration: Chairs 81)

Queen Anne Revival side chair, walnut & mahogany veneer, the arched crestrail continuing to curved stiles flanking a vase-form splat

w/mahogany veneer, trapezoidal upholstered seat on cabriole front legs ending in pads & joined to the back legs by a turned H-stretcher, ca. 1920s, 35" h. 170.00
(Illustration: Chairs 82)

Regency side chairs, carved mahogany, the gadrooned- and acanthus leaf-carved crest above pierced acanthus-carved backrail & cane seat now fitted w/loose cushion, on molded sabre legs, first half of 19th century, repairs, set of six 2,875.00
(Illustration: Chairs 83)

Regency dining chairs: two armchairs & six side chairs; mahogany, each w/turned crestrail above a tablet & crossed splat, flanked by reeded stiles, above padded, upholstered seat on ring-turned sabre

Chairs 84:
Regency Dining Armchair

legs, the armchairs w/reeded downswept arms on reeded tapering supports, stamped "IW," England, early 19th century, set of 8........................13,800.00
(Illustration: Chairs 84, one armchair)

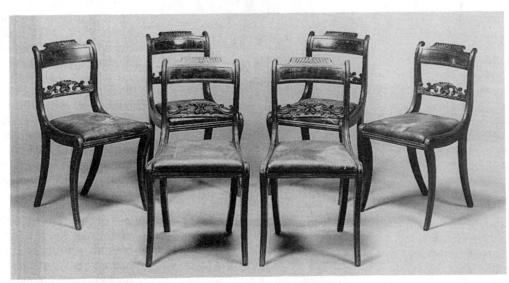

Chairs 83: Six Regency Side Chairs

Chairs 85:
Shaker Rocker with Bar

Chairs 86:
Shaker Side Chair

**Chairs 87: Turn of the Century
Rocking Chair**

Shaker rocker, turned
maple, the back comprised
of four slats w/between
stiles w/pointed lemon
finials, the rush seat raised
on turned stretchers ending
in rockers, appears to
retain original finish, New
Lebanon Community, New
York, first half 19th
century..........................6,900.00

**Shaker rocking chair
w/arms**, turned crestrail for
shawl or cushion above
four arched slats flanked by
round stiles, flat scrolled
arms w/mushroom
handholds on baluster-
turned arm supports
continuing to form round
legs joined by double front
& side stretchers, single
rear stretcher, on rockers,
original surface, old tape
seat, No. 6, New Lebanon,
New York, ca. 1890, 43" h.,

seat 14" h. 747.00
(Illustration: Chairs 85)

Shaker side chair, curly
maple, the back w/three
slats flanked by pointed

**Chairs 88: Turn of the Century
Office Chair**

ball-form finials, the rush
seat below on circular legs
joined by turned stretchers,
the rear legs fitted w/tilters,
Mount Lebanon, Massa-
chusetts, ca. 1830 ....6,325.00
(Illustration: Chairs 86)

**Turn of the century
"pressed-back" rocking
chair without arms**, oak,
the wide slightly shaped
crestrail pressed w/leafy
scrolls above six long
bobbin-turned spindles
flanked by simple turned
stiles w/knob finials, wide
caned square seat, simple
turned legs & bobbin-
turned front stretcher, ca.
1900, 34 ¾" h. 225.00
(Illustration: Chairs 87)

**Turn of the century office
chair**, oak, the shaped
crestrail w/rounded scroll-
carved ears & square stiles
flanking a tall oblong

Chairs 89: Turn of the Century Side Chair

Chairs 90: "Pressed-back" Turn of the Century Side Chairs

Chairs 91: Gothic Revival Armchair

leather-lined back panel, shaped arms w/carved handholds on S-scroll supports, leather seat, swiveling on a base w/four downswept legs on casters...........................750.00
(Illustration: Chairs 88)

Turn of the century "pressed-back" side chair, a wide smooth crestrail w/shaped edges & a pressed scroll band around the sides raised on ring- and baluster-turned stiles flanking seven spiral-turned spindles to the scroll-decorated lower slat, on a trapezoidal seat w/square cane insert, scalloped front seat apron, on simple turned & slightly curved front legs joined by three baluster- and ring-

turned rungs, 40" h. 225.00
(Illustration: Chairs 89)

Turn of the century "pressed-back" side chairs, oak, the wide shaped & stepped crestrail decorated w/a design of leafy scrolls above six slender fanned ring-turned spindles to the lower slat, trapezoidal seat w/square cane insert, shaped drop on front apron, on turned front legs w/ball feet joined by ring-turned double front rungs, ca. 1900-1910, 39 ⅜" h., set of 4 ....1,275.00
(Illustration: Chairs 90, two of four)

Victorian armchair, Gothic Revival substyle, walnut, the rectangular back w/crocket finials & crenellated top above

foliate-carved arms & padded seat, on X-frame supports headed by rams' heads & w/trefoils, w/embossed brown leather upholstery, England, mid-19th century.................1,725.00
(Illustration: Chairs 91)

Victorian armchair, Renaissance Revival substyle, rosewood, the carved crestrail centering a circular female portrait medallion & flanked by roundels over carved & gilt incurved stiles enclosing an upholstered tufted back, the upholstered armrests on carved male figurehead supports over a serpentine-shaped seat, on turned

trumpet-form legs on casters, attributed to John Jelliff, Newark, New Jersey, ca. 1870.......................1,320.00
(Illustration: Chairs 92)

Victorian armchair, Renaissance Revival substyle, walnut, parcel-gilt & ebonized, a circular padded back w/ribbon-carved crest flanked by reeded columnar stiles above an upholstered bowed seat, the backrail w/geometric carving, on reeded trumpet-form legs, ca. 1865-85, 40½" h. 1,610.00

Victorian armchair, Rococo substyle, carved hardwood, the high arched balloon

back pierce-carved overall w/leafy vines, the crestrail continuing down to form outswept arms w/S-scroll arm supports carved w/leafy vines, upholstered seat above a deep pierce-carved seatrail continuing to cabriole legs carved as leafy scrolls w/scroll feet, Burma, mid-19th century, 38 ½" h. 1,035.00
(Illustration: Chairs 93)

Victorian armchair, Rococo substyle, carved & laminated rosewood, the upholstered balloon back carved at the crest w/fruit & flowers, the foliate-carved & molded arms on down-scrolled supports enclosing

Chairs 93: Burmese Rococo Armchair

Chairs 92: Renaissance Revival Armchair

an upholstered serpentine seat on a conforming floral-carved rail, on demi-cabriole foliate-carved legs on casters, "Rosalie" patt., attributed to John Henry Belter, New York, mid-19th century..........................4,400.00
(Illustration: Chairs 94)

Victorian armchair, Rococo substyle, walnut, the pear-shaped balloon back w/a scroll-carved crest centered by a carved cartouche, padded open arms on shaped arm supports over the upholstered seat, serpentine molded seatrail & molded demi-cabriole front legs on casters, ca.

Chairs 95: Rococo Balloon Back Armchair

1860, 43 ½" h. 800.00
(Illustration: Chairs 95)

Victorian armchair, Rococo sub-style, carved walnut, the high ballon back w/a pierced scroll-carved crest centered by a cartouche, scroll-carved open arms above the serpentine seat, on demi-cabriole front legs & canted square back legs on casters, ca. 1850, 4' 8" h. 440.00
(Illustration: Chairs 96)

Victorian side chairs, Aesthetic Movement substyle, inlaid wood, rectangular molded crestrail w/mother-of-pearl & light wood ribbon-tied

Chairs 94: Rosalie Pattern Armchair

Chairs 96: Rococo Armchair

Chairs 97: Victorian Rococo Side Chairs

floral garlands flanked by squared incised stiles above a trapezoidal seat w/reeded seatrail, on turned tapering legs joined by a raised box stretcher, one w/padded seat & back, other unupholstered,

attributed to Herter Brothers, New York, ca. 1880-85, 34 ¼" h., pr. 575.00

Victorian side chairs, Rococo substyle, rosewood, the tufted upholstered balloon back w/carved surround over an upholstered serpentine seat, on cabriole front & splayed rear legs, mid-19th century, pr. 550.00
(Illustration: Chairs 97)

Victorian side chairs, Rococo substyle, walnut, an open balloon back w/finger-molded crestrail & arched slat above shaped & molded skirt guards on the upholstered seat, serpentine molded seatrail & simple cabriole front legs, ca. 1860, 35" h., set of 4.........................1,175.00
(Illustration: Chairs 98, one of four)

Victorian side chairs, Rococo substyle, mahogany, each w/shaped balloon back w/serpentine crest over a serpentine seat on carved cabriole front legs & curved square back legs, ca. 1860, set of 6 ....880.00
(Illustration: Chairs 99, one of six)

Wicker rocking chair w/arms, the high rounded balloon back w/three rolled panels & tightly woven arms flanking the oblong finely caned center back panel w/scrolled wicker trim, round caned seat, rounded woven seatrail w/arched apron, late 19th century, 41" h...................632.50
(Illustration: Chairs 100)

Wicker rocking chair w/arms, the ram's horn-shaped crestrail above a spindle & basket-weave back flanked by acorn-finial flared stiles & braided

Chairs 98: Rococo Walnut Side Chair

Chairs 99: Victorian Rococo Side Chair

armrests enclosing a petal-shaped seat w/spindle-decorated skirt, late 19th century.............................550.00
(Illustration: Chairs 101)

Wicker side chairs, the high balloon back w/three scrolled edge panels flanking the oval caned back panel w/a knob border & raised on wicker scrolls above the rectangular caned seat, scroll-trimmed legs & seat apron, late 19th century, 38" h., pr. 920.00
(Illustration: Chairs 102, one of two)

William & Mary armchair, carved maple, the molded arched crest w/outset ears above a caned back w/molded supports & molded stiles over downswept & out-turned molded arms w/scrolled handgrips above tapering ring-turned supports & molded seatrails centering a caned seat, on tapering cylinder- and block-turned legs w/elongated Spanish feet, joined by a ring-, baluster- and ball-turned front stretcher & turned side & medial stretchers, Philadelphia, 1715-1720, rear feet pieced 1 ½" , repair to crest at joint w/stile, 24 ¼" w., 16 ¾" d., 45" h. 27,600.00
(Illustration: Chairs 103)

William & Mary country-style corner chair, painted, a U-form shaped crestrail forming arms above three rod- and baluster-turned legs joined

Chairs 100: Balloon Back Wicker Rocker

Chairs 101: Spindled Wicker Rocker

Chairs 102: Ornate Wicker Side Chair

Chairs 103: William & Mary Armchair

Chairs 104: William & Mary Country-Style Corner Chair

century, 30" h................7,475.00
(Illustration: Chairs 104)

William & Mary "Crown" side chair, stained brown, shaped crestrail centering a pierced heart above four vertical molded bannisters flanked by baluster-turned stiles w/acorn finials, above a rush seat on turned legs w/flattened ball front feet, double box stretchers, Milford, Connecticut area, 1750-1770, 43 ½" h., seat 16 ½" h. 1,035.00
(Illustration: Chairs 105)

William & Mary "crooked back" side chairs, the tall serpentine-shaped back w/molded crestrail & molded stiles above a trapezoidal seat on block- and baluster-turned legs joined by stretchers, on carved feet, old dark surface, Boston area, 1720-1760, replaced double-nailed leather upholstery, imperfections,

Chairs 105: William & Mary "Crown" Chair

45" & 44 ½" h., seat 18 ½" h., pr. 10,925.00
(Illustration: Chairs 106)

William & Mary Revival side chair, walnut, a narrow arched crestrail

by shaped slats above the square old leather upholstered seat over original splint, baluster-turned front leg ending in pad foot, other legs w/knob feet, original black paint, New England, early 18th

Chairs 106: William & Mary Side Chairs

Chairs 107: William & Mary Revival Side Chair

Chairs 108: Windsor "Arrow-Back" Armchair

Chairs 109: Windsor Side Chairs

Chairs 110: Windsor "Bird-Cage" Armchair

above a long narrow shaped splat w/cane insert flanked by rod- and ball-turned stiles w/urn finials, wide trapezoidal caned seat, baluster- and block-turned front legs ending in simple Spanish feet & joined by a high bulbous turned stretcher, turned H-stretcher joins the four legs, ca. 1920s, 43" h. 225.00
(Illustration: Chairs 107)

Windsor "arrow-back" armchairs, painted & decorated, each w/U-shaped crestrail above four arrow-shaped spindles flanked by turned backswept stiles above cylindrical armrests & supports over a plank seat on bamboo-turned legs joined by flattened ball- and baluster-turned front stretchers & bamboo-

turned side & rear stretchers, original white paint w/red & black graining, foliate decoration & cornucopias w/fruit & flowers on crest in red, blue, brown, black & gold, 19th century, some wear, 33 ½" h., 18 ¼" h., pr. ...1,650.00
(Illustration: Chairs 108, one of two)

Windsor "bamboo-turned" side chairs, maple, each w/curved crestrail above seven tapering bamboo-turned spindles flanked by tapering stiles w/acorn finials above shaped seat, on raking bamboo-turned legs joined by stretchers, the front stretcher centering an elongated flattened oval, New England, early 19th century, old refinish, 33 ¾" h., seat 17" h., set of 6.........................1,955.00
(Illustration: Chairs 109, three of six)

Windsor "bird-cage" armchair, painted & decorated, bird-cage crest w/round medallion over six bamboo-turned spindles flanked by bamboo-turned stiles, arms & supports above a plank seat w/double beading on front edge, on bamboo-turned legs & box stretchers, putty-colored repaint w/yellow striping & rose-painted medallion over original green, Philadelphia, 34 ¾" h., seat 17¾" h. 770.00
(Illustration: Chairs 110)

Windsor "bow-back" armchair, painted brown, the bowed crestrail above seven spindles & scrolling arms w/bamboo-turned supports above a D-shaped plank seat, on bamboo-turned legs joined by a bamboo-turned H-

Chairs 111: Windsor "Bow-Back" Armchair

Chairs 112: "Bow-Back" Side Chair

Chairs 113: Branded Windsor Side Chair

stretcher, the entire surface painted brown w/black highlights, Pennsylvania, 1800-1810, 38 ½" h. 1,380.00
(Illustration: Chairs 111)

Windsor "bow-back" side chair, the incised bowed back above nine tapering spindles over a shaped plank seat, on bamboo-turned legs joined by a bamboo-turned swelled H-stretcher, possibly Pennsylvania, ca. 1810, 37" h. 460.00
(Illustration: Chairs 112)

Windsor "bow-back" side chair, old dark varnish stain, the arched crestrail above nine spindles, shaped saddle seat, on splayed bamboo-turned legs joined by H-stretcher, underside of seat branded "F. Trumble," Philadelphia, 1765-80, one bulbous stretcher varies from the

other, 39" h., seat 19 ½" h. 550.00
(Illustration: Chairs 113)

Windsor "bow-back" side chairs, each having an arched crest above seven

tapered spindles & shaped seat on bamboo-turned legs joined by stretchers, painted light green over white, ca. 1810, feet reduced in height, pr. 575.00
(Illustration: Chairs 114)

Chairs 114: Painted Windsor "Bow-back" Side Chairs

Windsor "bow-back" side chair, refinished, the arched crestrail above seven spindles, shaped saddle seat, on splayed bamboo-turned legs & H-stretcher, 37 ½" h., seat 17 ½" h., set of 6 (minor variations, several w/pieced repairs to seat) 2,145.00

Windsor "braced bow-back" armchair, walnut & mahogany, the incised bowed crestrail above seven baluster-turned spindles braced w/two baluster-turned spindles over serpentine mahogany arms w/scrolling handgrips above baluster- and ring-turned supports over a shaped plank seat, on baluster- and ring-turned legs joined by a swelled H-stretcher, Rhode Island, 1770-1800, repair to center spindle, 38" h.................1,380.00
(Illustration: Chairs 115)

Chairs 115: "Braced Bow-Back" Armchair

Windsor child's "sack-back" armchair, painted red, the arched crest above five tapered spindles, the U-shaped backrail forming slightly flared hand-holds, the plank seat below on vase-turned splayed legs joined by turned stretchers, Philadelphia, ca. 1785, feet slightly reduced 977.00
(Illustration: Chairs 116)

Chairs 116: Child's Windsor Armchair

Windsor "comb-back" armchair, ladies' size, painted, the arched crest above seven tapered spindles, the U-shaped backrail continuing to form slightly flared handholds, the peaked seat below on turned splayed legs joined by turned stretchers, painted dark green over light green, New England, ca. 1800.........................1,495.00
(Illustration: Chairs 117)

Chairs 117: "Comb-Back" Armchair

Windsor "comb-back" armchair, painted green, the serpentine crestrail w/carved ears above nine tapering spindles over a U-shaped arm rail terminating in out-turned handgrips w/baluster-turned supports above a D-shaped seat, on splayed baluster- and cylinder-turned legs ending in blunt arrow feet, joined by a baluster-turned H-stretcher, Philadelphia, 1765-1790, 42 ¼" h. 6,900.00

Windsor "continuous arm" armchair, painted, the bowed crestrail continuing to form arms on baluster-turned supports, enclosing nine tapered spindles over a saddle-shaped seat on raking baluster-turned legs & H-stretcher, old black paint over red, New England, probably

Chairs 118: Windsor "Continuous Arm" Armchair

Rhode Island, late 18th century, minor age cracks in seat, 36 ¾" h., seat 18" h. 7,150.00
(Illustration: Chairs 118)

Windsor "continuous arm" armchair, the bow crest continuing to form flared handholds above thirteen tapered spindles, the shaped plank seat below, on turned legs joined by turned stretchers, painted brown, ca. 1795, old repair to one arm 1,495.00
(Illustration: Chairs 119)

Windsor "continuous arm" armchair, painted, the arched crestrail above nine slender spindles continues down to form the narrow arms above spindles & ring- and baluster-turned canted arm supports, shaped saddle seat on ring- and baluster-turned canted legs joined by a swelled H-stretcher, old black paint, probably Rhode Island, ca. 1780, 36½" h. 1,610.00
(Illustration: Chairs 120, left)

Chairs 119: Painted "Continuous Arm" Armchair

Windsor "fan-back" side chair, the gently arched crestrail above seven slender spindles flanked by baluster-turned stiles,

Chairs 120: Windsor "Continuous Arm" Armchair, Windsor "Fan-Back" Side Chair, and Windsor "Sack-Back" Armchair

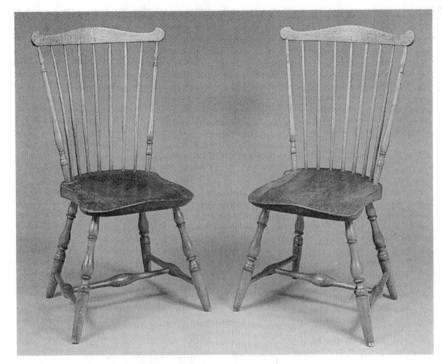

Chairs 121: Windsor "Fan-Back" Side Chairs

Chairs 122: Windsor "Sack-Back" Armchair

shaped saddle seat above ring- and baluster-turned canted legs joined by a swelled H-stretcher, late 18th century..................2,070.00
(Illustration: Chairs 120, center)

Windsor "fan-back" side chairs, each w/a serpentine crestrail w/upraised ears above seven spindles flanked by baluster-turned stiles over a shaped saddle seat, on baluster-turned legs joined by a swelled H-stretcher, possibly Connecticut, 1760-1790, 35 ¾" h., pr. 2,300.00
(Illustration: Chairs 121)

Windsor "sack-back" armchair, painted, the

bowed crestrail above seven spindles continuing down through a medial rail which forms flat shaped arms over spindles & ring- and baluster-turned arm supports, oblong shaped seat on ring- and baluster-turned canted legs joined by a swelled H-stretcher, old black painted w/contrasting red seat, New England, ca. 1780, 35" h. 11,500.00
(Illustration: Chairs 120, right)

Windsor "sack-back" armchair, painted black, the shaped crestrail above nine spindles held in place by a U-shaped armrail terminating in out-turned

handgrips over baluster-turned supports above a shaped seat, on baluster- and ring-turned legs joined by a swelled H-stretcher, the entire surface painted black w/gilt highlights, probably Philadelphia, 1765-1790, 38 ¼" h. 3,220.00
(Illustration: Chairs 122)

Windsor side chairs, each w/horizontal crest above seven spindles flanked by bamboo-turned stiles over a shaped seat, on splayed bamboo-turned legs joined by a bamboo-turned H-stretcher, Pennsylvania, 1820-1850, 31¼" h., assembled set of 4 ....460.00

Chests & Chests of Drawers

Art Nouveau chest of drawers, carved walnut & mahogany, *Les Lilas* patt., rectangular pink marble top w/molded edge above a shaped case of four long drawers carved w/lilac blossoms & leafage, the drawers w/gilt-bronze clover foliate mounts, designed by Louis Majorelle, France, ca. 1900, 23 ¼ x 46 ½", 34" h. ...18,400.00
(Illustration: Chests 1)

Blanket chest, child's country-style, grain-painted, the hinged rectangular lid w/flat molding opening to a well, the case w/molded edges & sides scroll-sawn to form bootjack feet, possibly Pennsylvania, ca. 1830, 24" w., 14" d., 19 ½" h. 977.00
(Illustration: Chests 2)

Blanket chest, Chippendale country-style, painted &

Chests 3: Painted Chippendale Blanket Chest

decorated pine, the rectangular hinged top w/applied molded edge opening to a compartment fitted w/a lidded till & secret drawers, the dovetailed case painted dark red, the front centering the initials "H.W." on a white-painted ground flanked by two green-painted reserves above a black-painted base molding, on bracket feet, the case sides fitted w/wrought-iron handles, Pennsylvania, 1770-1785, six inch loss to side molding of top, 51" w., 23 ¾" d., 23" h. 2,990.00
(Illustration: Chests 3)

Chests 1: Art Nouveau Chest of Drawers

Chests 2: Early Child's Blanket Chest

Chests 4: Chippendale Inlaid Blanket Chest

Blanket chest, Chippendale country-style, painted & decorated, the rectangular top w/applied molded edge centering a red-painted astragal reserve, the underside inscribed "Christian Eterly, 1782" in red chalk, opening to a compartment fitted w/a lidded till, the dovetailed case w/an applied frieze of four pilasters & three recessed arches, the reserves decorated w/red floral motifs on a white ground, the center panel inscribed "ANNO 1782," over a molded base, the case sides fitted w/wrought-iron handles, on casters, Lancaster County, Pennsylvania, 1782, 51¼" w., 25" d., 23¾" h. 4,025.00

Blanket chest, Chippendale country-style, inlaid walnut, the rectangular top w/molded edge opening to a deep well above a dovetailed case inlaid across the front w/three slender stylized flowers on stems above a mid-molding over two long & a short drawer across the bottom, molded base, scroll-cut bracket feet, Pennsylvania, ca. 1780, refinished, restoration, 21½ x 47", 29" h. 5,175.00
(Illustration: Chests 4)

Blanket chest, Chippendale, walnut, the rectangular hinged top w/thumb-molded edge opening to a compartment fitted w/a lidded till above a conforming dovetailed case over two short thumb-molded drawers above an applied base molding, on ogee bracket feet, Pennsylvania, ca. 1790, crack to left front foot, 50¾" w., 23¾" d., 29" h. 3,220.00
(Illustration: Chests 5)

Blanket chest, country-style, grain-painted poplar, hinged rectangular top w/applied molding opening to a compartment w/a lidded walnut till above a dovetailed case w/ applied base molding on turned feet, original brown flame graining, 19th century, 45¾" w., 19¾" d., 25" h. 660.00

Chests 5: Walnut Chippendale Blanket Chest

Blanket chest, country-style, painted & decorated poplar, hinged & molded rectangular top opening to a dovetailed compartment fitted w/a till, scalloped apron & dovetailed bracket feet, original red comb graining over a yellow ground, Pennsylvania, 19th century, 47 ½" w., 23" d., 28" h. 275.00

Blanket chest, country-style, painted & decorated pine, the rectangular top w/molded edge opening to a compartment w/lidded till, the dovetailed case w/gold stencilled "A.E." & "1843" on the front, above two short drawers w/porcelain pulls & ivory-inlaid keyhole escutcheons centering a panel w/cut-out hearts & circles, on a base w/applied molding & dovetailed bracket feet, old red & black repaint w/white trim, Soap Hollow, Pennsylvania, cracks in one corner of top, 47 ¼" w., 22 ½" d., 30 ½" h. 2,310.00
(Illustration: Chests 6)

Blanket chest, Federal country-style, grain-painted, the hinged rectangular top w/molded edge opening to a well, above a mid-molding over three short drawers on bracket feet, fanciful graining w/old brown & gold paint, probably Pennsylvania, early 19th century, 48" w., 24" d., 29 ½" h. 1,840.00
(Illustration: Chests 7)

Blanket chest, salmon paint-decorated pine, the rectangular hinged molded

Chests 6: Soap Hollow Blanket Chest

lid opening to a well, a molded long drawer below, the molded base on bracket feet, New England, 1800-20, 18 ½ x 43 ¼", 37 ¼" h. 2,587.00

Blanket chest, Queen Anne, walnut, the rectangular hinged molded lid opening to a well w/till, two molded

drawers below, on bracket feet, appears to retain original brasses, Pennsylvania, ca. 1750-80, 22 ½ x 49", 28 ½" h. 2,760.00
(Illustration: Chests 8)

Charles II chest of drawers, walnut, the rectangular top above two frieze drawers centered & flanked by pierced D-shap-

Chests 7: Federal Country-Style Blanket Chest

**Chests 8:
Queen Anne
Blanket Chest**

ed moldings, over one deep & two short drawers with molded cross & lozenge panels, molded base on block feet, England, third quarter 17th century, some restoration, 22 ¾ x 36 ½",

35 ¾" h. 4,600.00
(Illustration: Chests 9)

Chippendale "block-front" chest of drawers, mahogany, the rectangular molded top w/block front above a conforming case w/four graduated long

drawers w/cockbeaded surrounds, over a molded base w/central drop, on scroll-cut bracket feet, Massachusetts, ca. 1770, repairs to one foot, 21 ½ x 35 ¾", 30 ½" h. 29,900.00
(Illustration: Chests 10)

Chests 9: Charles II Chest of Drawers

Chests 10: Chippendale "Block-Front" Chest

**Chests 11:
Chippendale
"Bow-Front"
Chest of Drawers**

**Chests 12:
Mahogany Chippendale
"Bow-Front" Chest**

**Chests 13:
Cherry Chippendale
Chest of Drawers**

Chippendale "bow-front" chest of drawers, cherry, the rectangular top w/bowed front & barber-pole inlaid edge above a conforming case w/four cockbeaded long graduated drawers, flanked by fluted quarter columns, on bracket feet, Connecticut, ca. 1800, 25 x 41½", 36 ½" h. 4,370.00
(Illustration: Chests 11)

Chippendale "bow-front" chest of drawers, carved & figured mahogany, the oblong thumb-molded top w/bowed front above a case w/four long graduated cockbeaded drawers, the molded base continuing to claw-and-ball feet, Boston, ca. 1785, 24 x 41½", 35 ½" h. 7,475.00
(Illustration: Chests 12)

Chippendale chest of drawers, cherry, rectangular top above four long graduated drawers w/incised edges, fluted quarter columns flanking, molded base on ogee bracket feet, Connecticut, ca. 1790, 18 ½ x 41 ¼", 36 ¾" h. 2,875.00
(Illustration: Chests 13)

Chippendale chest of drawers, mahogany, the rectangular thumb-molded top above four long graduated drawers, each w/cockbeaded surrounds, on bracket feet, retains old, possibly original finish, Boston area, Massachusetts, ca. 1785, 22 ¼ x 40 ¼", 32 ½" h. 4,887.00

Chippendale "serpentine-front" chest of drawers, mahogany inlaid with mahogany veneer, thumb-molded top above four long graduated drawers w/incised edges, molded serpentine base on blocked ogee bracket feet, Massachusetts, ca. 1785, restoration to lower portion of three feet, 19 x 37 ⅛", 30 ½" h. 6,325.00
(Illustration: Chests 14)

Chippendale "serpentine-front" chest of drawers, mahogany, the oblong top w/thumb-molded edge above a conformingly-shaped case w/four long graduated drawers, the molded base continuing to ogee bracket feet, reddish brown color, Massachusetts, ca. 1780, two side foot facings replaced & patch to top of one drawer, 21 x 40", 33" h. 6,900.00
(Illustration: Chests 15)

Chippendale "serpentine-front" chest of drawers, inlaid mahogany, the oblong thumb-molded top w/serpentine-front above a conformingly-shaped case w/four long graduated line-inlaid cockbeaded drawers, line-inlaid canted corners flanking, on bracket feet, retains old, possibly original finish, Massachusetts or New Hampshire, ca. 1795, 23 ½ x 43 ½", 35 ½" h. 11,500.00

Chippendale tall chest of drawers, maple, the rectangular top w/a deep cove-molded cornice above

Chests 14: Massachusetts "Serpentine-Front" Chest of Drawers

Chests 15: Chippendale "Serpentine-front" Chest of Drawers

Chests 16: Chippendale Maple Tall Chest of Drawers

Chests 17: Chippendale Carved Maple Tall Chest of Drawers

Chests 18: Chippendale Cherry Tall Chest of Tall Drawers

Chests 19: Pennsylvania Chippendale Tall Chest of Drawers

Chests 20: Chippendale Tiger Maple Tall Chest of Drawers

a case of five long graduated drawers w/butterfly brasses, molded base, tall scroll-cut bracket feet, signed "W. Thorndike North Weare, N.H.," ca. 1780, original red stain, replaced brasses, minor imperfections, 17½ x 36", 45" h. 4,312.50
(Illustration: Chests 16)

Chippendale tall chest of drawers, carved maple, the molded cornice above five molded long drawers, the upper drawer faced to simulate five working drawers, the center panel carved w/a stylized fan, the molded base on bracket feet, now on casters, incised "Peter Hurd 1804," probably New Hampshire, ca. 1790, 19½ x 38½", 4' 7½" h. 4,715.00
(Illustration: Chests 17)

Chippendale tall chest of drawers, figured cherry, the molded cornice above five short & four long graduated molded drawers, fluted quarter-columns flanking, the molded base on ogee bracket feet, Pennsylvania, ca. 1780, repairs & patches to cornice moldings & feet, 24 x 41½ ", 5' 6" h. 4,600.00
(Illustration: Chests 18)

Chippendale tall chest of drawers, figured walnut, the molded cornice above five short & four long graduated molded drawers, fluted quarter-columns flanking the molded base raised on ogee bracket feet, Pennsylvania, ca. 1780, 24⅛ x 42⅞",

4' 10¼" h. 4,600.00
(Illustration: Chests 19)

Chippendale tall chest of drawers, tiger stripe maple, a rectangular top w/molded edge above a case w/a pair of small drawers above five long graduated drawers, all w/original butterfly brasses, molded base, tall cut-out bracket feet, old refinish, southeastern New England, ca. 1770, 17¾ x 36", 4' 3" h. 23,000.00
(Illustration: Chests 20)

Chippendale tall chest of drawers, walnut, a rectangular top w/deep coved cornice above a row of three short drawers above five long graduated drawers all w/original oval brasses, flanked by reeded chamfered front corners, molded base on tall scroll-cut ogee bracket feet, old mellow refinishing, Pennsylvania, late 18th century, minor edge damage, old minor repairs, 21¾ x 42 ½", 5' 6 ½" h. 8,250.00
(Illustration: Chests 21)

Chests 21: Chippendale Tall Chest of Drawers

Chests 22:
Chippendale Walnut Tall Chest of Drawers

Chests 23:
Chippendale "Block-Front" Chest

Chippendale tall chest of drawers, walnut, the molded cornice above three short drawers over three short & five long graduated drawers, on ogee bracket feet, Pennsylvania, ca. 1780, refinished, minor repairs & part of one back foot missing, 23½ x 44", 5' 10½ h., ...6,875.00
(Illustration: Chests 22)

Chippendale "block-front" chest-on-chest, carved & giltwood mahogany, two-part construc-tion: the upper section w/molded broken-arch pediment cen-tering & flanked by three flame-turned finials on sphere & tapered bases, above a case fitted w/three short drawers, the central drawer w/carved & gilt fan, over four long graduated drawers flanked by fluted

pilasters; the lower section w/mid-molding above four blocked long graduated drawers over a conforming molded base, on bracket feet w/spur returns, Massa-chusetts, 1760-1780, repairs to feet, replaced mid-molding, 43 ¾" w., 22 ½" d., 7' 11 ½" h.....47,150.00
(Illustration: Chests 23)

Chippendale chest-on-chest, figured maple, two-

 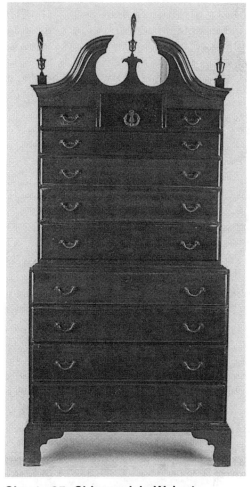

Chests 24: Chippendale "Bonnet-top" Chest on Chest

Chests 25: Chippendale Walnut "Bonnet-top" Chest on Chest

part construction: the upper section w/molded cornice above two short drawers over four thumb-molded long graduated drawers; the lower section w/three thumb-molded graduated drawers, on bracket feet, New England, 1780-1790, 42 ½" w., 22 ½" d., 6' 10 ½" h. 19,550.00

Chippendale "bonnet-top" chest on chest, cherry, two-part construction: the

upper section w/a broken pediment bonnet top w/three urn & flame-turned finials above a row of three drawers, the deep central drawer carved w/a large fan above four long graduated drawers w/butterfly pulls; the lower section w/a mid-molding above four long graduated drawers w/butterfly pulls, molded base, tall cut-out bracket feet, signed on top of bottom section "Made by

Joseph Hosmer Concord, Mass. 1782," replaced brasses, imperfections, 20 ½ x 39", 7' h. ....13,800.00 *(Illustration: Chests 24)*

Chippendale "bonnet-top" chest on chest, walnut, two-part construction: the upper section w/a broken scroll bonnet top w/carved sunburst terminals on the scrolls & three flame-turned finials above a row of three drawers, the deep central

Chests 26: Chippendale Chest-on-Frame

Chests 27: New York Classical Chest of Drawers

Chests 28: Classical Chest With Mirror

Chests 29: Classical Paw-foot Chest of Drawers

drawer ornately carved w/a large shell & scrolls above a pair of short drawers over three long graduated drawers, all flanked by chamfered reeded corners; the lower section w/a mid-molding above a pair of drawers over two long drawers all flanked by chamfered reeded corners, molded base & ogee bracket feet, Pennsylvania, late 18th century, replaced brasses, refinished, minor restoration, 23 x 42", 7' 9 ½" h. 28,750.00
(Illustration: Chests 25)

Chippendale chest-on-frame, maple, two-part construction: the upper section w/molded cornice above five molded long graduated drawers; the lower section w/shaped skirt & turned pendants continuing to cabriole legs ending in pad feet, New England, ca. 1785, 20 x 40 ¾", 55" h. 5,175.00
(Illustration: Chests 26)

Chippendale chest-on-frame, walnut, two-part construction: the upper section w/molded cornice above three short drawers over five graduated thumb-molded drawers flanked by fluted quarter columns; the lower section w/mid-molding above a shaped skirt, on shell-carved cabriole legs ending in trifid feet, Pennsylvania, ca. 1770, 22 ½ x 43 ½", 5' 10" h. 16,100.00

Classical chest of drawers, carved mahogany, the rectangular top

Chests 30: Pennsylvania Dower Chest

above a single frieze drawer & three recessed long drawers below, flanked by free-standing columns w/ormulo capitals, on acanthus leaf-carved animal paw feet, attributed to Duncan Phyfe, New York, ca. 1815-20, 21 x 36 ¼", 37 ½" h. 21,850.00
(Illustration: Chests 27)

Classical chest of drawers, gilt bronze-mounted mahogany, the upper section w/molded frame & berried laurel leaf surround enclosing a swiveling rectangular mirror plate, supported by acanthus-carved columns w/pineapple finials over three short drawers, the lower section w/black marble top over a case w/four long drawers, the top drawer mounted w/fan- and garland-draped urn set between fruit-laden baskets & anthemion, the lower drawers flanked by

half-round Corinthian columns, on gadrooned ball feet w/brass casters, mid-19th century, 42 ½" w., 5' 6" h. 3,740.00
(Illustration: Chests 28)

Classical chest of drawers, mahogany, the massively proportioned case w/splash-board surmounted by a plinth over a rectangular top above three small & one large projecting drawers, over three long drawers flanked by acanthus-carved columns, on paw front & vase-form rear feet, mid-19th century, 52" w., 22 ¼" d., 5' 1 ¼" h. 950.00
(Illustration: Chests 29)

Dower chest, painted & deco-rated, the rectangular hinged top w/molded edge centering two white-painted reserves opening to a compartment fitted w/a lidded till, the dovetailed case grain-painted in red &

Chests 31: Federal Inlaid Maple "Bow-front" Chest of Drawers

Chests 32: Federal "Bow-front" Chest of Drawers

Chests 33: Federal Inlaid Mahogany "Bow-front" Chest of Drawers

Chests 34: Federal Mahogany "Bow-front" Chest

brown, the front centering a white heart w/flowering tulips & inscribed "Ann Cattrina Schweitzer 1785" flanked by two white-painted & decorated reserves, over a molded base & bracket feet, the case sides fitted w/wrought-iron handles, Pennsylvania, 48 ¼" l., 23" d., 22 ½" h. 4,830.00
(Illustration: Chests 30)

Federal "bow-front" chest of drawers, inlaid maple, the rectangular top w/a bowed front above a case w/four long graduated drawers w/oval brasses & three brass keyhole escutcheons, molded base, ogee bracket feet, Massachusetts, ca. 1790, old finish, original brasses, minor imperfections, 21 x 38", 32" h. 2,990.00
(Illustration: Chests 31)

Federal "bow-front" chest of drawers, curly maple, the oblong top w/molded edge, above four cock-beaded & line-inlaid drawers, the upper drawer w/well dividers, the shaped skirt continuing to splayed French feet, New England, ca. 1815, 19 ½ x 40 ½", 34 ½" h. 4,600.00
(Illustration: Chests 32)

Federal "bow-front" chest of drawers, inlaid mahogany, the oblong top w/line-inlaid edge above four long graduated line-inlaid cockbeaded drawers, the shaped skirt below continuing to splayed bracket feet, appears to retain original acorn-decorated brasses, New England, ca. 1810, 22 x 40½", 36½ h. 4,025.000
(Illustration: Chests 33)

Federal "bow-front" chest of drawers, inlaid mahogany & maple, the bowed top w/inlaid edges above a conforming case w/four cockbeaded graduated long drawers in

Chests 35: Federal Walnut Child's Chest of Drawers

Chests 36: Federal Bird's-Eye Maple Chest

Chests 37: Federal Cherry Inlaid Chest of Drawers

figured maple w/mahogany crossbanding over a shaped inlaid skirt continuing to tall flared feet, Boston, possibly shop of John & Thomas Seymour, ca. 1800, 41" w., 22 ⅛" d., 40" h. 10,350.00

Federal "bow-front" chest of drawers, mahogany & mahogany veneer, the rectangular top w/bowed front & out-turned biscuit corners above a conforming case w/four long drawers w/applied edge beading & turned wooden knobs flanked by reeded quarter columns, on ring- and baluster-turned feet, old finish, ca. 1810, 42 ½" w., 21 ½" d., 40" h. (feet ended out) 1,045.00

Federal "bow-front" chest of drawers, inlaid mahogany, the oblong bowed top w/outset rounded corners above two short & three long crossbanded drawers, three-quarter round columns flanking, on ring-turned feet, Massachusetts, ca. 1820, 22 x 42 ½", 42 ½" h. 1,725.00
(Illustration: Chests 34)

Federal "bow-front" chests of drawers, figured mahogany, each having an oblong top above a conformingly-shaped case fitted w/long drawers, flanked by half-round columns, on turned vase-form feet, the drawers fitted w/lion's-head brasses, school of Joseph B. Barry, Philadelphia, ca. 1825,

22⅝ x 44⅝", 41¾ h., pr. 9,200.00

Federal child's chest of drawers, child's, inlaid walnut, the rectangular top above four long graduated cockbeaded line-inlaid drawers, line-inlaid canted corners flanking the shaped skirt continuing to line-inlaid flared bracket feet, appears to retain its original brasses, Pennsylvania, ca. 1820, 9 ½ x 18 ½", 19¾" h. 6,325.00
(Illustration: Chests 35)

Federal chest of drawers, bird's-eye maple & mahogany, a low scroll-cut & arched crestrail on a rectangular splashboard w/two oval inlaid panels flanked by oval-inlaid pilasters above the rectangular top above a projecting upper section w/two pairs of small drawers flanking a deep central drawer, all w/inlaid panels, the lower case w/three inlaid long graduated drawers flanked by spiral-turned columns, molded base on reeded baluster-turned short legs, turned wooden replaced knobs, old refinish, possibly New York, ca. 1820, 19 x 43 ½", 43" h. 1,495.00
(Illustration: Chests 36)

Federal chest of drawers, inlaid cherry, the rectangular top w/line-inlaid edges above a case of four long graduated drawers w/oval brasses & brass keyhole escutcheons, scroll-cut bracket feet,

Chests 38: Federal Inlaid Mahogany Chest of Drawers

Chests 39: Federal Satinwood-Inlaid Chest of Drawers

Chests 41: Rare Federal Chest of Drawers

signed "Daniel W. Wittemore, Springfield, July 7, 1810," replaced brasses, refinished, repairs to base, 19 x 38", 38" h. 1,610.00
(Illustration: Chests 37)

Federal chest of drawers, inlaid mahogany, the rectangular top above four long graduated line-inlaid drawers, the fan-inlaid base continuing to bracket feet, mid-Atlantic states, ca. 1815, some repairs to feet, 22 x 39", 38" h. 3,450.00
(Illustration: Chests 38)

Federal chest of drawers, satinwood-inlaid figured mahogany, the rec-tangular top above four line-inlaid long drawers, the upper drawer decorated w/satinwood diamond reserves centering inlaid oak leaves, the shaped skirt continuing to sightly splayed bracket feet, labeled Micheal Allison,

New York, ca.1810, minor repairs, 22 x 44¾", 44¼" h. 10,350.00
(Illustration: Chests 39)

Chests 40: Federal Chest of Drawers with Mirror

Federal chest of drawers w/mirror, carved mahogany & bird's-eye maple inlaid, a rectangular mirror within a narrow frame w/an arched crest swiveling between reeded uprights flanked by long slender scroll-cut supports atop a row of three small drawers set back on the rectangular top w/ovolu front corners above leaf-carved & reeded front corners flanking a pair of short drawers over two long drawers, turned tapering leaf-carved & reeded legs, Boston, ca. 1810-20, old brasses, old refinish, interior inscribed "Russell H. Wright," 21 x 39", 6' 4" h. 85,000.00
(Illustration: Chests 40)

Federal chest of drawers, walnut, the rectangular top w/molded edge above stop-fluted quarter columns flanking two long drawers over a central molded fan-

Chests 42: Federal "Serpentine-front" Chest of Drawers

Chests 43: Federal Poplar Tall Chest of Drawers

Chests 44: Federal Tall Chest of Drawers

carved frieze above a stop-fluted tambour door opening to a compartment & flanked by half-engaged columns, flanked on either side by two short drawers, on a molded base on ogee bracket feet, attributed to John Shearer, Martinsburg, West Virginia, ca. 1803, refinished, 40 ½" w., 24 ½" l., 41" h. ....63,000.00 *(Illustration: Chests 41)*

Federal "serpentine-front" chest of drawers, cherry & cherry veneer, a rectangular top w/a serpentine front above a

conforming case w/a long deep drawer w/an oval inlaid panel above three long graduated drawers, all w/oval brasses & brass keyhole escutcheons, scalloped apron & slender French feet, Connecticut or New York, ca. 1800, refinished, restoration, 26 x 40", 40" h. ....2,875.00 *(Illustration: Chests 42)*

Federal tall chest of drawers, poplar, the rectangular top w/dental-carved tympanum above four long graduated molded drawers on tapering turned

feet, the case painted on the stiles & cross members w/green & yellow flower-heads, each side panel painted w/a compass in blue, black & yellow, all on a red ground, Schwaben Creek Valley, Pennsylvania, ca. 1830, 21 x 41", 4' 3" h. ....31,050.00 *(Illustration: Chests 43)*

Federal tall chest of drawers, walnut, the rectangular molded cornice projecting over a conforming case w/three short over two short graduated thumb-molded

Chests 45: Federal Tall Chest of Drawers **Chests 46: Federal Chest-on-Chest**

drawers, over four long graduated thumb-molded drawers, flanked by chamfered columns above a shaped apron on flared bracket feet, eagle embossed brasses stamped "E Pluribus Unum," Pennsylvania, ca. 1800, 47 ½" l., 23" d., 5' 9 ⅞" h. 4,025.00
(Illustration: Chests 44)

Federal tall chest of drawers, cherry, cove-molded cornice above a case w/three short drawers over three short & five long

graduated drawers w/applied cockbeading & inlaid escutcheons, the case w/chamfered corners w/lamb's tongue, over a scrolled apron on flared bracket feet, ca. 1800, refinished, old repairs to feet & cornice, replaced brasses, 44" w., 22 ½ d., 5' 11 ¼ h., ...8,250.00
(Illustration: Chests 45)

Federal chest-on-chest, inlaid cherry, two-part construction: the upper section w/molded cornice above five short & three

long line-inlaid cock-beaded drawers, fluted quarter-columns flanking; the lower section w/three cockbeaded line-inlaid long graduated drawers, fluted quarter-columns flanking, the shaped skirt continuing to flared bracket feet, Pennsylvania, ca. 1810, 21 ⅛ x 41", 6' 6 ¾" h.....9,775.00
(Illustration: Chests 46)

George III "bow-front" chest of drawers, inlaid mahogany, the cross-banded bowed top above four conforming long

Chests 47: George III "Bow-Front" Chest

Chests 48: Hepplewhite Curly Maple Chest

graduated drawers, on tall flared feet, England, ca. 1800, 20 x 36", 36" h. ....4,313.00 *(Illustration: Chests 47)*

George III chest of drawers, mahogany, the rectangular thumb-molded-

edge top above four cockbeaded long graduated drawers, on bracket feet, England, ca. 1770, 17 ¾ x 35", 29" h. 2,530.00

Hepplewhite "bow-front" chest of drawers, cherry

inlaid w/curly maple, oblong bowed top above four long cockbeaded graduated & bowed drawers, shaped skirt ending in flared feet, Pennsylvania, ca. 1820, 23 ¼ x 41", 38" h. ....7,475.00 *(Illustration: Chests 48)*

Jacobean chest of drawers, oak, two-part construction: the rectangular overhanging upper section w/carved & molded top above a single drawer w/two molded panels & applied split balusters; the lower section w/three molded panel drawers flanked by split balusters, on a molded base on ball feet, England, early 17th century, 39" w., 22" d., 39" h. ....1,540.00 *(Illustration: Chests 49)*

Mission-style (Arts & Crafts movement) bride's

Chests 49: Jacobean Chest of Drawers

Chests 50: Gustav Stickley Bride's Chest

Chests 51: Mission Chest of Drawers w/Mirror

chest, oak, the rectangular two-panel top w/wide metal hinges & strap latch above a two-panel front w/incurved edge moldings & matching end panels, wide metal corner strap mounts, short square legs continuing from stiles, original finish, Gustav Stickley, early 20th century......................13,200.00
(Illustration: Chests 50)

Mission-style (Arts & Crafts movement) chest of drawers, a large rectangular mirror w/gently arched frame swiveling between square, slightly tapering uprights joined to the base w/butterfly joints, the rectangular top overhanging a case w/a pair of small drawers over a long deep drawer over a shallower lower drawer, a wide arched apron, round wooden pulls, corner stiles form short legs on casters, designed by Harvey Ellis, original medium brown finish, some top stains, red decal mark of Gustav Stickley, Model No. 911, early 20th century, 22 x 48", 5' 7 ½" h. 3,025.00
(Illustration: Chests 51)

Mission-style (Arts & Crafts movement) tall chest of drawers, oak, a rectangular top w/a low crestrail above a tall case w/five long drawers each w/two polished copper & brass bail pulls, slightly arched skirt, square legs joined by a floor stretcher, recent medium finish, burnt-in mark of Charles Limbert Company, Grand Rapids, Michigan, Model

Chests 52: Limbert Tall Chest of Drawers

Chests 53: Early Mule Chest

No. 487 ¼, early 20th century, 20 x 36", 4' 2" h. 1,870.00
(Illustration: Chests 52)

Mule chest (box chest w/one or more drawers below a storage compartment), Chippendale country-style, pine & poplar, the rectangular top w/molded edge opening to a compartment faced w/two false long drawers, over three cockbeaded long drawers, on a molded base w/tall bracket feet, old dark finish, original brasses (two bails missing), late 18th - early 19th century, age cracks & one back foot reattached, 38 ¾ w., 19" d., 48 ¼" h. 1,595.00
(Illustration: Chests 53)

Mule chest, pine, the rectangular top w/molded edge opening to a storage compartment faced w/two false drawers over two long drawers, on cut-out feet, 19th century, 44 w., 17 ¾" d., 41 ¼" h. (replaced back foot, refinished)......................429.00

Pilgrim Century chest, carved & painted, the thumb-molded hinged rectangular top opening to a well fitted w/a lidded till, the front w/reeded frieze over three panels carved in low relief on a punch-

Chests 54: Pilgrim Century Chest

Chests 55: Pilgrim Century Chest

Chests 56: Pilgrim Century Chest-over-Drawers

decorated ground, the ends panels w/stylized tulips & leaves flanking a center panel w/a sunflower & scrolling leaves, the panels flanked by applied single split balusters on the outside stiles & double column- and urn-turned split balusters on the two central stiles, the sides applied bosses set in a molded surround, on an applied molded base on plain block feet, attributed to Peter Blin, Wethersfield, Connecticut, 1675-1725, feet pieced 5¼", 21 x 48", 23¾" h. 11,500.00
(Illustration: Chests 54)

Pilgrim Century chest, oak, the rectangular top above a case w/three molded panels, the center one w/a

geometric coffered panel & applied split balusters flanked by broken-arch-molded panels, the skirt w/two molded panels centering split appliques, the stiles continuing to form feet, Essex County, Massachusetts, 1660-1690, 21 x 45 ¼", 30 ½" h. ...63,000.00
(Illustration: Chests 55)

Pilgrim Century chest-over-drawers, carved oak & pine, the rectangular top opening to a well above a carved frieze & three carved panels, the center panel w/"S.K.," over two carved long drawers, flanked by carved stiles continuing to form rectangular feet, Connecticut, probably Hadley area, 1670-1710, old refinish, top

replaced, 41" w., 17 ½" d., 45" h. 19,550.00
(Illustration: Chests 56)

Queen Anne "block-front" chest of drawers, mahogany, the oblong top w/thumb-molded edge above a conformingly shaped case w/four blocked long graduated drawers, the molded base continuing to blocked bracket feet, Boston, Massachusetts, ca. 1760, restoration to feet & patches to top & case, 20 x 36", 31" h. 19,550.00
(Illustration: Chests 57)

Queen Anne diminutive chest of drawers, walnut, the rectangular thumb-molded top above four long graduated drawers, each

Chests 57: Queen Anne "Block-front" Chest of Drawers

Chests 58: Queen Anne Diminutive Chest of Drawers

w/incised edges, the molded base on bracket feet, appears to retain its original brasses, Pennsylvania or Middle Atlantic States, ca. 1740-60, 16 x 32", 29" h. 6,325.00
(Illustration: Chests 58)

Queen Anne tall chest of drawers, maple, the molded cornice above two short & four long drawers, on bracket feet, retains old finish, Rhode Island, 1760-80, minor repairs to drawer lips, 19¼ x 38¼", 47" h. 3,450.00
(Illustration: Chests 59)

Queen Anne chest-on-frame, maple, two-part construction: the upper section w/rectangular top w/molded edge lifting above a deep compart-

Chests 59: Rhode Island Queen Anne Tall Chest of Drawers

Chests 60: Queen Anne Chest-on-Frame

1760, 21 ½ x 42",
5' 9 ½" h. (some restoration
to bottom drawer, slight
repairs to drawer lips & two
feet) 4,887.00

**Queen Anne chest on
frame,** figured walnut,
two-part construction, the
upper section w/molded
cornice above five short
& four long graduated
molded drawers, the frame
below w/shaped skirt
continuing to angular
cabriole legs ending in
trifid feet, Pennsylvania,
ca. 1790, 23 ½ x 43 ½,
6' 1" h. 8,050.00
(Illustration: Chests 61)

ment, the case w/two false
over two working long
drawers; the base
w/scalloped skirt on short
cabriole legs ending in pad
feet, New England, 18th
century, old refinish,
replaced brasses, 36" w.,
18" d., 50 ½" h. 6,900.00
(Illustration: Chests 60)

**Queen Anne flat-top chest-
on-frame**, walnut, two-part
construction: the upper
section w/molded cornice
above three short drawers
over two drawers over
three long drawers, all
w/thumb molding; the lower
section w/mid-molding
above a long drawer, the
scalloped skirt continuing to
cabriole legs ending in trifid
feet, Pennsylvania, ca.

Chests 61: Queen Anne Chest-on-Frame

Chests 62: Pine Victorian Chest

Chests 63: Aesthetic Chest with Mirror

Regency "bow-front" chest-on-frame, carved mahogany, two-part construction: the upper section w/arched molded cornice above a bowed case w/two short & three long graduated drawers, flanked by palmetto-carved capitals above reeded columns; the lower section w/reeded mid-molding above three long graduated drawers w/a reeded skirt, flanked by spiral-carved columns, on slightly tapered palmetto-carved front legs ending in brass paw front feet & block rear feet, England early 19th century, 46 ¾" w., 23" d., 6' 11" h. 6,050.00

Shaker tall chest of drawers, pine, the molded cornice above five long graduated molded drawers, the molded base continuing to bracket feet, Harvard, Massachusetts, ca. 1840, 20 ⅛ x 42", 5' h. 2,300.00

Victorian country-style chest of drawers, pine, the rectangular top w/thumb-molded edge above two short drawers over two long drawers, solid sides, on ball feet, England, ca. 1850, 33" w., 19" d., 30" h.............................412.00
(Illustration: Chests 62)

Victorian chest of drawers w/mirror, Aesthetic Movement substyle, maple, the tall superstructure w/a pedimented cornice above a pierced arcaded row of short spindles above chevron-carved bands across the top & sides flanking the tall rectangular mirror, outset lower sides w/spindle-galleried candle shelves above baluster-turned supports above the rectangular white marble top over a case w/three long graduated incised drawers w/teardrop pulls, plinth base on casters, late 19th century, 22 ½ x 50 ¼", 7' h. 1,725.00
(Illustration: Chests 63)

Victorian "lockside" tall chest of drawers, Aesthetic Movement substyle, walnut, the galleried rectangular top w/scroll-carved pediment & molded edge over one projecting long drawer above

Chests 64: Victorian "Lockside" Chest of Drawers

Chests 65: Victorian Renaissance Revival Rosewood Chest of Drawers

five bead-carved long drawers flanked by reeded stiles headed w/foliate carving, paneled sides, on a molded base on block feet on casters, late 19th century, 35 ½" w., 20" d., 5' 4" h. 1,430.00
(Illustration: Chests 64)

Victorian chest of drawers,
Renaissance Revival substyle, rosewood, broken arch pediment w/three urn-shaped finials above a swag-carved frieze over a rectangular mirror flanked by carved square columns & scrolled supports, the lower section w/marble top over four carved long graduated drawers flanked by fluted columns, the case sides w/towel bars on bun feet, ca. 1860 ....1,485.00
(Illustration: Chests 65)

Victorian chest of drawers,
Renaissance Revival substyle, walnut, the superstructure w/pediment cresting in a shell w/flanking wheat sheaves, scrolls, volutes & applied burl walnut veneer panels above an arched rectangular mirror plate flanked by reeded drop-finial candle shelves, the lower section w/rounded-corner rectangular white marble top above a conforming case w/three molded long graduated drawers w/carved oval band panels & carved fruit pulls over one base drawer, on stepped disk feet, 47" w., 22 ¼" d., 8' 3 ½" h. 1,320.00
(Illustration: Chests 66)

Victorian "serpentine-front" chest of drawers, Rococo substyle, rosewood, the superstructure w/an arched tall

Chests 68: William & Mary Blanket Chest

Chests 69: English William & Mary Chest

Chests 66: Renaissance Revival Walnut Chest of Drawers

Chests 67: Belter Chest of Drawers

mirror plate within a conforming
frame topped by a crest carved w/a
cartouche flanked by cherubs &
scrolls & swiveling between tall scroll-
carved supports, the base w/a
serpentine top above a conforming
case of four long graduated drawers
adorned w/foliate & scroll carving,
flanked by columns, on a serpentine
plinth base, attributed to John Henry
Belter, New York, ca. 1850,
48" w., 24" d., 7' 6" h. 18,700.00
(Illustration: Chests 67)

William & Mary blanket chest,
tiger stripe maple, rectangular top
w/molded cornice edge lifting
above a well w/two false drawer
fronts above two long working
drawers all w/brass teardrop pulls,
wide molded base on turnip-turned
feet, some original brasses,
refinished, minor imperfections,
Rhode Island, early 18th century,
18 x 37", 38 ¾" h............................. 4,600.00
(Illustration: Chests 68)

William & Mary chest of drawers,
walnut & marquetry, the rectangular
top w/central floral-spray oval
panel & similar spandrels, the
case w/two short over three long
graduated paneled drawers, the
sides w/flower-filled vase panels,
on molded base on later bun feet,
England, late 17th century, 37" w.,
24" d., 36 ½" h. 23,000.00
(Illustration: Chests 69)

William & Mary chest of drawers,
oyster-veneered walnut, rectangular top
inlaid w/concentric designs above a
case w/two short drawers over three
long graduated drawers similarly inlaid,
on later bracket feet, w/fruitwood
banding, England, late 17th c., 22 x 37",
34" h..10,350.00

Chests 70: William IV Chiffonier

William IV chiffonier, black & gold
japanning, the superstructure
w/scrolled crest & scrolled shelf
supports above a rounded-corner
rectangular top over a frieze
drawer & cupboard door w/round
pleated silk panel flanked by
tapering turned columns on
turned feet, England, second
quarter 19th century, restorations
to decoration, 30" w., 16" d.",
4' 5" h. 2,990.00
(Illustration: Chests 70)

Cupboards

Corner cupboard,
Chippendale bonnet-top, painted off-white, two-part construction: the upper section w/swan's-neck crest centering an urn-form finial, the arched glazed mullioned door below opening to a green-painted shelved interior; the lower section w/ double-paneled door opening to shelves, on ogee bracket feet, probably Pennsylvania or Middle Atlantic states, approximately 1 ½" of feet replaced, ca. 1785, 24 ½ x 44 ¼", 7' 5 ¼" h. 6,325.00
(Illustration: Cupboards 1)

Corner cupboard,
Chippendale, walnut, two-part construction: the upper section w/molded cornice above a pair of paneled cupboard doors opening to two shelves over an arched open pie shelf; the lower section w/mid-molding above a pair of paneled cupboard doors opening to a single shelf, over a base molding, Chester County, Pennsylvania, ca. 1770, 55" w., 28 ¼" d., 6' 9 ¼" h. 3,680.00
(Illustration: Cupboards 2)

Corner cupboard,
Chippendale country-style, painted green, the molded cornice above a tall paneled cupboard door w/wrought-iron butterfly hinges opening to a compartment fitted w/three scalloped shelves over an

Cupboards 1: Chippendale Bonnet-Top Corner Cupboard

Cupboards 2: Chippendale Walnut Corner Cupboard

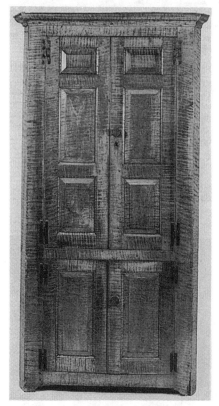

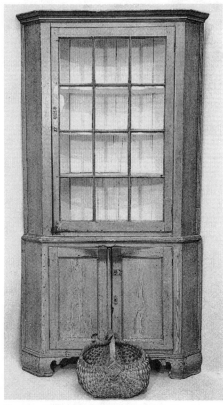

Cupboards 3: Chippendale Tiger Maple Corner Cupboard

Cupboards 4: Chippendale Pine Corner Cupboard

Cupboards 5: Chippendale Grain-Painted Corner Cupboard

applied mid-molding, above a paneled cupboard door w/wrought-iron butterfly hinges opening to a single shelf, on a molded base, Pennsylvania, ca. 1760, 28 ¾" w., 15 ¾" d., 6' ¾" h. 8,050.00

Corner cupboard,
Chippendale country-style, tiger stripe maple, one-piece construction, an ogee molded cornice above a pair of tall triple raised-panel cupboard doors w/shorter panels above & below long central panel, a pair of raised panel lower doors, doors opening to

turkey-breast shelves, fitted w/H-hinges, on short bracket feet, last half 18th century, 20 x 41", 6' 9" h. 14,300.00
(Illustration: Cupboards 3)

Corner cupboard,
Chippendale country-style, pine, the molded cornice above a cupboard door w/two fielded panels & a beaded, molded surround opening to shaped shelves, above a mid-molding over a cupboard door w/fielded panel & cock-beaded surround above a molded base, New England, last half 18th century, old

refinish, 42" w., 22" d., 6' 11" h..........................2,530.00
(Illustration: Cupboards 4)

Corner cupboard,
Chippendale country-style, barrel-back type, painted poplar or cherry, two-part construction: the upper section w/molded cornice above a single 12-pane glazed door opening to three scalloped shelves in a perimeter-molded case; the lower section w/mid-molding above a pair of paneled cupboard doors, on a molded base & ogee bracket feet, the lower section also w/applied

**Cupboards 7:
Chippendale Hanging
Corner Cupboard**

**Cupboards 6: Decorated
Chippendale Corner Cupboard**

perimeter molding, old yellow grained repaint over old red w/white interiors, late 18th - early 19th century, wear & damage to feet, one glass cracked, pieced repair to molding, 45 ½" w., 6' 11 ½" h. 4,950.00
(Illustration: Cupboards 5)

Corner cupboard, Chippendale country-style, painted pine, two-part construction: the upper section w/molded cornice & dentil-molded frieze above two arched, glazed mullioned doors opening to butterfly shelves & surrounded by an applied

molded keystone arch continuing to molded square columns; the lower section w/mid-molding above two paneled doors flanked by square molded columns on a molded plinth base, old cream & salmon repaint, late 18th century, some edge & molding damage, hinges & hardware replaced, two panes in one door broken, 60" w., 8' 5" h. 2,970.00
(Illustration: Cupboards 6)

Corner cupboard, hanging-type, Chippendale country-style, painted brown, the shaped pediment above a

molded cornice over a raised panel cupboard door w/wrought-iron rat-tail hinges & wrought-iron escutcheon opening to a single shelf, above a thumb-molded drawer & applied frontal base molding, the entire surface painted dark brown, Pennsylvania, 1760-1800, 26" w., 16 ½" d., 41 ¼" h. 4,025.00
(Illustration: Cupboards 7)

Corner cupboard, Federal country-style, painted walnut, one-piece construction, a molded cornice over a pair of doors in beaded frames, each w/a small panel over a long panel, over a mid-molding above a pair of paneled cupboard doors, on cut-out feet, cleaned down to traces of old blue paint, Ohio, early 19th century, 55 ½" w., 7' h. (repairs to one bottom door & small sections of cornice, hardware removed) 1,760.00

Corner cupboard, Federal country-style, burl graining, two-part construction: the upper section w/a wide ogee cornice above a pair of 8-pane glazed arched cupboard doors flanking a central band of almond-glazed panes opening to a white-painted interior w/three shelves, one w/spoon slots, the doors flanked by small quarter columns; the lower section w/a mid-molding above a pair of raised roundels w/wooden knobs flanking a pair of shaped drawers w/wooden knobs above a

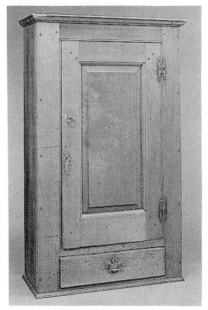

Cupboards 11: Chippendale Hanging Cupboard

Cupboards 10: Chippendale Hanging Cupboard

Cupboards 9: Federal Architectural Corner Cupboard

Cupboards 8: Federal Decorated Corner Cupboard

Cupboards 12: Country Chippendale Hanging Cupboard

pair of paneled cupboard doors, scalloped apron & bracket feet, overall fine black burl graining, western Pennsylvania, early 19th century, one drawer repaired, cornice 57 ¾ x 61 ¾", 7'½" h. 7,150.00
(Illustration: Cupboards 8)

Corner cupboard, Federal country-style, painted poplar, one-piece construction, molded cornice over a pair of tall paneled doors over two paneled doors in the bottom section w/cockbeaded frame, perimeter moldings on case, on simple cut-out feet, old worn cream-colored repaint, 19th century, 47" w., 7' 1" h. (one piece of end cornice molding replaced) 3,465.00

Corner cupboard, Federal country-style, painted pine, architectural one-piece construction, the molded fluted cornice above a pair of arched, glazed & mullioned doors opening to a painted shelved interior, two paneled doors below opening to a shelf, molded square columns flanking, ca. 1780, 21 x 55", 8' 1" h. 2,587.00
(Illustration: Cupboards 9)

Hanging cupboard, early American country-style, pine, a rectangular top overhanging a coved molding over a rectangular raised panel door w/strap hinges, scroll-cut lower ends flanking a narrow set-back shelf, New England, 18th century, old refinish, minor imperfections, 18 ½ x 25", 35¾" h. 4,025.00
(Illustration: Cupboards 10)

Hanging cupboard, Chippendale, walnut, the molded cornice above a rectangular paneled cupboard door w/wrought-iron H-hinges opening to two shelves, over a thumb-molded drawer above a base molding, Pennsylvania, ca. 1770, 24 ¼" w., 9 ¼" d., 40 ¼" h. 3,220.00
(Illustration: Cupboards 11)

Hanging cupboard, Chippendale country-style, red-painted pine, the rectangular molded cornice above a dovetailed case w/chamfered corners over a cockbeaded rectangular two-panel cupboard door opening to three shelves, above an applied base molding, the entire surface painted dark red, probably Pennsylvania, 1780-1800, 36" w., 14⅓" d., 41¼" h. 4,830.00
(Illustration: Cupboards 12)

Linen press, Chippendale, mahogany, two-part construction: the upper section w/molded & dentil-carved cornice above paneled doors opening to a yellow-painted shelved interior; the lower section w/four long graduated cock-beaded drawers, on

Cupboards 13: Chippendale Linen Press

Cupboards 14: Georgian Linen Press

bracket feet, labeled by Matthew Egerton, New Brunswick, New Jersey, ca. 1790, some repairs to feet & slightly reduced, 21 x 48 ¼", 6' 8 ¼" h...14,950.00
(Illustration: Cupboards 13)

Linen press, Georgian, mahogany, the rectangular top w/a narrow cornice above a pair of tall paneled cupboard doors above a mid-molding over a pair of small drawers over two long drawers, molded base, shaped bracket feet, England, ca. 1780,

22 x 48", 7' h.................4,400.00
(Illustration: Cupboards 14)

Linen press, Victorian country-style, pine, the rectangular upper section w/projecting cornice above two tall cupboard doors, the lower section w/two short drawers over two long drawers, on a plinth base, England, 19th century, 50" w., 19" d., 7' 6" h. 990.00
(Illustration: Cupboards 15)

Pewter cupboard, early American country-style,

pine, rectangular top above three graduated open shelves all framed by edge molding above the slightly stepped-out lower section w/a large raised-panel cupboard door w/exposed hinged & wooden thumb latch, lower case framed by molding, flat base, New England, late 18th century, old refinish, imperfections, 22¾ x 46¾", 5' 10½" h. 2,070.00
(Illustration: Cupboards 16)

Cupboards 15: Pine Linen Press

Cupboards 16: Early Pewter Cupboard

Pewter cupboard, poplar, one-piece construction, the rectangular top w/cove-molded cornice over three open shelves w/plate rails w/beaded edges above a stepped-out base w/single small drawer flanked by paneled cupboard doors, above a shaped apron & square post feet, old worn patina w/traces of reddish brown on sides, early 19th century, age cracks, wear & edge damage, one door hinge an old surface-mounted replacement, 48" w., 19 ¼" d., 6' 3" h. 7,370.00
(Illustration: Cupboards 17)

Pewter cupboard, painted pine, one-piece construction, the top w/molded cornice over three molded-edge open shelves w/plate bars, above a projecting lower section w/two short

Cupboards 17: Poplar Pewter Cupboard

Cupboards 20: Painted Poplar Pie Safe

Cupboards 19: Walnut Pie Safe

Cupboards 18: Painted Pine Pewter Cupboard

drawers over a pair of paneled cupboard doors, on a molded base w/bracket feet, red repaint, attributed to Hudson River Valley, 18th century, repairs to feet & back feet replaced, edge repairs to top & ends of cornice replaced, 55" w., 22" d., 7' 3" h. ....10,175.00 *(Illustration: Cupboards 18)*

Pie safe, poplar w/blue repaint, rectangular top above a pair of cupboard doors, each w/three tin panels punched in a circle & star design, above a single long drawer over two

paneled doors over a scalloped apron, sides each w/three similarly punched tin panels, square feet, back signed "L.A. Cars, Buffalo, W.Va.," 41 ¼" w., 17 ¼" d. 506.00

Pie safe, walnut, rectangular top w/wide cove-molded cornice over a single door w/five punched tin panels w/scalloped starbursts & corner crescents, simple cut-out feet, 19th century, 37 ¼" w., 17 ¾" d., 6' 4 ½" h. ....2,860.00 *(Illustration: Cupboards 19)*

Pie safe, painted poplar, simple board cornice above a pair of doors each w/three punched tin panels w/a center diamond & corner circles over a long drawer over two paneled cupboard doors, solid board sides, high cut-out feet, old black paint, 19th century, 43 ½" w., 16 ¼" d., 7' ½" h. ....990.00 *(Illustration: Cupboards 20)*

Step-back wall cupboard, Chippendale country-style, walnut, two-part construction: the rectangular upper section w/molded cornice above two glazed cupboard doors w/wrought-iron rat-tail hinges opening to an interior fitted w/two shelves above an open pie shelf; the lower section w/reeded edge above two short thumb-molded drawers over two paneled cupboard doors opening to a single shelf above a molded base, on bracket feet, Pennsylvania, ca. 1790, 50 ¼" w., 19 ⅜" d., 7' 1 ½" h. 14,950.00

Step-back wall cupboard, country-style, painted pine, two-part construction: the

upper section w/a rectangular top w/projecting molded cornice above a pair of 3-pane glazed doors w/scalloped top rails; the projecting lower section w/two overhanging drawers over two paneled cupboard doors w/applied molding, on a molded base w/scrolled skirt on bracket feet w/a tapered central foot, original red sponge graining on case & curly maple graining on doors & drawers, Ohio, mid-19th century, minor paint wear & edge damage, 56 ½" w., 23" d., 7' 6 ¼" h. 3,080.00
(Illustration: Cupboards 21)

Step-back wall cupboard, country-style, walnut, two-piece construction: the upper section w/a rectangular top w/flaring cornice above a pair of 8-pane glazed cupboard doors opening to shelves; the projecting lower section w/three short drawers above a pair of raised panel cupboard doors, 19th century, 45" w., 21" d., 6' 11 ¼" h. (bottom edge molding of top & brasses replaced) 1,650.00

Step-back wall cupboard, Federal country-style, maple, two-part construction: the upper section w/a

Cupboards 21: Decorated Step-back Wall Cupboard

Cupboards 22: Federal Step-back Wall Cupboard

Cupboards 23: Victorian Walnut Step-back Wall Cupboard

Cupboards 24: Victorian Cherry Step-back Wall Cupboard

rectangular top w/wide cove-molded cornice projecting above two 9-pane glazed cupboard doors opening to three shelves above an open pie shelf; the stepped-out lower section w/five short drawers above a pair of paneled cupboard doors over a scalloped apron & simple cut-out feet, old cherry-colored finish, interior w/old flaking white paint, original brasses, Pennsylvania, 19th century, minor edge damage & age cracks, 67 ½" w., 18" d., 6' 11 ¼" h. 16,500.00
(Illustration: Cupboards 22)

Step-back wall cupboard, Victorian country-style, walnut, two-part construction: the upper section w/a rectangular top over a deep ogee cornice over a pair of 3-pane glazed cupboard doors opening to two shelves; the stepped-out lower section w/a pair of drawers w/scroll-carved pulls above a pair of paneled cupboard doors, on double -ball turned feet, mid-19th century, 18 x 43", 6' 10" h. 3,500.00
(Illustration: Cupboards 23)

Step-back wall cupboard, Victorian country-style,

cherry, molded cornice above two pairs of cabinet doors w/raised panels & chamfered stiles & rails, the projecting lower section w/two pairs of similarly paneled doors, on a molded plinth base, one end of cornice & one end of base molding replaced, refinished, 75" w., 25 ¼" d., 7' 2" h. 1,980.00
(Illustration: Cupboards 24)

Storage cupboard over drawers, Shaker, butternut, two-part construction: the upper section w/thumb-molded cornice above paneled cupboard

doors opening to shelves, above two short drawers; the lower section w/four graduated long drawers w/inlaid bone diamond-shape keyhole escutcheons, on bracket feet, Harvard, Massachusetts, ca. 1840, 16 x 36 ⅛", 5' 6 ½" h.....................26,450.00
(Illustration: Cupboards 25)

Wall cupboard, Early American country style, painted pine, the molded cornice above a top section w/butterfly-hinged door opening to a single-shelved interior over a mid-molding above a similar lower section w/molded bottom edge, on turned turnip feet, red paint, New England, 18th century, restorations, 41 ¼" w., 20" d., 5' 3 ½" h........................6,900.00
(Illustration: Cupboards 26)

Wall cupboard, French Provincial, carved fruitwood, two-part construction: both sections w/canted corners, the upper section w/ogee-molded cornice above two raised panel cupboard doors; the lower section w/two short molded-edge frieze drawers above a pair of raised panel cupboard doors, on ogee block feet, 52" w., 24 ½" d., 7' 2" h. 1,210.00
(Illustration: Cupboards 27)

Wall cupboard, Queen Anne, painted pine, one-piece construction, a rectangular top w/a deep molded & dentil-carved cornice above a large four-panel cupboard door

Cupboards 25: Shaker Cupboard over Drawers

Cupboards 27: French Provincial Wall Cupboard

Cupboards 26: Early American Wall Cupboard

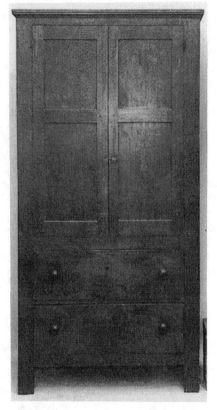

Cupboards 28: Queen Anne Wall Cupboard

Cupboards 29: Shaker Wall Cupboard

opening to shelves above a mid-molding over a double-paneled cupboard door, molded base on tapering bracket feet, brown-painted yellow, one side unfinished, inscription on unfinished side, Virginia, late 18th century, 24 ½ x 31", 5' 9 ½" h. 4,025.00
(Illustration: Cupboards 28)

Wall cupboard, Shaker, walnut, one-piece construction, molded cornice above a pair of two-panel cupboard doors over two long drawers, one-board ends, on cut-out feet, original dark finish &

wooden pulls, attributed to Union Village, Ohio, ca. 1815, crack in stile of one door near hinge, 46" w., 20 ¾" d., 7' 5" h. 3,740.00
(Illustration: Cupboards 29)

Wall cupboard, walnut, rectangular top w/narrow applied molding above a wide paneled door set in a beaded frame, interior w/old reddish orange paint on the shelves, center shelf w/concave cut-out, applied base molding, mellow re-finishing, Pennsylvania, probably early 19th c., 13½ x 23", 26½" h. 2,090.00

Wall cupboard, walnut, two-piece construction: the upper section w/a rectangular top w/a flat flaring cornice above a pair of tall 8-pane glazed cupboard doors opening to three shelves; the lower section w/a slightly stepped-out top above three small drawers above a pair of tall raised panel cupboard doors, slender bracket feet, old mellow refinishing, found in northwestern Pennsylvania, 19th century, cornice 17 x 45", 6' 11 ¼" h. (replaced brasses)........1,650.00

Welsh cupboard, George III style, oak, two-part construction: the upper section w/a stepped widely flaring cornice above a pair of tall double-paneled cupboard doors w/H-hinges; the lower section w/a mid-molding above a row of three drawers over a pair of long drawers, each w/pierced brass butterfly pulls, short straight legs, repairs & some replacements, England, late 18th - early 19th century, 24 x 63", 6' 8" h........................5,175.00
(Illustration: Cupboards 30)

Welsh cupboard, Queen Anne-Style, oak, the long narrow rectangular top w/stepped-out ends above a conforming open superstructure w/three short shelves in the end sections & four long shelves in the center section, the lower section w/a wide rectangular top w/molded edges above a case w/three deep drawers each w/two 'butterfly' brasses & keyhole escutcheons, a scroll-cut apron & cabriole front legs ending in snake feet, England, late 19th century, 20 x 71", 5' 10" h.....................1,265.00
(Illustration: Cupboards 31)

**Cupboards 30:
English Welsh
Cupboard**

**Cupboards 31:
Queen Anne-Style
Welsh Cupboard**

Desks

Arts & Crafts desk, oak, rectangular top overhanging a case w/a pair of long drawers over a pair of scroll-carved short drawers flanking the kneehole opening w/acanthus leaf-carved brackets, the legs & frame carved w/bands of acanthus leaves, the lower legs flared & reeded, foliate-cast metal drawer pulls, in the manner of Charles Rohlfs, ca. 1910, 29 ¾ X 48", 30 ½" h.. $2,070.00 *(Illustration: Desks 1)*

Child's desk, country-style, painted brown, the rectangular slanted hinged top opening to a compartment, on tapering cylindrical-turned legs, early 19th century, 19 ½" w., 13 ½" d., 29 ½" h. .... 460.00 *(Illustration: Desks 2)*

**Desks 2:
Early Child's Desk**

Chippendale country-style slant-top schoolmaster's desk, walnut, the rectangular top w/molded edge lifting above an interior fitted w/five pigeonholes over three short drawers, the case w/applied molding, on block- and baluster-turned legs joined by a block- and baluster-turned H-stretcher, Pennsylvania, ca. 1770, 36" w., 24" d., 35 ½ " h. .... 5,175.00 *(Illustration: Desks 3)*

Chippendale slant-front desk, birch, a narrow rectangular top above a rectangular slant lid opening to an interior fitted w/small drawers & pigeonholes above a case w/four long graduated drawers w/oval brasses, a molded base on simple cut-out bracket feet,

**Desks 1:
Arts & Crafts Desk**

**Desks 3:
Chippendale Schoolmaster's Desk**

Desks 4: Massachusetts Chippendale Desk

Desks 5: Chippendale Curly Maple Desk

probably Massachusetts, ca. 1780, original brasses, old refinish, 21 x 42", 43" h. 2,760.00
(Illustration: Desks 4)

Chippendale slant-front desk, curly maple, the rectangular hinged, molded lid opening to a stepped interior fitted w/pigeonholes & blocked drawers centering a blocked prospect door opening to two blocked doors, above a case w/four long graduated drawers, molded base, bracket feet, Massachusetts, ca. 1760, repairs to hinge areas of lid, 20 ½ x 35 ¾", 41 ½" h. 11,500.00
(Illustration: Desks 5)

Chippendale slant-front desk, walnut, the thumb-molded hinged lid

opening to an interior fitted with valanced pigeonholes & small drawers, centering a prospect section w/door above four long graduated

molded drawers, on ogee bracket feet, Southern U.S., ca. 1780, feet replaced, 18 ½ x 34 ¼", 39 ¾" 3,737.00
(Illustration: Desks 6)

**Desks 6:
Southern Chippendale Walnut Desk**

Chippendale slant-front desk, walnut, the molded slant lid opening to interior fitted w/central prospect door enclosing five shaped drawers flanked by molded document drawers centered by two pigeonholes above two short drawers, flanked by four short stepped drawers, the case fitted w/four thumb-molded long graduated drawers flanked by fluted quarter columns, on a molded base on ogee bracket feet w/spur returns, Philadelphia, ca. 1770, 36 ¾" w., 21 ⅝" d., 42" h. 9,775.00

Classical country-style clerk's desk, refinished poplar, two-part construction: the upper section w/a rectangular top above a paneled fall-front opening to an interior fitted w/pigeonholes & single

Desks 7: Plantation Desk

drawer; the stepped-out lower section w/single long drawer on turned & paneled legs, 38 ½" w., 23 ½" d., 4' 4 ¾" h. 715.00

Classical country-style "plantation" desk, walnut, two-part construction: the upper section w/molded cornice above two glazed 3-pane cupboard doors opening to shelves, above two short drawers over a fall-front drawer opening to an interior fitted w/pigeonholes; the projecting lower section w/hinged, thumb-molded lid opening to a well, raised on turned & paneled legs, damage to one end of cornice, early 19th century, 44" w., 40 ¾" d., 7' 1" h. 1,430.00
(Illustration: Desks 7)

Federal drop-front desk, inlaid curly maple, the rectangular top above two

Desks 8: Federal Drop-Front Desk

Desks 9: Federal Lady's Desk

**Desks 10: Federal
Inlaid Mahogany
Lady's Desk**

short drawers & a pull-out
writing section w/hinged
drop-front panel opening to
an interior fitted w/small
drawers over valanced
pigeonholes centering a
hinged prospect door
inlaid at the center
w/Masonic emblems,
opening to a pull-out box
w/two valanced
pigeonholes, all above
three long graduated
drawers w/oval brasses,
the shaped skirt continuing
to French feet, all drawer
edges inlaid w/light & dark
checkered line decoration,
attributed to William
Cummings, East Dorset,
Bennington County,

Vermont, ca. 1815,
21 1/8 x 44 1/4", 4'1" h....11,500.00
(Illustration: Desks 8)

**Federal lady's writing
desk**, carved mahogany,
the rectangular top opening
to three drawers above a
baize-lined hinged writing
surface, opening to a well,
two cockbeaded drawers
below flanked by leaf- and
punchwork-decorated dies,
on reeded tapering legs
ending in peg feet, Salem,
Massachusetts, ca. 1815,
18 3/4 X 29 3/4", 34"h.......5,175.00
(Illustration: Desks 9)

Federal lady's desk,
inlaid mahogany, two-part

construction: the upper
section w/a rectangular
top above a row of three
narrow line-inlaid drawers
above a pair of folding
tambour doors flanking a
central inlaid door; the
lower section w/a fold-out
writing surface above
slides & three long
graduated line-inlaid
drawers w/oval pulls
& keyhole escutcheons,
on square tapering
line-inlaid legs, Massa-
chusetts, ca. 1790,
original pulls, old refinish,
inscription on interior
drawer, 22 x 42",
4' 5 1/4" h. 4,600.00
(Illustration: Desks 10)

Desks 13: George III Pedestal Desk

George I slant-front desk, walnut, the rectangular banded lid over a banded slant lid enclosing a fitted interior above four banded long graduated drawers, on a molded base w/bracket feet, England, early 18th century, 36" w., 20" d., 40" h. ....4,600.00 *(Illustration: Desks 11)*

George III *bonheur du jour* (writing desk), mahogany, the line-inlaid superstructure w/arched crest above two open shelves flanked by scrolled sides, over a base w/scroll-inlaid fold-over top & leather-lined interior above a line-inlaid frieze drawer mounted w/enamel pulls, on square tapering legs w/cuffs, joined by an incurved platform stretcher, England, late 18th century, 26 ¾" w., 17" d., 49" h. ....5,750.00 *(Illustration: Desks 12)*

George III pedestal desk, mahogany, the rectangular reeded leather-lined top above four working & two false drawers on each side, one end w/three drawers, the other w/kneehole flanked by two drawers, on four paneled pedestals opening to shelves or folio divides, plinth bases, England, ca. 1800, 8' 2" w., 54 ¼" d., 30" h. ....7,475.00 *(Illustration: Desks 13)*

Desks 11: George I Slant-Front Desk

Desks 12: George III *Bonheur du Jour*

Desks 14: Small Mission Desk

Desks 15: Mission Drop-Front Desk

George III writing table, mahogany, the banded rectangular top w/reeded edge above a central short drawer over an arched kneehole, flanked by two pairs of short drawers, on square tapering legs on casters, England, late 18th century, 49" w., 27" d., 31" h. 6,670.00

Mission-style (Arts & Crafts movement) slant-front desk, oak, rectangular top w/slant front opening to an interior fitted w/pigeonholes over a single short drawer, on square legs joined by a rear stretcher & medial shelf, each side w/two vertical slats, ca. 1910, 31" w................................275.00
(Illustration: Desks 14)

Mission-style (Arts & Crafts movement) drop-front desk, oak, a low

crestrail on the narrow rectangular top above the wide slant-front opening to a fitted interior above a pair of short drawers over a

Desks 16: Stickley Desk

long drawer each w/original copper hardware, tall square legs joined by a galleried medial shelf, original medium brown finish, branded Gustav Stickley mark, Model No. 731, early 20th century, 15 X 30", 42" h. 1,760.00
(Illustration: Desks 15)

Mission-style (Arts & Crafts movement) drop-front desk, oak, galleried rectangular top above a drop-front w/five vertical chamfered slat panel & hammered copper strap hinges opening to a fitted compartment, over two closed shelves, paneled sides, through-tenon construction, on square feet, later overcoat removed from original finish, red decal mark of Gustav Stickley, Model No. 518, 26" w., 10" d., 4' 3 ¼" h. 4,675.00
(Illustration: Desks 16)

Desks 17: Mission Oak Lifetime Desk

Mission-style (Arts & Crafts movement) desk, oak, the flat rectangular top above two short drawers & a short cupboard door over a flat medial shelf & side stretchers, on square legs, through-tenon construction, hammered copper hardware, decal & paper label of Lifetime Furniture Company, Grand Rapids, Michigan, Model No. 927, ca. 1910, edge roughness, 54" w., 30" d., 29 ½" h. 1,265.00
(Illustration: Desks 17)

Queen Anne slant-front desk-on-frame, red-painted maple, two-part construction: the upper section w/hinged molded lid opening to an interior fitted w/valanced pigeonholes over drawers, over a single molded long drawer; the lower section w/shaped skirt on circular tapering legs ending in pad feet, Connecticut, ca. 1750, 32 ¾" w., 17" d.,

41 ½" h. 25,875.00
(Illustration: Desks 18)

Regency "Carlton House" desk, satinwood, the curved superstructure w/pierced brass gallery

fitted w/an arrangement of stepped drawers above a hinged ratcheted leather-lined writing surface over w/three frieze drawers, on turned tapering legs on casters, locks & casters

Desks 18: Queen Anne Desk

Desks 19: Regency Carlton House Desk

Desks 20: Victorian "Davenport" Desk

patent-marked, one drawer w/paper armorial label, England, early 19th century, 25 x 41¾", 38" h. 90,500.00
(Illustration: Desks 19)

Turn of the century "rolltop" desk, oak, the S-scroll rolltop opens to an interior fitted w/small drawers & cubbyholes above the rectangular top over a center drawer over the kneehole flanked on one side by a fold-down door to a pull-out typewriter shelf over two small drawers & on the other side by a stack of four drawers,

metal tag marked "The Gunn Desk - Grand Rapids," 35" w., 60" l. ...4,950.00

Victorian "Davenport" desk, carved rosewood, a small three-quarter gallery above the slant-top hinged lid above a case w/paneled sides, one side a hinged door opening to fitted drawers, scroll supports at the front raised on flaring cushion feet on casters, the lid opening to four satin-wood drawers & a secret button to open the side pen drawer, England, ca. 1850, 24 x 25 ½", 36 h. 3,080.00
(Illustration: Desks 20)

Victorian lady's writing desk, Aesthetic Movement substyle, ebonized cherry, the super-structure w/a diamond lattice gallery w/outcurved corner posts above a rectangular shelf supported on shaped pierced brackets flanking a pair of pierced square lattice panels flanking a band of Oriental leafage above three thin drawers over a writing surface above pierced end brackets flanking a case w/three long drawers each w/a central rectangular panel w/Oriental leafage & diamond-form metal pulls,

pierced lattice brackets at top corners of outcurved square legs, late 19th century, 20 ¼ x 30", 4' h.................................1,150.00
(Illustration: Desks 21)

Victorian "patent" desk, Renaissance Revival substyle, Wooton Standard Grade, walnut, the carved architectural gallery above a hinged drop frieze drawer over hinged side compartments w/burl panels, fitted w/pigeonholes, document shelves & original green letter boxes, flanking an interior fitted w/pigeonholes, document shelves, short drawers w/bird's-eye maple veneers & hinged drop-front writing surface, on molded trestle legs on casters, ca. 1875, minor

Desks 21: Aesthetic Movement Desk

gallery elements missing, 42 ½" w., 31 ½" d., 5' 6 ½" h....................11,000.00
(Illustration: Desks 22)

Victorian pedestal partner's desk, mahogany, the rectangular molded leather-lined top above a long frieze drawer flanked by short drawers on each side, each pedestal w/cupboard door flanked by open shelves on squared supports, on plinths, England, mid-19th century, 67" w., 42 ½" d., 31 ½" h....................21,850.00
(Illustration: Desks 23)

Victorian writing table, mahogany, the green gilt-tooled rectangular leather top w/thumb-molded edge over a gadroon-molded

Desks 22: Wooton "Patent" Desk

Desks 23: English Victorian Partner's Desk

frieze w/a pair of cock-beaded short drawers, raised on baluster-turned legs, England, late 19th century, 46" w., 29 ½" h...990.00

William & Mary kneehole desk, veneered walnut, the rectangular quarter-veneered top w/molded edge above a long frieze drawer, the arched kneehole headed by a slender drawer & forward-sliding compartment, flanked by three drawers to each side, on bun feet, England, ca. 1690, 20 ½ x 35 ½", 32" h.....11,500.00 (Illustration: Desks 24)

Desks 24: William & Mary Kneehole Desk

Dining Room Suites

Art Deco: dining table, four armchairs & four side chairs; nickled-bronze mounted *ebené de Macassar*, the table w/a rectangular top w/draw-ends veneered in *ebené de Macassar* & inlaid w/a pattern of squares in amboyna, raised on a trestle base, the ends conjoined by five nickled-bronze rods; the chairs w/frames in *ebené de Macassar*, upholstered in the original textured green horsehair, two armchairs w/curved arms & two armchairs w/square arms, Leon Jallot, France, ca. 1928, table 42 x 108", 29 ¾" h., the set..........24,150.00
(Illustration: Dining 1, table & five chairs)

Dining 1: Art Deco Dining Set

Art Moderne: dining table, six side chairs & a large side cabinet; burled walnut, the table w/a rectangular top w/incurvate corners above a conforming black-painted apron raised on shaped heavy pedestal supports; the chairs each w/lobed arched back above an over-upholstered seat raised on tapering black-painted legs; the side cabinet w/center drop-front fitted section above a pair of cabinet doors flanked by large side cabinets, England, ca. 1935, table 38 x 74", 30 ¼" h., the set................................2,300.00
(Illustration: Dining 2, table & four chairs)

Jacobean Revival: dining table, two armchairs & four side chairs; walnut & walnut veneer, the rectangular table w/cut corners & deep molded apron raised on six heavy reeded ball-and urn-turned legs joined by shaped stretchers; the chairs w/arched crests above a vase-form splat, on ball- and urn-turned reeded front legs, ca. 1920s, 7 pcs. 1,995.00
(Illustration: Dining 3, two chairs)

Queen Anne Revival: oval dining table, one armchair & five side chairs; oak, the oval top opening to accept leaves, raised on simple cabriole

Dining 2: Art Moderne Dining Set

legs ending in pad feet on casters, each chair w/a simple arched crestrail above a vase-form splat, on simple cabriole legs ending in pad feet, legs joined by an H-stretcher, ca. 1920s, table w/three leaves, table 45 x 58", chairs each 40 ½" h., 7 pcs............................4,350.00
(Illustration: Dining 4, table & two chairs)

Victorian Baroque style: round dining table & 15 matching chairs; carved oak, the table w/a deep ornately carved apron featuring scroll bands & ribbon-tied leafy vines, raised on four large winged caryatid paw-foot legs centered by a heavy baluster-turned pedestal, late 19th century, the set..............................38,000.00
(Illustration: Dining 5, table)

Dining 3: Jacobean Revival Dining Chairs

Dining 4: Queen Anne Revival Dining Set

Dining 5: Ornate Victorian Baroque Dining Table

Dry Sinks

Painted pine, rectangular top w/zinc-lined shallow well w/molded edge above paneled ends & a pair of doors w/wide applied molding over a scalloped base & cut-out feet, old yellow graining over earlier dark finish, 19th century, 42 ¾" w., 22 ½" d., 31 ¾" h. 1,430.00

Painted pine, rectangular top well above a pair of paneled cupboard doors w/cast-iron latches, simple cut-out feet, old worn grey repaint over brown graining & other colors, 19th century, 17 ¾ x 48", 36" h. 1,045.00
(Illustration: Dry Sinks 1)

Pine, a low rounded crestrail above the rectangular top w/a rectangular well at one end & a rectangular work surface at the other above a single drawer w/wooden knob, a pair of paneled

Dry Sinks 1: Painted Pine Dry Sink

doors below w/molding trim, flat base, refinished, back-boards incomplete, crest replaced, 19th century, 17 ¾ x 49", 32 ¼" h. 990.00
(Illustration: Dry Sinks 2)

Poplar, rectangular w/galleried top w/shelf over well

w/rectangular work surface at one end above small drawer, the base w/two paneled cupboard doors raised on cut-out feet, 19th century, refinished, old replaced iron thumb latch, 48 ¼" w., 20 ¾" d., 4' 6" h. 1,375.00
(Illustration: Dry Sinks 3)

Walnut, rectangular w/scalloped crest above a gallery shelf & projecting zinc-lined well over two paneled doors w/applied molding over a scalloped base & cut-out feet, 19th century, repair to zinc lining & age cracks, 49" w., 29½" d., 45" h...1,540.00

Dry Sinks 2: Refinished Pine Dry Sink

Dry Sinks 3: Early Poplar Dry Sink

Garden & Lawn

All pieces are cast iron unless otherwise noted.

Armchairs, rustic-style, stoneware, the crestrail, splat & stiles in the form of branches, the seat & base in the form of a tree trunk, stamped "Whitehill, 1879," 19" w., 15" d., 34" h., pr. 4,840.00
(Illustration: Garden 1, one of two)

Love seat, the shaped back w/foliage & berry-filled arches continuing to griffin arms over an incurved scrollwork seat, on cabriole legs, layers of white re-paint, 19th century, 44" w. (old welded repairs).........990.00

Love seat, Rococo style, the back w/floral serpentine crest above interlacing arches over a pierced &

Garden 3: Gothic Garden Settee

scroll-decorated seat flanked by pierced floral-decorated downscrolled arms, raised on scrolling cabriole legs, painted

black, labeled "James W. Carr," Richmond, Virginia, 19th century, 44" w., 35 ½" h. 825.00
(Illustration: Garden 2)

Garden 1: Stoneware Garden Chair

Garden 2: Rococo Garden Love Seat

Garden 4: Fern Garden Set

Settee, Gothic Revival substyle, the back decorated w/armorial crest & pierced trefoil & quatrefoil designs flanked by pierced downswept arms above an iron rod seat, raised on downswept legs, signed "Wood and Perot, Makers, Phila.," mid-19th century, 59 ½" l. ....3,080.00 *(Illustration: Garden 3)*

Settee, the back composed of loosely entwined slender branches w/some leaves & acorns, loosly entwined branch design in seat & curved twig arms & legs, 47½" l., 32" h. (pitted, rust) 1,155.00

Settee, a scalloped crestrail above six tall panels of pierced leafy branches, curved scroll-pierced seat, back curves to form arms w/the arm supports & front legs formed as a winged griffin on a single paw foot, layers of white repaint, 19th century, 44" l. (old weld repairs) 990.00

Settee, the arched back centered by an urn w/flowers finial flanked by scrolling leafy pierced vines & scrolls above a central Minerva head mask above the pierced back composed of overlapping oval rings, scrolled arms, the seat pierced w/a three-wheel design, leafy scroll front legs, 45" l., 41½" h. (some damage, cracks, welded repairs, rebolted, pitted, finial incomplete) 1,760.00

Settee & two armchairs, each w/openwork fern back curving around to similar arms above a strapwork-scrolled seat, on shaped fern legs, white paint, New York, 1870-1900, 3 pcs. ....4,025.00 *(Illustration: Garden 4)*

Side chairs, shield-shaped back w/polychrome floral decoration within a scrolling pierced surround above a trapezoidal seat w/serpentine seatrail, on scrolling legs joined by a scrolling X-form stretcher, painted white, 19th century, 37 ¼" h., pr. 460.00

Hall Racks & Trees

Hall rack, Art Deco, wrought iron, the side panels decorated w/overlapping bands of leaves & clusters of berries, a large rectangular mirror in the center w/three coat hooks at the top, the lower section w/an umbrella holder w/a pierced leafy scroll front design, in the manner of Edgar Brandt, France, ca. 1930, 9 ¾ x 31 ¼", 6' 2" h. 10,350.00
(Illustration: Hall Racks 1)

Hall rack, Art Deco, wrought iron & marble, a flat crestrail above w/panel of leafy scrolls flanked by zigzag bands continuing down to flank the long octagonal mirror, raised on scrolls & bars centered by a raised square marble shelf flanked by two umbrella holders at the sides, in the manner of Raymond Subes, France, ca. 1925, 13 x 35 ½", 6' 6 ½" h. 6,325.00
(Illustration: Hall Racks 2)

Hall rack, turn of the century, oak, a shell & scroll-carved crest atop a wide flat diamond-form frame holding a beveled mirror & mounted w/three metal coat hooks, on a tall vase-form back above a fixed rectangular seat flanked by flat arms on scrolled arm supports, a deep apron & flat shaped front legs, ca. 1900, 26 ½" w., 6' 5 ½" h. 1,295.00
(Illustration: Hall Racks 3)

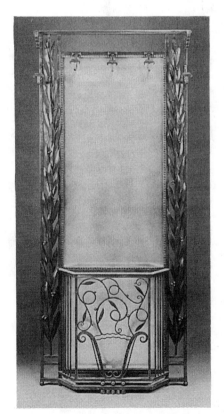

Hall racks 1: French Art Deco Hall Rack

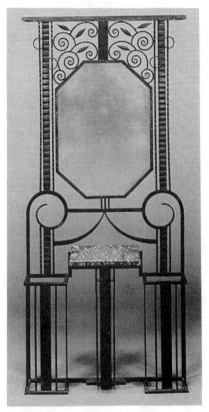

Hall racks 2: Art Deco Hall Rack with Marble

Hall racks 3: Turn of the Century Hall Rack

Hall rack, turn of the
century, oak, the tall back
w/a scroll-carved crest
above a wide C-scroll band
above two coat hooks over
an oval mirror flanked by
further hooks & scroll
bands, carved scrolls
above the rectangular
lift-seat flanked by open
arms, deep apron
w/carved scrolls,
short scroll front legs,
ca. 1900.....1,400.00 to 1,600.00
(Illustration: Hall Racks 4)

Hall tree, turn of the century,
oak, the tall slender turned
post w/a knob- and
baluster-turned finial above
six bobbin-turned pegs,
raised on four widely
canted baluster-turned legs
w/knob feet, 5' 5" h. 215.00
(Illustration: Hall Racks 5)

Hall racks 4:
Ornate Oak Hall Rack

Hall racks 5:
Turn of the Century
Hall Tree

Highboys

Chippendale "bonnet-top" highboy, walnut, two-part construction: the upper section w/molded scrolled pediment terminating in floral rosettes & surmounted by three flame-carved & urn finials, above two short drawers centering a shell- and foliate-carved central drawer, over two short & three long graduated drawers, all thumb-molded & flanked by fluted quarter columns; the lower section w/mid-molding above one long & two short drawers, all thumb-molded & flanked by fluted quarter columns, over a shaped skirt w/central carved shell, on shell-carved cabriole legs ending in claw-and-ball feet, Philadelphia, ca. 1770, 44" w., 23 ½" d., 7' 10" h. 107,000.00
(Illustration: Highboys 1)

Chippendale "bonnet-top" highboy, carved mahogany, two-part construction: the upper section w/swan's-neck crest ending in carved floral rosettes & centering a pierced scroll- and leaf-

Highboys 1: Rare Chippendale Highboy

Highboys 2: Fine Chippendale Highboy

carved cartouche, three-part flame- and urn-form finials flanking on fluted plinths, the scrollboard elaborately carved w/projecting pierced shell flanked by scroll-carved grasses long & ruffles above five short & three long graduated drawers, thumb-molded, flanked by fluted quarter-columns; the lower section w/frieze drawer above three short drawers, the central one carved w/shell & grasses, the skirt shell- and C-scroll carved, continuing to acanthus-carved cabriole legs, ending in claw-and-ball feet on brass casters, Philadelphia, ca. 1775, cartouche & some applied leaf carving replaced, minor patches to moldings & drawer lips, appears to retain original brasses, 23 ¼ x 44 ½", 8' 1" h. ....151,000.00 *(Illustration: Highboys 2)*

Chippendale highboy base, carved walnut, the rectangular top w/molded underedge & canted corners above a thumb-molded frieze drawer & three small drawers, the center one w/carved shell & flanking applied grasses, fluted canted corners, the scalloped skirt continuing to acanthus- and flower-carved cabriole legs ending in claw-and-ball feet, Philadelphia area, ca. 1755, 23 ¼ x 45 ½", 37 ¼" h. 6,900.00

Queen Anne "bonnet-top" highboy, curly maple, two-part construction: the upper

Highboys 3: New England Queen Anne Highboy

section w/molded swan's-neck pediment w/three urn- and flame-form finials, above a case w/three small drawers, the central drawer carved w/circular shell motif above five long graduated drawers; the lower section w/a long drawer above three short drawers, the central drawer carved w/circular shell motif, above a shaped apron on cabriole legs ending in pad feet, New England, ca. 1760, small patch to one drawer, 41 ¼" w., 7' 11 ½" h......11,500.00 *(Illustration: Highboys 3)*

Queen Anne "flat-top" highboy, curly maple, two-

Highboys 4: Queen Anne Curly Maple Highboy

part construction: the upper section w/molded cornice above two short & three long molded graduated drawers; the lower section w/one long & three short molded drawers, the shaped skirt w/acorn pendants continuing to cabriole legs ending in slipper feet, Rhode Island, ca. 1760, 20 x 35", 5' 7" h. ....10,350.00 *(Illustration: Highboys 4)*

Queen Anne "flat-top" highboy, carved cherry, two-part construction: the upper section w/molded cornice above three short drawers, the center drawer fan-carved, four long

Highboys 5: Queen Anne Cherry Highboy

graduated molded drawers below; the lower section w/one long & three short molded drawers, the center drawer fan-carved, the shaped skirt w/acorn pendants continuing to cabriole legs ending in pad feet, retains old, probably original finish, Connecticut, lacks one leg return, ca. 1760, 19 x 37 ½",
6' ¼" h. 36,800.00
(Illustration: Highboys 5)

Queen Anne "flat-top" highboy, cherry, two-part construction: the upper section w/flat rectangular top w/molded edge above a fan-carved central short drawer flanked by a pair of short drawers over four long molded-edge graduated drawers; the lower section w/one long

Highboys 6: Connecticut Queen Anne Highboy

drawer over three short drawers, the central drawer fan-carved, above a scrolled apron on cabriole legs ending in pad feet, Connecticut, refinished, two knee returns on legs replaced, base has old changes in drawer configuration, drawer construction varies, 37 ½ x 19 ¼",
6' 3 ¾" h. 9,900.00
(Illustration: Highboys 6)

William & Mary "flat-top" highboy, walnut & walnut burl veneer, two-part construction: the upper section w/a rectangular top w/a narrow cornice above a pair of small drawers over three long graduated drawers, each w/florette & pendant pulls; the lower

Highboy 7: William & Mary Highboy

section w/a mid-molding & molded edge above two deep drawers flanking a shallow center drawer above a triple-arch apron, on six trumpet-form turned legs joined by flat shaped stretchers above 'turnip' feet, New England, early 18th century, refinished, restored, 20 x 35 ½",
5' h. 5,175.00
(Illustration: Highboys 7)

Lowboys

Chippendale lowboy, carved mahogany, the rectangular molded top above a skirt fitted w/a cockbeaded long drawer over two smaller drawers flanking a central section carved w/scrolls & a pierced circular & geometric device, the shaped apron continuing to shell-carved cabriole legs

**Lowboys 1:
Chippendale Mahogany Lowboy**

Lowboys 2: Chippendale Curly Maple Lowboy

ending in claw-and-ball feet, 18th century, 22 x 35 ½", 28 ½" h. 1,725.00
(Illustration: Lowboys 1)

Chippendale lowboy, curly maple, rectangular thumb-molded top above two long graduated drawers, the lower drawer faced to simulate three working drawers w/the center panel fan-carved, the shaped skirt below continuing to frontal angular cabriole legs ending in claw-and-ball feet, the rear legs ending in raised pad feet, appears to retain original brasses, Massachusetts, ca. 1770, 21 ½ x 42 ⅛", 33 ¼" h. 13,800.00
(Illustration: Lowboys 2)

Queen Anne lowboy, burl-veneered walnut, the rectangular top w/molded edge centering a canvas-lined writing surface within

a crossbanded surround, the case below w/one long over three short drawers, the deeply scalloped shaped cockbeaded skirt continuing to cabriole legs ending in pad feet, retains

a deep reddish brown old patina, old repair to front left foot, probably retains original brasses, Boston, Massachusetts, 1730-60, 22 x 34 ¼", 30 ¾" h. 9,775.00
(Illustration: Lowboys 3)

Lowboys 3: Queen Anne Lowboy

LOVE SEATS, SOFAS & SETTEES

Chaise longue, Egyptian Revival style, painted wood, the high backrest carved as a large eagle w/the curved wings forming arms, the frame painted w/Egyptian designs, on six square legs w/flaring feet, upholstered seat, ca. 1925, 72" l. 8,050.00
(Illustration: Love Seats 1)

Chaise longue, Victorian Eastlake substyle, the stepped crestrail machine-cut w/bars & sunbursts w/line-incised decoration above the low upholstered back & angled back support & long seat, line-incised back support rail & seatrail, on short flat curved legs on casters, red velvet upholstery, ca. 1880, 72" l. 1,295.00
(Illustration: Love Seats 2)

Daybed, Art Deco, gilt & black lacquer, the fluted corner posts w/foliate carved & gilded tops enclosing upholstered sides, the apron carved w/swags & gilded, uphol-stered in grey silk, France, ca. 1925, 29 x 70", 28½" h. 4,025.00

Daybed, French Empire, walnut, the upholstered head- and footboards w/round rails capped

Love Seats 2: Victorian Eastlake Chaise Longue

Love Seats 1: Egyptian Revival Chaise Longue

w/brass plates on bronze-mounted half-column uprights, on square legs ending in blocked feet, w/down-curved siderails, France, early 19th century, 71" l., " 40½" d., 41½" h. 1,540.00
(Illustration: Love Seats 3)

Daybed, Mission-style (Arts & Crafts Movement), oak, the low ends w/four wide slats between tapering posts w/through-tenons, original spring seat w/new leather, original medium brown finish, Handicraft mark of L. & J.G. Stickley, Model No. 292, 30 x 80", 28" h. 2,970.00
(Illustration: Love Seats 4)

Daybed, William & Mary, carved beech, the adjustable back w/carved molded arched crest terminating in scrolled volutes over pierced carved foliage & molded rails centering caning, flanked by block- and ring-turned stiles over a long caned seat, on block- and baluster-turned legs w/turned feet, joined by pierced, molded & foliate-carved arched side stretchers & ball- and ring-turned medial stretchers, England, 1690-1710, 60" d., 21½" w., 40¾" h. 4,025.00
(Illustration: Love Seats 5)

Love seats, George III-Style, walnut, a narrow crestrail centered by a scroll carving above a pierced fretwork back & arms, caned seat, raised on Marlboro legs joined by

Love Seats 3: French Empire Daybed

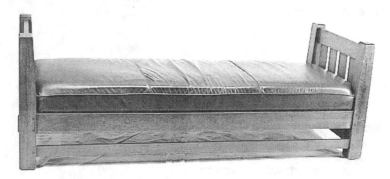
Love Seats 4: Mission Daybed

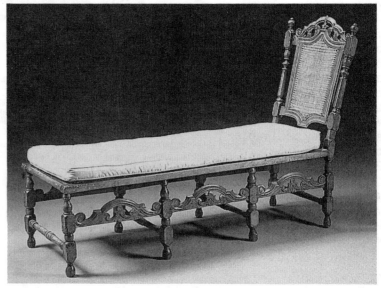
Love Seats 5: William & Mary Daybed

**Love Seats 6:
George III-Style
Love Seat**

**Love Seats 7:
Louis XV-Style
Love Seat**

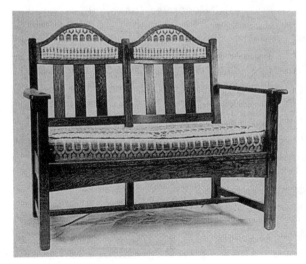

**Love Seats 8:
Mission Oak
Love Seat**

box stretchers, England, late 19th century, 40" l., 34" h., pr. (Illustration: one of two)..........................2,530.00
(Illustration: Love Seats 6)

Love seat, Louis XV-Style, carved giltwood, the gently arched back & downswept arms ornately pierce-carved w/leafy garlands & scrolls, ribbon bows & shells, a tufted upholstered seat, on scroll-carved cabriole legs, late 19th - early 20th century, 44" l. 1,840.00
(Illustration: Love Seats 7)

Love seat, Mission-style (Arts & Crafts Movement), oak, 'ebonoak' line, the double chair back w/two arched crestrails above upholstered panels over three-slat backs & three flat stiles above flat shaped arms over the upholstered cushion seat, arched seatrail & five legs joined by stretchers, the posts inlaid w/dark wood bands, original color, new finish, branded mark of the Charles Limbert Furniture Company, Grand Rapids, Michigan, 24½ x 24½", 37" h. 1,870.00
(Illustration: Love Seats 8)

Love seat, wicker, the high back w/a pair of large oval frames w/ornate caned panels above pairs of scrolls flanking square frames w/spindles, the tall knobbed stiles above low scroll arms over the woven seat, wide apron w/turned bobbins & scrolls, wrapped & knobbed legs, Wakefield

Love Seats 9: Ornate Wicker Love Seat

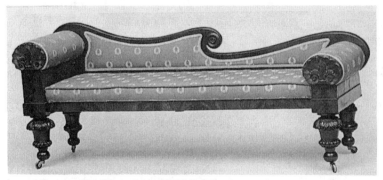

Love Seats 10: Classical Meridienne

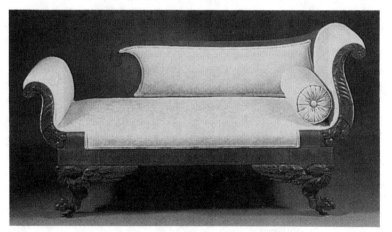

Love Seats 11: Classical Recamier with Eagles

Rattan Company, ca. 1895, damages, 19¾ x 42", 44½"............................2,070.00
(Illustration: Love Seats 9)

Meridienne, Classical, mahogany, the scrolled crestrail above an up-holstered back & two cylindrical upholstered arms of different height w/shell-carved ends on plinth supports, recessed upholstered seat, on tapering acanthus-carved & gadrooned turned feet on casters, Philadelphia, ca. 1825, 72" l., 20" d., 18" h. 2,860.00
(Illustration: Love Seats 10)

Recamier, Classical, mahogany, the serpentine ends of different height & carved w/rosettes & cornucopia, the sloping back terminating in a carved rosette, on legs carved w/an eagle w/ebony eye, ending in hairy paw feet, New York, 1810-1820, 6½" l., 29½" h. 9,200.00
(Illustration: Love Seats 11)

Recamier, Classical, carved mahogany, the sloping serpentine upholstered back above a scrolled arm at one end w/leaves & a blossom carved on the arm support, straight rounded seatrail above winged paw feet on casters, Boston, ca. 1830, no upholstery, 26 x 80", 34½" h........................1,100.00
(Illustration: Love Seats 12)

Recamier, Classical, bird's-eye maple inlaid & carved mahogany, the acanthus-

Love Seats 13: Classical Recamier with Bird's-Eye Maple

carved & shaped crest flanked by out-scrolled arms, the arm supports in the form of carved cornucopia & acanthus leaves, the figured seatrail w/rectangular bird's-eye maple-inlaid panels, on acanthus-, swag- and feather-carved scroll legs, Boston, Massachusetts, ca. 1820, 84" l. ....5,463.00 *(Illustration: Love Seats 13)*

Recamier, Victorian Rococo substyle, rosewood, the arched crestrail w/carved floral spray above an upholstered back & serpentine seat w/carved seatrail, foliate-carved arm supports, on demi-cabriole legs, England, mid-19th century, 80" l..................2,200.00 *(Illustration: Love Seats 14)*

Settee, Biedermeier, satinwood, the serpentine crestrail over an upholstered back flanked by outswept scrolling upholstered arms enclosing a loose cushion seat, over a rounded seatrail flanked by

Love Seats 12: American Classical Recamier

Love Seats 14: Victorian Recamier

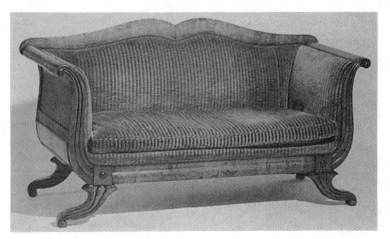

Love Seats 15: Biedermeier Settee

rosette-centered square panels, raised on stylized cornucopia downswept legs terminating in rosettes, Continental, ca. 1830, 76 ½" l., 28 ½" d., 40" h. 5,500.00
(Illustration: Love Seats 15)

Settee, Classical, tiger stripe & bird's-eye maple, the high arched crestrail w/flat crest over a caned back flanked by block- and baluster-turned stiles flanking the out-scrolled

Love Seats 17: Ornate Classical Settee

panel ends above the caned seat, serpentine deep seatrail, turned legs on casters, cane damaged, Mid-Atlantic States, early 19th century, 55 ¾" l., 34 ½" h. 3,450.00
(Illustration: Love Seats 16)

Settee, Classical, carved mahogany, the flat crestrail flanked by acanthus-carved scrolls above out-scrolled arms w/high feathery leaf-carved S-scroll supports flanking the upholstered

Love Seats 16: Classical Maple Settee

seat, flat seatrail raised on large carved dolphins above animal paw feet, some veneer patches, New England, ca. 1835, 57" l. 1,840.00
(Illustration: Love Seats 17)

Settee, Edwardian, Classical-Style, satinwood-inlaid mahogany, the inlaid straight crestrail over a caned back curving down to inward scrolled inlaid armrests terminating in rosettes, the seatrail w/paneled inlay, on downswept legs on brass casters, England, late 19th century, 56" l.........1,210.00 *(Illustration: Love Seats 18)*

Settee, Federal country-style, painted white, the shaped crest above a half-spindle back & down-scrolled arms over a plank seat, on splayed cylindrical legs joined by stretchers, Pennsylvania, 19th century, 75 ¼" l.,

Love Seats 18: Edwardian Classical Settee

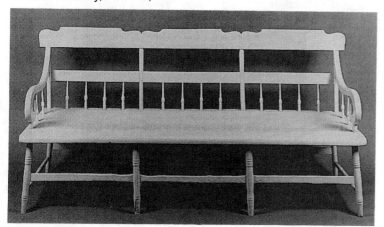

Love Seats 19: Federal Country-Style Settee

23" d., 35 ½" h. ....518.00 *(Illustration: Love Seats 19)*

Settee, Federal country-style, painted & decorated, three-section back w/wide scrolled crestrail above medial rails, scrolled arms on turned supports, shaped plank seat, on turned legs w/flat front & rear stretchers, turned side stretchers, original brown flame graining w/green & white striping & gilt foliage accented w/black, repair

to one arm at stile, Pennsylvania, ca. 1840, 76" w...........................1,870.00 *(Illustration: Love Seats 20)*

Settee, Federal, carved mahogany, a slightly stepped crestrail on the upholstered back flanked by downswept upholstered arms w/reeded baluster-turned arm supports, upholstered seat w/flat seatrail w/tack trim, on reeded turned & tapering

Love Seats 20: Federal Decorated Settee

front legs, Pennsylvania,
ca. 1805, old refinish,
striped silk upholstery,
17 ½ x 66", 35 ½" h. 6,900.00
(Illustration: Love Seats 21)

Settee, George I double
chair-back type, walnut,
the serpentine cresting
above two solid vase-form
backsplats & drop-in seat,
flanked by out-scrolled
open arms, raised on
cabriole legs ending in pad
feet, England, early 18th
century, 54" l................8,625.00
(Illustration: Love Seats 22)

Settee, George III, painted
& parcel-gilt, the arched
crestrail above a padded
backrest & serpentine
loose-cushioned seat
flanked by out-scrolled
arms, raised on stop-fluted
legs, England, last quarter
18th century, 69" l........4,600.00
(Illustration: Love Seats 23)

Settee, Mission-style (Arts
& Crafts movement), oak,
the flat crestrail above
broad splats, straight
rectangular arm supports
above an upholstered seat,
plain deep seatrail, on
square legs, original
medium-dark finish &
leather upholstery,
unsigned Lifetime
Furniture Company, Grand
Rapids, Michigan, Model
No. 688 C\v, ca. 1910, 72"
w., 32¼" d., 34" h. 2,990.00
(Illustration: Love Seats 24)

Settee, wicker, the wide
oblong tightly woven back
w/an openwork band of
alternating green & white
painted beadwork above a
lacy panel of scrolls, out-

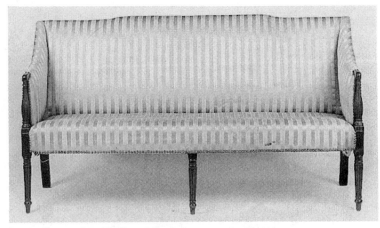

Love Seats 21: Federal Settee

Love Seats 22: George I Settee

Love Seats 23: George III Settee

Love Seats 24: Mission Oak Settee

Love Seats 25: Painted Wicker Settee

Love Seats 26: Windsor "Rod-Back" Settee

scrolled arms above the oval seat, deep tightly woven gently arched seatrail on short bead-trimmed legs, painted white, late 19th - early 20th century, 49½" l., 39½" h...........................690.00
(Illustration: Love Seats 25)

Settee, Windsor "rod-back," maple, ash & pine, the bamboo-turned crestrail above a 'bird-cage' style back w/slender bamboo-turned spindles, bamboo-turned end arms, long shaped plank seat on five pairs of turned legs joined by bamboo-turned stretchers, refinished, imperfections, stamped "J. Burden, Phila.," Phila-delphia, early 19th century, 77" l., 34½" h...............3,740.00
(Illustration: Love Seats 26)

Settee, Windsor, a long flat board crestrail above numerous plain spindles spaced by slender baluster-turned spindles, angled downswept arms above plain spindles & canted baluster-turned arm supports, thick slightly shaped plank seat, on ten bamboo-turned legs joined by bamboo-turned stretchers, old greenish grey repaint, late 18th - early 19th c., 88" l., 35" h. 20,900.00

Settle, country-style, painted pine, curved back w/beaded panels & partly projecting hood, shaped one-board ends, above a curved seat over a conforming apron w/two short drawers, sides

Love Seats 27: Early Country Settle

Love Seats 28: New England High Back Settle

continuing to form feet, black repaint, repair to one drawer & base molding added, ca. 1800, 61" w., 17" d., 5' h. 1,870.00
(Illustration: Love Seats 27)

Settle, early American country-style, the high back w/tongue & groove boards flanked by tapering ends w/low arms, plank seat, old refinish, minor imperfections, New England, 1750-1800, 15½ x 64½", 5' 1½" h. 1,840.00
(Illustration: Love Seats 28)

Sofa, Chippendale "camelback," mahogany, the serpentine upholstered back above out-scrolled downcurving arms above an over-upholstered seat on square molded legs joined by stretchers, 91" l. 11,500.00
(Illustration: Love Seats 29)

Sofa, Classical, mahogany, the scrolled brass string-inlaid flat crestrail sweeping down to upholstered anthemion-carved cylindrical armrests enclosing an upholstered back & seat above a molded & gadrooned seatrail, raised on foliate-carved scrolled legs ending in paw feet on casters, Philadelphia, ca. 1830, 77" l., 30" d., 33" h. 1,300.00
(Illustration: Love Seats 30)

Sofa, Classical, carved mahogany, the flat rounded crestrail flanked by foliate-carved scrolls terminating in rosettes above a padded upholstered back & circular

padded arms carved w/coiled dolphins surrounding small foliate-carved round drawers, over an upholstered seat & molded seatrail, on fruit- and foliate-carved legs w/paw feet, New York, 1820-1830, 76¾" l., 33½" h. 6,670.00
(Illustration: Love Seats 31)

Sofa, Federal, carved mahogany, the flat tri-paneled crestrail carved w/panels of thunderbolts tied w/bow-knots centering a panel of drapery swags similarly tied, the uphol-stered back & seat below flanked by incurved closed arms & arm supports w/turned & reeded spindle at the front above the bowed seatrail, on reeded tapering legs ending in brass casters, in the New York City manner, early 19th century, 73" l.........4,025.00
(Illustration: Love Seats 32)

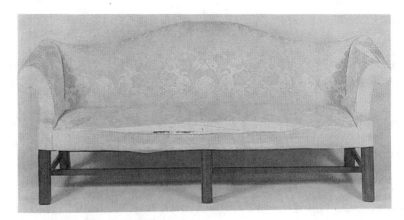

Love Seats 29: Chippendale Sofa

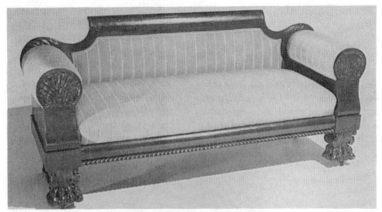

Love Seats 30: Classical Philadelphia Sofa

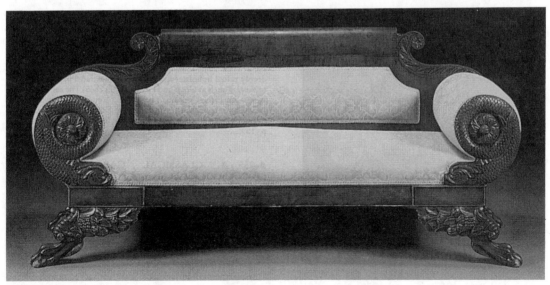

Love Seats 31: New York Classical Sofa

Sofa, Federal, mahogany, upholstered back over downswept arms & carved handgrips on reeded baluster-turned supports above a loose cushion seat, on reeded tapering front & plain back legs, early 19th century, front feet ended out, 78" l. ....2,530.00 *(Illustration: Love Seats 33)*

Sofa, Federal, cherry, the gently arched upholstered back flanked by outswept open arms w/slats over a loose cushion seat, flat seatrail on square tapering legs, 20th century moire silk upholstery, New York, ca. 1810, refinished, 82" l., 30" h. ....3,575.00 *(Illustration: Love Seats 34)*

Sofa, Victorian Rococo substyle, mahogany, the triple-arch back w/scroll- and floral-carved crests, the upholstered arms

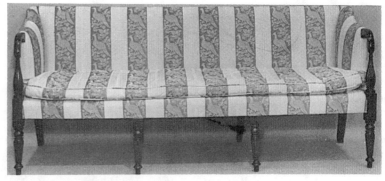

Love Seats 33: Federal Mahogany Sofa

Love Seats 34: Federal Cherry Sofa

Love Seats 32: Federal New York Style Sofa

Love Seats 35: Victorian Rococo Sofa

w/carved & scrolled arm supports above a carved undulating seatrail, on demi-cabriole front legs on casters, mid-19th century, 66" l., 18" d., 40" h........1,320.00
(Illustration: Love Seats 35)

Sofa, Victorian Rococo substyle, laminated rosewood, the serpentine crestrail centered w/a raised section w/a center carved cartouche flanked by beaded bands over pierced scroll carving, further pierced scroll carving at the ends, the high tufted upholstered back flanked by half-arms w/serpentine arm supports continuing to demi-cabriole legs & a cartouche-carved serpentine seatrail, Stanton Hall patt., J. & J. Meeks, New York, New York, ca. 1850s.......................5,225.00
(Illustration: Love Seats 36)

Sofa, willow wicker, the long low flat back w/a tightly-woven wide band above an open lattice lower section flanked by broad flat arms, flat tightly woven seatrail over an open lattice band, pale moss green finish, w/canvas-covered cushions, attributed to Gustav Stickley, Model No. 72, ca. 1909, 30 x 80", 33 ¼" h. 11,500.00

Wagon seat, country-style, painted wood, the double chair back w/horizontal crest above a horizontal slat flanked by cylindrical stiles over a rush seat, on turned legs joined by double box stretchers, the entire surface painted black w/gilt highlights, Pennsyl-vania, ca. 1830, 34" h...1,725.00
(Illustration: Love Seats 37)

Love Seats 36: Stanton Hall Sofa

Love Seats 37: Early Wagon Seat

MIRRORS

Art Deco wall mirror, wrought iron, a simple narrow oval frame w/overlapping pairs of leaves at the center of each side, inner dentil beading enclosing a beveled mirror, France, ca. 1925, unsigned, 23 x 32" 4,600.00

Art Nouveau wall mirror, carved wood, the rectangular mirror plate w/gently arched top & bottom within a molded surround carved at the top w/stylized poppy blossoms & leafage, unsigned, France, ca. 1900, 25 ¾ x 34 ¾" 1,725.00

Baroque wall mirror, giltwood, the rectangular beveled mirror plate within an elaborate foliate & C-scrolled border w/acanthus leaves & flowerheads, Italy, first quarter 18th century, 55½" w., 5' 10" h. 10,925.00
(Illustration: Mirrors 1)

Biedermeier mirror on stand, table model, walnut, the oval beveled plate within a banded frame, the support headed by down-curved swans' heads, above a breakfront plinth base fitted w/three short drawers, raised on down-scrolled legs, Continental, 19th century, 23" w.,

14½" d., 35" h. 770.00
(Illustration: Mirrors 2)

Chippendale wall mirror, mahogany, the arched & scrolled pediment flanked by scrolled ears above a rectangular mirror plate within a molded frame over a shaped pendant w/scroll-ed ears, probably Pennsyl-vania, crack to left top ear, ca. 1770, 20" h. 748.00
(Illustration: Mirrors 3)

Chippendale wall mirror, mahogany, the scrolled pediment centering a pierced gilt eagle above a rectangular mirror plate w/gilt molding over a

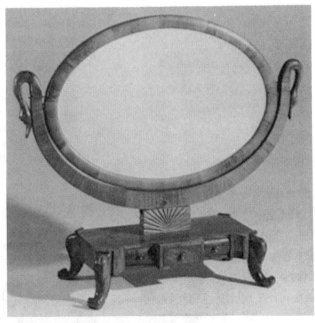

Mirrors 2: Biedermeier Table Mirror

Mirrors 1: Italian Baroque Wall Mirror

Mirrors 3: Chippendale Mahogany Wall Mirror

scrolled pendant, ca. 1760, 33¼" h..........................1,093.00

Mirrors 5: Ornate Federal "Girandole" Mirror

Chippendale wall mirror, mahogany, the shaped crest centering a pierced, carved gilt shell, above a rectangular mirror plate w/carved gilt surround over a shaped pendant, American or English, ca. 1760, 15" w., 44½" h. ...5,520.00
(Illustration: Mirrors 4)

Federal "girandole" wall mirror, giltwood, two-light, surmounted by a spread-winged eagle finial suspending a ball & chain from its beak, the circular convex mirror plate below w/a spherule-mounted ebonized surround, two scrolled candlearms below hung w/prisms, above a shaped scroll pendant, first half 19th century, 21¾" w., 42" h. 7,475.00
(Illustration: Mirrors 5)

Federal "girandole" wall mirror, giltwood, two-light, surmounted by an eagle on a rocky plinth flanked by carved rosettes & acanthus leaves above a circular molded frame w/gilt spherules enclosing a convex mirror plate w/reeded ebonized surround, flanked by acanthus- and rosette-decorated candlearms, over an acanthus & pineapple pendant drop, English or American, late 18th century, 26 x 43½" 2,530.00
(Illustration: Mirrors 6)

Federal "girandole" wall mirror, giltwood, spread-winged eagle finial above a circular molded ebonized frame mounted w/sphe-

Mirrors 4: Chippendale Mirror with Gilt Shell

rules centering a convex mirror plate, the pendant below in the form of a sea horse, American or English, first quarter 19th century,

Mirrors 6: Federal "Girandole" Mirror

Mirrors 7: "Girandole" Mirror with Sea Horse

Mirrors 8: Federal Shaving Mirror

Mirrors 9: Federal Inlaid Wall Mirror

restorations, 25½" w.,
47" h. 3,450.00
(Illustration: Mirrors 7)

Federal shaving mirror,
table model, mahogany,
the rectangular mirror plate
swiveling between two
block- and baluster-turned
supports w/acorn finials,
above a bowed case w/two
short drawers, on ogee
bracket feet, New England,
ca. 1800, 19" w., 7¼" d.,
20" h. 460.00
(Illustration: Mirrors 8)

Federal wall mirror, satinwood-inlaid mahogany, the
shaped crest centering an
inlaid conch shell, the
rectan-gular mirror plate
below, over a shaped
pendant, American or
English, minor repairs, ca.

1785, 18" w.,
33½" h..........................2,588.00
(Illustration: Mirrors 9)

Federal wall mirror,
mahogany & gilt gesso, a
high arched & scroll-cut

Mirrors 10: Federal Mirror with Peacock

crest centered by a gilt
gesso spread-winged eagle
above a rectangular mirror
plate w/molded borders,
scroll-cut bottom border,
probably American, ca.
1780, old finish,
18½ x 38 " 1,610.00
(Illustration: Mirrors 23, center)

Federal wall mirror, painted
pine & églomisé, the
molded cornice above a
blue, green & yellow
églomisé panel centering a
peacock looking over his
shoulder amid sprays of
green leaves, over a
rectangular mirror plate
flanked by applied reeded
pilasters above a molded
base, Pennsylvania,
1820-1830, 22¼" h.......1,265.00
(Illustration: Mirrors 10)

Federal wall mirror,
mahogany, églomisé, the
molded cornice above a

Mirrors 11: Federal Mirror with Farmhouse

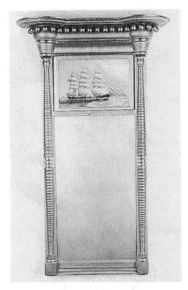

Mirrors 12: Federal Mirror with Ship Portrait

Mirrors 13: George II Wall Mirror

polychrome églomisé panel depicting a farmhouse & ship, over a rectangular mirror plate flanked by applied reeded pilasters above a molded base, Mid-Atlantic States, 1820-1830, 34 ¾" h. 805.00
(Illustration: Mirrors 11)

Federal wall mirror, gilt gesso, the oblong flat top w/outset rounded ends above a band of spherules above ringed capitals above tall slender ringed half-columns flanking a replaced tablet w/an oil portrait of a sailing ship above the rectangular mirror, ship portrait signed by H.R. Bartlett, Bristol, 1874, mirror labeled by A.A. Waterhouse, Albany, New York, ca. 1820, 25½ x 40½" 1,840.00
(Illustration: Mirrors 12)

Federal wall mirror, two-part, pine & mahogany veneer, the pediment w/out-turned corners above a frieze over an églomisé panel painted w/a land-scape over a rectangular

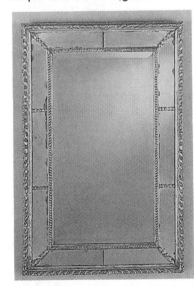

Mirrors 14: George III Giltwood Wall Mirror

mirror plate, flanked by spiral-turned columns, some flaking, early 19th century, 19" w., 35 ¾" h. 264.00

George II wall mirror, parcel-gilt walnut, the cartouche-shaped plate centered at the top w/a shell, the sides & apron w/foliate scroll & rocaille decoration, re-gilt, England, mid-18th century, 30 x 55" 7,475.00
(Illustration: Mirrors 13)

George III wall mirror, giltwood, the rectangular beveled plate & outer slips divided by rope-twist borders within a gadrooned frame, Eng-land, late 18th century, lacking peripheral elements, 24 ½" w., 34 ½" h. 2,990.00
(Illustration: Mirrors 14)

Mirrors 15: Ornate George III Wall Mirror

George III wall mirror, giltwood, the rectangular mirror plate w/waved & architectural surround

Mirrors 17: Engraved Georgian Mirror

w/temple & foliate crest & confronting C-scroll base, England, ca. 1760, re-gilt, 21" w., 38 ½" h. 2,070.00
(Illustration: Mirrors 15)

George III wall mirror, giltwood, the asymmetrical foliate-carved surround surmounted by a spray, centering divided mirror plates, England, third quarter 18th century, 17" w., 43 ½" h. 16,100.00

Georgian wall mirror, walnut, the arched scroll-cut crest above a rectangular mirror plate w/rounded upper corners & molded borders, scroll-cut bottom border, England, late 18th century, minor restoration, 17 x 30" 460.00
(Illustration: Mirrors 23, right)

Georgian wall mirror, walnut, the high arched crest w/scroll-cut edges above a small rectangular mirror within a wide ogee molded frame, probably England, 18th century, old refinishing, restoration, 17 x 30" 1,955.00
(Illustration: Mirrors 16)

Georgian wall mirror, walnut, the high arched crest w/small scroll above an arched molding over a conforming crown-engraved mirror plate over a long rectangular mirror framed by an ogee molding, beveled mirrors, England, 18th century, old refinish, imperfections................2,530.00
(Illustration: Mirrors 17)

George III-Style wall mirrors, giltwood, each

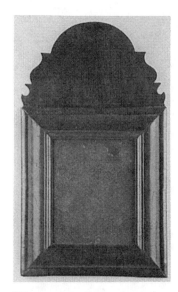

Mirrors 16: Georgian Wall Mirror

w/oval mirror plate w/outer slips carved w/anthemion & scrolling foliage, w/stylized anthemion crest flanked by upright long leaves continuing to enclose the sides, w/pendant husk

Mirrors 18: George III-Style Mirror

Mirrors 19: Louis XV Giltwood Wall Mirror

Mirrors 20: Louis XVI-Style Pier Mirror

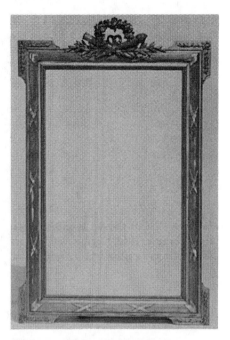

Mirrors 21: Louis XVI-Style Wall Mirror

base, England, late 19th century, re-gilt, 30 ½" w., 55" h. (Illustration: one of two)............................14,375.00
(Illustration: Mirrors 18)

Louis XV wall mirror, giltwood, the rectangular mirror plate surmounted by a cartouche & foliate C-scrolls continuing to the sides w/trailing vines, France, mid-18th century, re-backed, 29 ¼" w., 4' 11" h........................6,325.00
(Illustration: Mirrors 19)

Louis XVI-Style pier mirror, giltwood, the arched rectangular mirror plate within a foliate-carved frame w/a rocaille crest, mid-19th century, 35" w., 6' 4" h. 1,430.00
(Illustration: Mirrors 20)

Louis XVI-Style wall mirror, carved giltwood, the rectangular mirror plate w/ribbon-crossed reeded surround & husk-carved out-thrust corners sur-

mounted by a crest w/wreath above a quiver & torch over foliage, late 19th century, 34 ½" w., 4' 5 ½" h. 1,650.00
(Illustration: Mirrors 21)

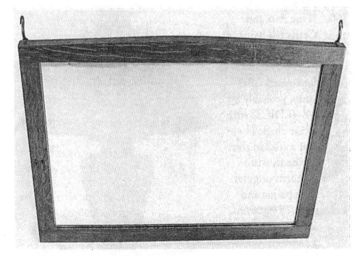

Mirrors 22: Mission Oak Wall Mirror

Mirrors 23: Queen Anne, Federal and Georgian Mirrors

**Mission-style (Arts &
Crafts movement) wall
mirror**, oak, an inverted
"V" crestrail above a
rectangular framed mirror
plate, original copper
mounting hooks at the top,
original dark brown finish,
red decal mark of Gustav
Stickley, Model No. 910,
early 20th century,
23 x 28 ½" 1,540.00
(Illustration: Mirrors 22)

Queen Anne wall mirror,
mahogany, the arched
crest w/small scrolls above
the rectangular mirror plate
w/rounded upper corners,
scroll-cut bottom border
labeled "John Elliot Chestnut Street Philadelphia,"
ca. 1753-62, old finish,
19 x 42 ½" 4,312.50
(Illustration: Mirrors 23, left)

Queen Anne wall mirror,
carved walnut, the arched
& scalloped crest flanked
by scrolled ears above a
rectangular beveled plate
within a molded surround,
Pennsylvania, 1750-1780,
23⅔" h..........................1,610.00
(Illustration: Mirrors 24)

Queen Anne wall mirror,
parcel-gilt walnut, the
arched shaped crest
centering a gilt shell
reserve, the oblong mirror
plate below w/gilt slip,

**Mirrors 24: Queen Anne
Wall Mirror**

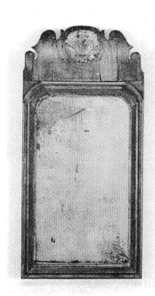

**Mirrors 25: Parcel-Gilt
Queen Anne Mirror**

Mirrors 26: Italian Rococo Wall Mirror

Mirrors 27: William & Mary Wall Mirror

American or English,
ca. 1730-1760, repair to
two scrolls, 11½" w.,
23 ⅞" h. 2,300.00
(Illustration: Mirrors 25)

Rococo wall mirror,
giltwood, the rectangular
mirror plate within double
border of mirror plate
surmounted by a mirrored
cartouche within foliate
scrolls, terminating in
foliate scrolls, Italy, mid-
18th century, rebacked,
37" w., 5' 1" h..............10,350.00
(Illustration: Mirrors 26)

William & Mary wall mirror,
walnut, the fret-carved
crest centering a crown
flanked by a unicorn & lion,

above a rectangular mirror
plate within a molded slip,
surrounded by a convex-
molded frame, England,
ca. 1690, restorations,
26 ½" w., 40 ¾" h........14,950.00
(Illustration: Mirrors 27)

William IV wall mirror,
giltwood, the cartouche-
shaped mirror plate within
a surround of bulrushes,
flowers & C-scrolls
w/flower-filled basket crest
& confronting scroll base,
England, second quarter
19th century, 25" w.,
47" h. 5,520.00
(Illustration: Mirrors 28)

Mirrors 28: William IV Giltwood Mirror

Louis XV-Style: settee & two armchairs; giltwood, each w/upholstered shield-shaped back w/Black Forest scenes within a molded frame, the crest molded w/flowers & scrolling fleur-de-lis, molded floral curved arms & legs, Black Forest region, Germany, 3 pcs. 2,350.00
(Illustration: Parlor 1, settee)

Mission-style (Arts & Crafts movement): love seat, armchair & rocker; oak, barrel-shaped pieces each w/a U-form crestrail above full-length vertical slats & drop-in spring seats, original dark finish, remnant of paper labels of the Plail Brothers, early 20th c., love seat 21 x 46", 32 ½" h., 3 pcs............13,200.00
(Illustration: Parlor 2)

Parlor 1: Louis XV-Style Settee

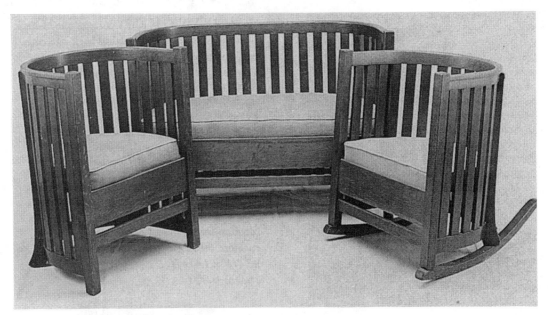

Parlor 2: Mission Oak Parlor Suite

Parlor 3:
Gothic Revival Settee

settee & chairs each
stenciled "A E K," third
quarter 19th century, some
restoration, settee 60" w.,
33 ½" h., 4 pcs.................747.00
(Illustration: Parlor 3, settee)

**Victorian Renaissance
Revival substyle: sofa,
armchair & three side
chairs**; carved walnut, the
triple-back sofa w/central
medallion carved crestrail

**Victorian Gothic Revival
substyle**: settee & three
side chairs; walnut, the
settee w/ upholstered
three-panel back sur-
mounted by flattened ball
finials, on Gothic arch supports over an upholstered
seat w/pierced panel
apron, flanked by uphol-
stered armrests on turned
supports, on turned feet,

Parlor 4:
Renaissance Revival Sofa

w/bust, padded armrests
on bust-carved supports,
over a serpentine seat on
trumpet-shaped legs on
casters, attributed to John
Jelliff, New Jersey, ca.
1870, sofa 80" w.,
5 pcs............................3,300.00
(Illustration: Parlor 4, sofa)

**Victorian Rococo
substyle: sofa & three
side chairs**; carved &
laminated rosewood, the
sofa w/a serpentine wide

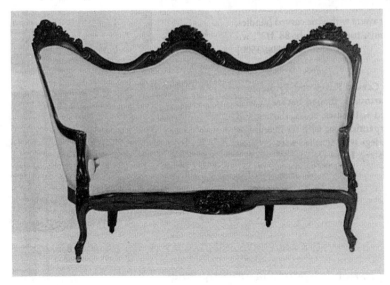

Parlor 6:
Rosalie Pattern Sofa

Parlor 5: Rococo Rosewood Sofa & Chairs

crestrail pierced & carved w/a center floral bouquet & trailing vines, flowers & C-scrolls above the tufted upholstered back & closed arms, the serpentine seat w/a molded & carved seatrail continuing to demi-cabriole legs, the side chairs w/matching carving around the oval padded back panel, ca. 1850s, the set........................11,500.00
(Illustration: Parlor 5, sofa & two chairs)

Victorian Rococo substyle: sofa, two armchairs, & two side chairs; carved & laminated rosewood, Rosalie patt., the triple-back sofa w/fruit- and floral-carved crestrail continuing to form scrolled arms on demi-cabriole legs on casters, carved serpentine seatrail, chairs similarly carved, attributed to John Henry Belter,

New York, ca. 1850-1860, 5 pcs..........................16,500.00
(Illustration: Parlor 6, sofa)

Victorian Rococo substyle: sofa, pair of armchairs & pair of side chairs; carved mahogany, each w/crestrail carved w/sprays of roses, uphol-stered back, seat & arms,

serpentine arms supports, on short slender cabriole legs, ca. 1850-1860, sofa 70 ½" l., 5 pcs...............3,300.00
(Illustration: Parlor 7, sofa)

Victorian Rococo substyle: pair of love seats, pair of armchairs & four side chairs; carved & laminated rosewood, the

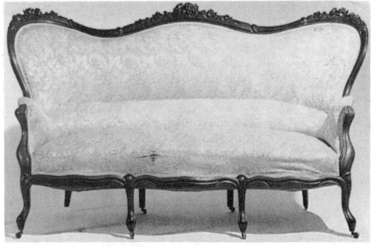

Parlor 7: Rococo Mahogany Sofa

Parlor 8: Rococo Armchairs

Parlor 9: Wicker Armchair

love seats w/pierced & carved triple-arched crestrail continuing to padded armrests on carved, scrolled supports, enclosing an upholstered back & seat w/carved serpentine seatrail, on carved demi-cabriole legs on casters, the chairs similarly carved, attributed to John Henry Belter, New York, ca. 1855, love seats 64" w., 24" d., 48" h., 8 pcs...........................10,725.00
(Illustration: Parlor 8, armchairs)

Wicker: two settees, a bench & an armchair; Empire-style w/a raised rolled panel in the center of the crestrails above the tightly woven back flanked by high rolled arms continuing down to form the seatrail, on tightly woven scrolled legs, painted white, England, early 20th century, 63" l., 32" h., 4 pcs. 977.50
(Illustration: Parlor 9, armchair)

Fire screen, Art Nouveau style, mahogany & leaded glass, the frame carved w/pierced whiplash designs, the central section w/panels of clear & mottled glass in shades of violet, pink, grey, white & sky blue, stamped "A. Landry," Abel Landry, France, ca. 1900, some restoration, 30 ½" w., 39" h..............3,737.50
(Illustration: Screens 1)

Fire screen, Louis XV-Style, gilt bronze, the cartouche shape w/foliate scrollwork, on four scrolling legs, late 19th century, 32" w., 30 ¼" h. 1,265.00
(Illustration: Screens 2)

Fire screen, Victorian, mahogany, floral fruitwood inlay surround w/shaped crest centering a glazed

Screens 1: Art Nouveau Fire Screen

panel w/floral needlework, raised on inlaid supports w/urn finials, on arched downscrolled legs joined

Screens 3: Victorian Dutch Fire Screen

by a turned inlaid stretcher, Holland, mid-19th century.............................880.00
(Illustration: Screens 3)

Screens 2: Louis XV-Style Fire Screen

Screens 4: Victorian Japanned Fire Screen

Screens 5: Mission Oak Screen

Screens 6: Victorian Three-Fold Screen

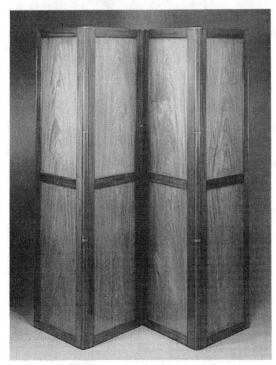

Screens 7: Victorian Mahogany Screen

Fire screen, Victorian, silk & japanned wood, the surround w/pagoda-shaped crest & decorated w/Oriental figures & scenes enclosing a floral silk-embroidered panel, w/floral-decorated turned supports on arched scrolled legs w/pendants, joined by a decorated block- and baluster-turned stretcher, England, late 19th century, 32" w., 45" h. 1,495.00
(Illustration: Screens 4)

Folding screen, three-fold, Mission-style (Arts & Crafts movement), oak, the central panel w/an arched crestrail, each panel w/an embroidered linen panel w/a Glasgow rose design in the center one, red decal mark of Gustav Stickley, Model No. 81, original dark finish, new linen, early 20th century, 57" w., 4' 11" h..1,760.00
(Illustration: Screens 5)

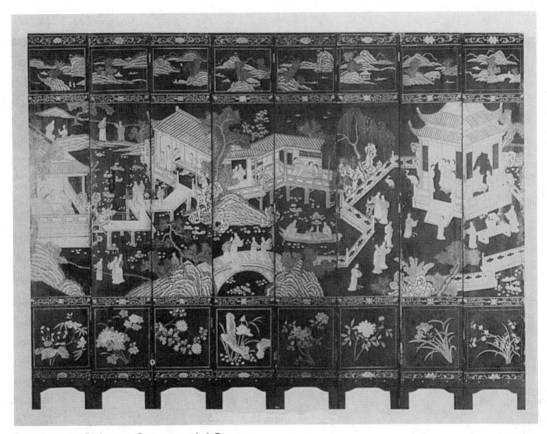

Screens 8: Chinese Coromandel Screen

Folding screen, three-fold, Victorian, each section decorated w/decoupage Victorian genre scenes w/animals & people, the reverse w/Chinese court scenes, England, late 19th century, each panel 25" w., 6' 1" h. 1,430.00
(Illustration: Screens 6)

Folding screen, four-fold, Victorian, mahogany, each fold w/two plain panels, England, mid-19th century, each panel 25 ½" w., 7' 6" h. 6,325.00
(Illustration: Screens 7)

Folding screen, 12-fold, Coromandel-type, painted w/a continuous scene of court officials in terraced pavilions w/figures, the upper borders w/antique symbols & flora & fauna, the reverse decorated w/blossoming trees & flowers, China, late 19th century, altered, each panel 18 ½" w., 9' 2" h. 5,175.00
(Illustration: Screens 8, eight of twelve panels)

Chinese Export secretary-bookcase, black & gold japanned, two-part construction: the upper section w/molded frieze above a pair of glazed doors w/arched divides opening to three shelves & mirrored back, flanked by pilasters; the lower section w/paneled doors flanked by pilasters, on rounded feet, decorated overall w/Chinese figures in landscapes, birds amid blossoming trees & scrolling foliage, China, second quarter 19th century, decoration restored, 14 ½ x 42", 5' 5" h. 6,325.00
(Illustration: Secretaries 1)

Chippendale secretary-bookcase, walnut, two-part construction: the upper section w/rectangular top w/molded & dentil-carved cornice above a blind fret-carved frieze, above cupboard doors w/shaped panels, candle slide below; the lower section w/hinged rectangular slant lid opening to an interior fitted w/pigeonholes w/pierced valances over small drawers, centering a scalloped paneled prospect door opening to two small drawers, four graduated molded long drawers below, stop-fluted quarter-columns flanking, the molded base on ogee bracket feet, Southern U.S., ca. 1790, lower feet replaced, 22 ¼ x 43", 7' 7 ½" h. 14,950.00
(Illustration: Secretaries 2)

Federal secretary, mahogany, wavy birch & inlaid rosewood, two-part

Secretaries 1: Chinese Export Secretary

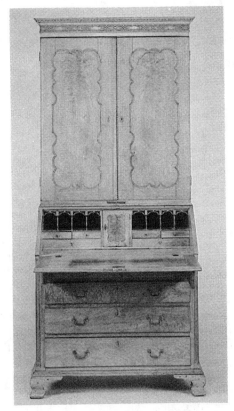

Secretaries 2: Chippendale Secretary

Secretaries 3: Fine Federal Secretary

Secretaries 4. Tiger Maple Federal Secretary

construction: the upper section w/a rectangular top w/narrow molded cornice above a pair of doors w/triple arched panes opening to rows of small drawers over pigeonholes; the stepped-out lower section w/a fold-out writing leaf above a pair of slides & three long drawers w/round brass knobs on ring- and baluster-turned legs, Massachusetts or New Hampshire, early 19th century, old refinish, brasses appear original,

19 x 37", 4' 6" h. 6,325.00
(Illustration: Secretaries 3)

Federal secretary-bookcase, tiger stripe maple, two-part construction: the upper section w/a pointed cornice above a pair of paneled cupboard doors opening to shelves; the lower section w/a slant-front lid opening to a fitted interior above a case of four long graduated drawers w/simple bail pulls, shaped apron & simple bracket feet, southeastern

New England, ca. 1790, old refinish, top of different origin, restoration, 18 ½ x 38", 6 2" h. 4,025.00
(Illustration: Secretaries 4)

Federal "bow-front" secretary-bookcase, flame-birch-veneered mahogany, two-part construction: the upper section w/molded cornice above geometrically glazed doors opening to shelves, the rectangular hinged writing surface below opening to small

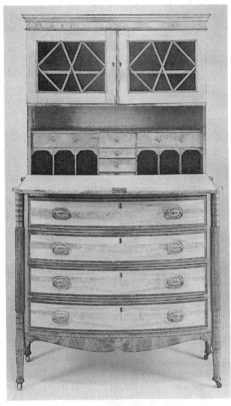

Secretaries 5:
Federal "Bow-Front" Secretary

Secretaries 6:
Three-part Federal Secretary

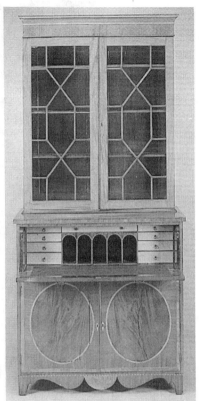

Secretaries 7:
Labeled Federal Secretary

drawers & valanced pigeonholes; the lower section of bowed form w/four cockbeaded long drawers, reeded three-quarter-round columns flanking, on turned feet, ending in casters; New England, ca. 1810, 21½ x 43½", 6' 3" h. 6,325.00
(Illustration: Secretaries 5)

Federal secretary-bookcase, inlaid mahogany, three-part construction: the upper

section w/swan's-neck pediment terminating in inlaid rosettes centering an eagle & urn finial on plinth, over a dentil-molded line-inlaid frieze above two geometrically-glazed doors opening to shelves on molded base; the middle section w/pair of tambour doors, each opening to two short drawers over valanced pigeonholes, flanked & divided by vertical inlay, on molded base; the

bottom section w/hinged drop writing surface above two cockbeaded line-inlaid long drawers flanked by inlaid calligraphy scrolls, on tapering square legs w/pendant floral inlay & crossbanded cuffs, branded "E.M. Clark," Portsmouth, New Hampshire, late 18th - early 19th century, old refinish, 37" w., 20 ¼" d., 7' ½" h. 46,000.00
(Illustration: Secretaries 6)

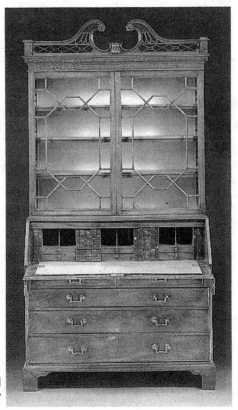

**Secretaries 8:
George III
Secretary**

Thomas Seymour, Boston,
ca. 1800-1815, 21 x 41⅜",
7' 3" h. 27,600.00

Federal secretary-bookcase, inlaid
mahogany, three-part construction:
the removable molded cornice
w/interlaced line inlay; the upper
section w/ geometrically-glazed &
mullioned cupboard doors opening to
an interior w/adjustable shelves; the
projecting lower section w/pullout
drawer opening to a baize-lined
writing surface & fitted w/pigeonholes
& satinwood small drawers, a pair of
inlaid cupboard doors below opening
to a shelf, the scalloped apron
supported on short bracket feet,
labeled by Stitcher & Clemmens,
Baltimore, ca. 1804, feet reduced
approximately 2", 22 x 41½",
7' 5" h. 8,625.00
(Illustration: Secretaries 7)

Federal secretary-bookcase,
satinwood-inlaid mahogany, three-
part construction: the top w/shaped
pediment centering a rectangular
panel flanked by two smaller plinths
above a dentil-molded frieze over
Gothic pattern glazed doors
w/ebonized line inlay enclosing three
shelves; the middle section comprised
of a rectangular case w/three cross-
banded line-inlaid short drawers over
three cross-banded line-inlaid doors
w/ivory escutcheons; the lower
section w/banded & inlaid hinged
writing flap over a case w/banded &
inlaid long drawer over two similar
cupboard doors flanked by bottle
drawers, all w/ivory escutcheons &
flanked by line-inlaid & satinwood
panels, on elongated spade feet;
attributed to the shop of John &

**Secretaries 9:
Queen Anne
Secretary**

George III secretary-bookcase, mahogany, two-part construction: the upper section w/pierced swan's-neck pediment above a dentilled cornice & blind-fret frieze over geometrically-glazed mullioned doors; the lower section w/slant lid opening to a fitted interior, above two short & three long drawers, raised on bracket feet, England, late 18th century, 23 x 52", 7' 1" h. 14,950.00
(Illustration: Secretaries 8)

George III "breakfront" secretary-bookcase, mahogany, the overhanging molded cornice above two pairs of glazed doors opening to adjustable shelves, the lower part w/central secretary drawer above three drawers, flanked by cupboards, on a conforming plinth, England, ca. 1790, 5' 7 ½" w., 18 ½" l., 8' h. 20,700.00

Queen Anne secretary-bookcase, black-japanned & gilt-decorated, two-part construction: the upper section w/double-arched molded cornice above beveled mirror-inset doors opening to an interior fitted w/shelves above drawers & candle slides; the lower section w/ slant-front lid opening to a leather-lined writing surface & interior fitted w/pigeonholes above drawers flanked by stepped sides, fitted w/sliding panel opening to a well; all over two short over two long graduated drawers, raised on bracket feet, chinoiserie decoration in gold red & orange, England, 25 x 40", 7' 2" h. (decoration restored, interior of upper section rebuilt) 27,600.00

Queen Anne secretary-book-case, walnut, two-part construction: the upper section w/double-domed cornice surmounted by giltwood urn-form finials, over mirror-inset doors opening to pigeonholes, folio slides, a mirrored door & small drawers, over candle slides; the lower section w/slant lid opening to a fitted interior w/a well, over two short & two long drawers, raised on bracket feet, upper section of later date, England, early 18th century, 23 ½ x 39 ½", 7' 3" h. 14,950.00
(Illustration: Secretaries 9)

Queen Anne secretary-bookcase, walnut, two-part construction: the upper section w/molded broken arch pediment above a pair of beveled mirror-inset doors opening to an interior fitted w/small drawers, folio divides, document slides &

Secretaries 10: Rare Queen Anne Secretary

Secretaries 11:
Renaissance Revival Secretary

Secretaries 12:
Victorian Rococo Secretary

central inlaid door, over a
pair of candle slides,
flanked by square columns;
the lower section w/slant lid
opening to a similarly fitted
interior, over one long, two
short & two long banded
drawers, on a molded base
on bracket feet, England,
ca. 1715, mirror plates
replaced, 41" w., 23 ¾" d.,
7' 5" h. 123,500.00
(Illustration: Secretaries 10)

**Victorian secretary-
bookcase**, Renaissance

Revival substyle, walnut
w/bird's-eye maple interior
& drawer fronts, two-part
construction: the upper
section w/a rectangular top
w/a molded arched cornice
above a pair of glazed
cupboard doors w/small
wooden knobs opening to
shelves; the lower section
w/a paneled cylinder rolltop opening to an interior
fitted w/pigeonholes &
small drawers above a long
drawer over a pair of
paneled cupboard doors,

molded base w/decorative
finials, ca. 1870, 8' h.....3,500.00
(Illustration: Secretaries 11)

**Victorian secretary-
bookcase**, Rococo
substyle, mahogany, two-
part construction: the upper
section w/ogee-molded
cornice w/undulating scroll-
carved crest centering a
scalloped shell, over a
scroll-carved frieze above
C-scroll-carved arched-top
glazed doors opening to
shelves over two short

Secretaries 13: Very Tall Victorian Rococo Mahogany Secretary

ogee drawers; the lower section w/drop-front opening to green felt-lined writing surface above projecting ogee-molded drawer over two long drawers w/scalloped base on bracket feet on casters, mid-19th century, 42 ½" w., 20 ¾" d., 7' 4" h. 1,980.00
(Illustration: Secretaries 12)

Victorian secretary-bookcase, Rococo substyle, mahogany, two-part construction: the upper section w/ogee cornice above a frieze w/applied foliate carving over a pair of glazed doors w/applied foliate carving opening to shelves; the lower section w/a slant front opening to pigeonholes & short ogee-molded drawers flanking a shaped shelf, the case w/a serpentine drawer over two long drawers, all w/applied foliate carving, on a similarly carved bracket base, ca. 1840, 44 ½" w., 20" d., 7' 10 ½" h. 3,520.00
(Illustration: Secretaries 13)

Floor shelves, country-style, cherry, six rectangular graduated open shelves each raised on four baluster-turned supports w/ring-turned top & bottom section, good old finish, bottom shelf 11½ x 36", 4' 7" h. (some edge damage, three shelves cracked) 935.00

Floor shelves, country-style, painted pine, a pointed crestrail flanked by rounded ends above four shelves, the sides w/boot-jack feet, traces of red paint, Pennsylvania, early 19th century, 13 ¾ x 37 ½", 4' h. 2,070.00
(Illustration: Shelves 1)

Floor shelves, country-style, painted walnut, two-tier, square nail construction, rectangular top above two graduated shelves flanked by canted sides w/cut-out feet, old red paint, found in Miami County, Ohio. 11 ¾" deep, 27 ½" w., 36" h. 605.00

Hanging shelf, Art Nouveau style, carved walnut, the rounded top shelf carved w/a central bouquet of roses above a semi-clad maiden enclosed in a floral & leaf-surrounded niche, signed "R. Carabin," Rupert Carabin, France, ca. 1900, 27" h. 11,500.00
(Illustration: Shelves 2)

Hanging shelf, Arts & Crafts style, carved & stained oak, carved to suggest a long, slender stringed musical instrument w/pierced back

Shelves 1: Country-Style Floor Shelves

Shelves 2: Art Nouveau Hanging Shelf

panels above a rectangular shelf on a carved support, by Charles Rohlfs, impressed monogram "R 1902," 13" w., 4' 3" h.................3,910.00

Hanging shelf, country-style, walnut, a small half-round shelf supported by a cut bracket on a shaped backboard w/rope-carved loops at the top & rope carving w/tassels at edge of sides under shelf flanking long center tassel drop, square nail construction, late 19th century, old soft finish, 12 ½" w., 11 ¼" h. ..115.50

Hanging shelves, Art Nouveau style, carved & marquetry, open rectangular form w/central shelf, the back inlaid w/butterflies, one side inlaid w/fuchsia, the other w/fuchsia blossoms & a single butterfly, w/inlaid signature, Emile Gallé, France, late 19th - early 20th century, 10 x 42", 24" h. 1,840.00

Hanging shelves, country-style, painted pine, the three-tier, arched crest above three graduated shelves, traces of red & green paint, 19th century, 19 ½" h. 460.00

Shelves 3: Rococo Hanging Shelves

Hanging shelves, country-style, walnut, three-tier, well scalloped sides supporting three graduated shelves, scrubbed grey finish, found in Wayne County, Ohio, 23 ½" w., 36 ½" h. (glued split along back edge of one end)..1,210.00

Hanging shelves, Rococo style, pine & parcel-gilt, four-tier, a swan's-neck cresting above scroll sides & shaped uprights supporting four shaped & graduated open shelves, 19th century, 7 x 54", 4' ½" h.........................4,025.00
(Illustration: Shelves 3)

Hanging shelves, Victorian, carved walnut, a half-round thin board above a large carved spread-winged eagle w/head turned to the side above a flattened backplate suspending a large fruit- and leaf-carved drop, old varnish finish, eagles w/glass eyes, 19th century, 14 ¾" w., 17" h., facing pair....................1,760.00

Art Deco sideboard, rosewood & bronze, the long curved shaped top over a conforming case w/a central glazed door w/bronze surround flanked by large curved doors, France, ca. 1935, 19 x 105", 32 ½" h. 5,750.00
(Illustration: Sideboards 1)

Art Nouveau sideboard, carved mahogany & marquetry, in three tiers, the high & wide arched backsplash carved at the center w/a fanned floral cluster surrounded by a fishscale design in marquetry above the rectangular red marble top above a long narrow center drawer flanked by bold buttress supports carved w/chicory leaves, an open shelf w/rounded corners in the center above a pair of paneled cupboard doors w/mountainous autumnal landscape scenes in marquetry & flanked by open shelves, on a molded, stepped base, designed by Louis Majorelle, France, ca. 1900, 16 ½ x 65", 4' 7 ¾" h. 12,650.00

Art Nouveau sideboard, gilt-bronze mounted mahogany, the super-structure w/an arched crestrail over a paneled band above a large glazed door w/a forked mullion opening to shelves & flanked by shaped sides & small open shelves all raised on curved supports

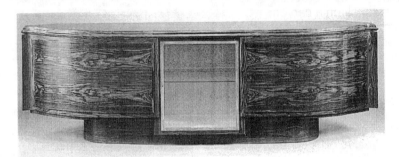

Sideboards 1: Art Deco Sideboard

over the open rectangular stepped-out base w/a pair of drawers over a pair of cupboard doors w/arched & floral-carved panels, the lower case flanked by stepped-back shaped sides w/open shelves, raised on short flared feet continuing to a shaped apron, cast

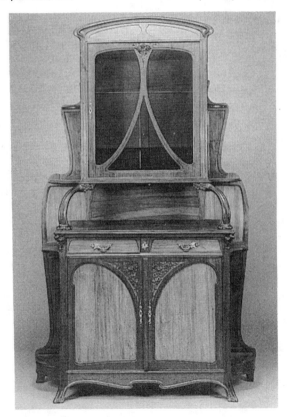

Sideboards 2: Art Nouveau Sideboard

Sideboards 3: Classical Server

Sideboards 4: Classical Sideboard

gilt-bronze foliate escutcheons & pulls, designed by Louis Majorelle, France, ca. 1900, 21 x 60", 8' 1 ½" h......................2,760.00
(Illustration: Sideboards 2)

Classical server, mahogany, the scroll-supported shelf above a backboard on a rectangular top, above a short central drawer flanked by two half-round drawers projecting over a long drawer over raised panel cabinet doors, flanked by turned columns, on scrolled front & bracket rear feet, mid-19th century, 47 ¼" w., 23" d., 4' 9" h. ..770.00
(Illustration: Sideboards 3)

Classical sideboard, mahogany, the splashback w/a rectangular center section flanked by scroll-carved ends above the rectangular top w/stepped-out ends above a conforming case w/a long central drawer flanked by shorter stepped-out end drawers above an open central recess flanked by paneled cupboard doors w/stamped brass banding, each flanked by a pair of columns w/brass capitals & bases, raised on short gadrooned acorn-form feet, stenciled label of "Emmons and Archibald No. 39 Orange Street, Boston, Cabinet, Chair and Upholstery Manufactory," Boston, Massachusetts, 1818-25, minor veneer & beading loss, 24 ½ x 74", 41 ½" h..........................8,800.00
(Illustration: Sideboards 4)

Sideboards 5: Empire Revival Sideboard

Sideboards 6: Federal Huntboard

Empire Revival style sideboard, oak, a superstructure w/a thick rectangular narrow shelf above a long rectangular beveled mirror flanked by C-scroll supports resting on the rectangular top over a case w/a pair of long round-front drawers w/two wooden knobs overhanging a pair of plain cupboard doors over a long drawer w/wooden knobs at the bottom, the case flanked by long ogee pilasters & raised on C-scroll front legs on casters, ca. 1910, 21 x 48", overall 4' 7½" h. 795.00
(Illustration: Sideboards 5)

Federal country-style huntboard, yellow pine, the rectangular top above two pairs of graduated short drawers, raised panel ends, on tapered square legs, Southern, early 19th century, refinished, repairs to drawers, age cracks, 53¼ " w., 22" d., 46½" h. 3,300.00
(Illustration: Sideboards 6)

Federal "serpentine-front" sideboard, satinwood-

Sideboards 7: Federal "Serpentine-Front" Sideboard

Sideboards 8: Inlaid Federal Sideboard

Sideboards 9: Kidney-Shaped Federal Sideboard

inlaid mahogany, the serpentine-shaped top w/line inlays above a conforming case centering a bowed, cockbeaded & line-inlaid long drawer flanked by inswept cockbeaded & line-inlaid short drawers over cockbeaded & line-inlaid central cupboard doors flanked by line-inlaid panels flanked by inswept line-inlaid bottle drawers, on pendant-flower & line-inlaid square tapering legs, Massachusetts, ca. 1800, 27 ¼ x 66 ¼", 41⅛" h. 21,850.00 *(Illustration: Sideboards 7)*

Federal sideboard, inlaid mahogany, the rectangular top w/a serpentine top above a conforming case w/large doors w/round inlaid panels at each end flanking a long central drawer above a pair of small cupboard doors w/oval inlaid panels, on six square tapering legs w/line inlay, possibly New York, ca. 1790, old refinish, restored, 24 x 63", 39" h. ....4,600.00 *(Illustration: Sideboards 8)*

Federal sideboard, inlaid mahogany, the kidney-shaped inlaid top above a conforming case w/central long drawer over two cupboard doors flanked by rounded cupboard doors, all w/line inlay, on square tapering line-inlaid legs w/crossbanded cuffs, Philadelphia, ca. 1800, holes for brass gallery

Sideboards 10:
Federal "Fan-inlaid" Sideboard

filled-in on top, 26 ½" w.,
73" d., 40 ¼" h. 6,900.00
(Illustration: Sideboards 9)

**Federal "serpentine-front"
sideboard**, satinwood-
inlaid mahogany, the
oblong top w/serpentine
front above a conforming
case w/four drawers above
a pair of concave bottle
drawers w/fan-shaped
corner & band inlays
flanking a recessed center
section w/a pair of convex
doors w/similar inlay, each
door & drawer separated
by book-end-inlaid dies, on
line-inlaid square tapering
legs ending in crossbanded
cuffs, New York, ca. 1800,
30 x 74 ¾", 41" h. 17,250.00
(Illustration: SIdeboards 10)

**Federal "serpentine-front"
sideboard**, inlaid
mahogany, the oblong top
w/serpentine center section
above a conformingly-
shaped case w/pair of
concave doors centering a
pair of serpentine doors,
oval-inlaid dies flanking,
on square tapering legs
ending in Marlboro feet,
Baltimore, ca. 1800,
27 ½ x 75 ¾", 39 ¼" h.
(minor repairs to
veneer) 9,775.00

Federal sideboard,
mahogany, the drop-center
w/arched splashboard
flanked by raised cavetto-
molded plinth sides, each
w/cockbeaded drawer
above an arched-panel ve-
neered cupboard door, the
bow-front central long
drawer over a pair of
recessed cupboard doors,
flanked by compartmented

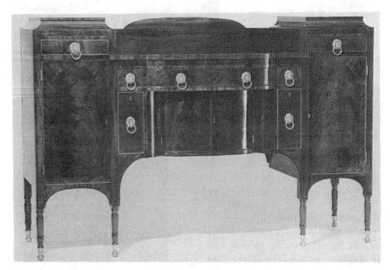

Sideboards 11: Drop-Center Federal Sideboard

bottle drawers, raised on
reeded turned legs ending
in brass feet, New York, ca.
1800, 78" w., 27" d.,
4' 3 ½" h. 5,775.00
(Illustration: Sideboards 11)

**George III "demi-lune"
side-board**, satinwood-
cross-banded inlaid

mahogany, the demi-lune
top above a frieze drawer
over an arched recess
flanked on each side
by a deep drawer &
cupboard door, raised
on square tapering
legs, England, ca. 1790,
30 x 72", 37" h. 5,175.00
(Illustration: Sideboards 12)

Sideboards 12: George III "Demi-lune" Sideboard

Sideboards 13: George III Sideboard

George III sideboard, inlaid mahogany, rectangular top w/serpentine front above a conforming case w/a long central drawer flanked by a bottle drawer & two graduated drawers, raised on square tapering paneled legs ending in modified spade feet, patarae & line inlay, England, late 18th century, 30 ½ x 72", 37 ½" h. 9,200.00
(Illustration: Sideboards 13)

George III "bow-front" sideboard, inlaid mahogany, the bow-fronted top fitted w/brass splash rail over two inlaid cockbeaded frieze drawers over tambour drawers flanked by deep drawers, raised on square tapering legs w/line inlay, England, last quarter 18th century, 29 ½ x 83", 4' 10" h. ...10,350.00
(Illustration: Sideboards 14)

Louis XV Provincial-Style server, walnut, a serpentine top above a pair of short serpentine-front scroll-paneled cupboard doors above the serpentine-front top over a pair of cupboard doors w/bold cartouche-form scroll-panel doors w/long pierced brass keyhole escutcheons & long hinges, a scroll-carved apron & short scroll legs on knobs, France, late 19th century, 27 x 61 ½", 43 ¾" h. 2,530.00
(Illustration: Sideboards 15)

Mission-style (Arts & Crafts movement) sideboard, oak, rectan-

Sideboards 14: George III "Bow-Front" Sideboard

Sideboards 15: Louis XV-Style Server

Sideboards 16: Lifetime Mission Sideboard

Sideboards 17: Lifetime Mirrored Sideboard

gular top surmounted by a splashboard w/beveled mirror plate, over two short drawers over a long drawer above a pair of cabinet doors, on square legs, original finish & hammered copper hardware, decal mark of Lifetime Furniture Company, Grand Rapids, Michigan, Model No. 5039, 48" w., 19" d., 4' 3" h. ..1,045.00
(Illustration: Sideboards 16)

Mission-style (Arts & Crafts movement) sideboard, oak, the high backboard w/a flat crestrail over an open shelf above a long rectangular mirror above the rectangular top slightly over-hanging a case w/a pair of square doors flanking three small drawers in the center above one long drawer at the bottom, square legs on casters, faceted brass pulls, original medium brown finish, decal in one drawer for the Lifetime Furniture Company, 20 x 54", 4' 7" h. 990.00
(Illustration: Sideboards 17)

Mission-style (Arts & Crafts movement) sideboard, oak, paneled & strapped splash-board above a rectangular top over four short drawers flanked by two cabinet doors, over a long drawer, on tall square feet, original finish & hammered copper hardware, L. & J.G. Stickley, Model No. 735, ca. 1910, veneer chips at sides, 56" w., 22" d., 46 ¼" h. 2,300.00
(Illustration: Sideboards 18)

Sheraton-Style sideboard, mahogany, the rectangular top w/serpentine front above a conforming case w/a long & two short drawers above short doors at the ends flanking an arched central opening, bellflower-carved bands dividing the front, square tapering legs ending in block feet & also carved w/bellflower bands, England, second half 19th century, 51 ½" l. ....3,575.00 *(Illustration: Sideboards 19)*

Turn of the century sideboard, maple, the tall superstructure w/an arched scroll-carved crestrail centered by a shell finial above a rounded frieze bar & scroll-carved ends above a long rectangular shelf raised on reeded columns flanking small open shelves & a large oval mirror, the lower stepped-out base w/a rectangular top w/molded edge over a long & two short round-fronted drawers over a pair of square cupboard doors w/scroll-carved panels above a long drawer, all flanked by long S-scrolls down the sides, on a molded base raised on carved claw front feet, ca. 1900, 23 x 44", overall 6' 11 ¼" h. ....1,090.00 *(Illustration: Sideboards 20)*

Sideboards 18: L. & J.G. Stickley Sideboard

Sideboards 19: Sheraton-Style Sideboard

Sideboards 20: Maple Sideboard

STANDS

Book stand, Mission-style (Arts & Crafts movement), oak, rotating-type, square top above two open shelves w/three slats at each side, rotating on a central post above the X-form base on casters, new dark brown finish, Danner company decal mark, early 20th century, 20" sq., 34½" h. 605.00

Candlestand, Chippendale tilt-top type, cherry, a squared top w/serpentine edges tilting above a slender columnar standard raised on a tripod base w/cabriole legs ending in pad feet, probably Massachusetts, ca. 1780, refinished, 17¾ x 18", 27¼" h. 1,955.00
(Illustration: Stands 1)

Candlestand, Chippendale tilt-top type, mahogany, the circular dished top tilting & revolving above a birdcage support & urn-form standard, on cabriole legs ending in peaked snake feet, Philadelphia, ca. 1780, 21" d., 27½" h. 2,875.00
(Illustration: Stands 2)

Candlestand, Classical tilt-top type, mahogany, the oblong octagonal top tilting above an acanthus-carved vase-form standard on reeded down-curving legs, New York, repair to block on underside of top, ca. 1815, 18¼ x 26¾", 28¾" h. 2,300.00
(Illustration: Stands 3)

Stands 1: Chippendale Cherry Candlestand

Candlestand, country-style, cherry, oval one-board top above a vase-form standard on flat down-

Stands 2: Chippendale Mahogany Candlestand

curving legs, early 19th century, 16 x 19 ½", 28 ½" h. (top w/minor stains) 412.00

Stands 3: Classical Candlestand

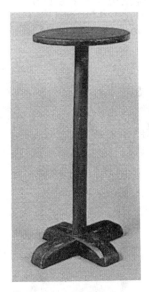

Stands 4: Grained Candlestand

Stands 5: Turned Maple Candlestand

Stands 6: Painted Candlestand

Stands 7: Round Stand

Stands 8: Federal Cherry Candlestand

Candlestand, country-style, grain-painted oak, the circular top w/molded edge above a cylindrical standard, on an X-form base, 19th century, 13 ¼" d., 29 ½" h. 230.00
(Illustration: Stands 4)

Candlestand, country-style, maple, the square top w/canted corners above a tapering cylindrical standard ending in a ring-turned ball, on splayed baluster-turned tripod legs, 19th century, 16" w., 15 ¾" d., 24 ½" h. 633.00
(Illustration: Stands 5)

Candlestand, country-style, painted blue, the rectangular top w/rounded corners above a swelled & ring-turned columnar standard, on an X-form base, possibly Pennsylvania, 18th - 19th century, 19 ¾" w., 17 ½" d.,

29" h. 1,265.00
(Illustration: Stands 6)

Candlestand, country-style, painted wood, the molded edge circular top above a tapering ring- and baluster-turned standard over a

Stands 9: Federal Octagonal Candlestand

turned circular base on tripod baluster-turned splayed legs, Mid-Atlantic States, 19th century, 10" d., 26 ½" h. 2,875.00
(Illustration: Stands 7)

Candlestand, Federal tilt-top type, cherry, the shaped rectangular top tilting above a ring-turned urn-shaped pedestal, on arched tripod legs, Pennsylvania, ca. 1790, 23 ½" w., 16 ¾" d., 30" h. 1,495.00
(Illustration: Stands 8)

Candlestand, Federal, maple, the octagonal top above an urn-form standard on cabriole legs ending in peaked snake feet, painted red, New England, probably New Hampshire, ca. 1795, 16 x 16 ⅜", 26 ½" h. 3,738.00
(Illustration: Stands 9)

Stands 10: Federal Mahogany Candlestand

Candlestand, Federal, curly maple, rectangular top w/foliate inlay & rounded corners over a turned pedestal above a spider-leg base, early 19th century, 19 ¾" w., 16 ½" d.,

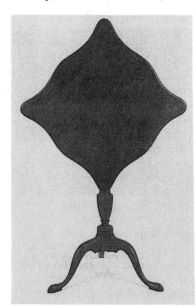

Stands 12: Federal Mahogany Candlestand

28 ¼" h. (age cracks in top & base of pedestal w/old stabilizing repairs) 440.00

Candlestand, Federal tilt-top type, mahogany, the molded square top tilting above a birdcage support over a tapering ring- and urn-turned standard, on cabriole legs ending in snake feet, New England, ca. 1770, 16 ¾ x 17", 29 ½" h. 5,750.00
(Illustration: Stands 10)

Candlestand, Federal, inlaid mahogany, rectangular top w/cut corners & line-inlaid banding tilting above a turned standard on a tripod base w/snake feet, Massachusetts, ca. 1800, old finish, minor imperfections, 15 ½ x 20", 29 ½" h..........................1,150.00
(Illustration: Stands 11)

Candlestand, Federal, mahogany, the squared top w/serpentine edges tilting above a turned standard above a tripod base w/cabriole legs ending in snake feet, original finish, Massachusetts, ca. 1790, 19 ¾ x 20", 28" h. 7,475.00
(Illustration: Stands 12)

Candlestand, Federal, walnut, the rectangular top above a baluster-turned pedestal, on arched tripod legs, New England, ca. 1800, 19 ¼" w., 15 ¼" d., 28 ½" h. 575.00
(Illustration: Stands 13)

Candlestand, Queen Anne country-style, cherry, the rectangular top on a baluster-turned standard

Stands 11: Inlaid Federal Candlestand

on a tripod base w/cabriole legs ending in snake feet, New England, late 18th century, old refinish, 14 ½" w., 14" d., 25 ½" h. 690.00
(Illustration: Stands 14)

Stands 13: Federal Walnut Candlestand

Stands 14: Queen Anne Cherry Candlestand

Candlestand, Queen Anne, mahogany, the circular top above a baluster-turned standard on cabriole legs ending in snake feet, Newport, Rhode Island, ca.

1750, 22" d., 26 ¾" h. 1,725.00
(Illustration: Stands 15)

Canterbury (music stand), George III-Style, mahogany, the four turned endposts w/ball finials enclosing four sectional compartments w/down-curved rails, the scalloped handle w/kidney-shaped opening, on a base w/single drawer on turned legs w/brass casters, 19th century, 20 ¼" w., 14 ½" d., 19 ¾" h. 550.00

Crock stand, country-style, painted & decorated pine, three half-round graduated tiers on a tripod frame of flat stepped braces, old yellow comb graining, 48" w., 36" h. (repaired break to bottom shelf) 137.00

Crock stand, country-style, painted soft wood, three half-round graduated shelves supported by a

Stands 15: Queen Anne Mahogany Candlestand

tripod frame comprised of wide shaped boards, cleaned down to old red paint, age cracks & open knothole in one shelf, 58" w., 28" d., 32 ½" h. ...275.00
(Illustration: Stands 16)

Stands 16: Country Crock Stand

Stands 17: George III Dumbwaiter

Stands 18: Mission Oak Magazine Stand

Stands 19: Stickley Magazine Stand

Stands 21: Art Deco Nightstand

Stands 20: Wicker Music Stand

Dumbwaiter, George III, mahogany, three graduated dished tiers raised on a spiral-turned support, on a tripod base w/cabriole legs ending in snake feet, England, late 18th century, 21 ¼" d., 41 ¼" h. 690.00
(Illustration: Stands 17)

Magazine stand, Mission-style (Arts & Crafts movement), oak, square top projecting over plain apron & four open shelves, the top & bottom shelves w/keyed through-tenons, sides w/two slats, on square feet, original finish, unmarked, 16 ¼" sq., 33" h. 660.00
(Illustration: Stands 18)

Magazine stand, Mission-style (Arts & Crafts movement), oak, flat rectangular top w/arched apron above three shelves, solid sides, on tall cut-out feet joined by side

stretchers, designed by Harvey Ellis, unsigned Gustav Stickley, Model No. 72, ca. 1910, some refinishing, 22" w., 13" d., 42 ¼" h. 1,725.00
(Illustration: Stands 19)

Music stand, Victorian wicker, a scrolled slanted top compartment flanked by stiles above three wicker-decorated open shelves w/knobbed front legs & scroll trim, late 19th

Stands 22: Federal Nightstand

Stands 23: Aesthetic Plant Stand

Stands 24: Rustic Plant Stand

Stands 25: George III Urn Stand

century, 4' ½" h. 920.00
(Illustration: Stands 20)

Nightstands, Art Deco, rosewood, a partial shaped gallery above two rectangular shelves w/rounded corners, on half-round shoe feet, France, ca. 1930, 11 ½ x 15 ¼", 20 ¾" h., pr. 1,840.00
(Illustration: Stands 21, one of two)

Nightstand, Federal, mahogany & flame birch veneer, a rectangular top w/reeded edge lifting above a deep well w/a veneered false drawer front w/oval bail above a pair of cupboard doors, old brass bail handles at sides, w/a scalloped apron & tall French feet, old refinish, imperfections, Massachusetts or New Hampshire, ca. 1800, 18 x 24", 25 ½" h. 1,840.00
(Illustration: Stands 22)

Plant stand, Victorian Aesthetic Movement substyle, cast brass, a square dished top above four scrolled bars & a center bar above a wide segment over four long bars centered by a large column w/cap finial, on four angled bar legs w/triangular fins at the base of the center posts, ca. 1880-85, 13 ½" w., 32 ¾" h. 920.00
(Illustration: Stands 23)

Plant stand, Victorian Adirondack- or Rustic-style, walnut & antlers, the circular walnut top on a clustered moose & deer antler base, late 19th century, 18" d., 30" h. ...1,320.00
(Illustration: Stands 24)

Portfolio stand, Victorian Aesthetic Movement substyle, inlaid & ebonized, the galleried gently canted top above mirrored sides w/inset Minton plaques, the

two-tiered front & back compartments fitted w/shaped dividers, flanked by stylized turned & inlaid pilasters, on reeded outswept feet, original condition, England, ca. 1880, 27 ¾" w., 33" d., 46" h. 3,850.00

Urn stand, George III, mahogany & marquetry, the square top w/scrolled gallery & entwined berried vine above an apron w/candleslide, on square tapering legs headed by pendant husks & joined by a pierced X-form stretcher, England, ca. 1770, 11 ¾" sq., 26" h. 3,680.00

Urn stand, George III, mahogany, the circular dished top above a turned & spiral-fluted standard on a tripod base w/cabriole legs ending in snake feet, England, mid-18th century,

16" d., 22" h. 5,520.00
(Illustration: Stands 25)

Washstand, Federal corner-style, bird's-eye maple-veneered mahogany, the shaped splashboard w/triangular shelf above a top shelf pierced w/a large & two small holes w/turned wooden cuffs above a bowed medial shelf fitted w/a small drawer above downswept legs joined by a shaped stretcher, Boston, Massachusetts, ca. 1805, 16 x 22 ¾", 40 ½" h. 6,325.00
(Illustration: Stands 26)

Washstand, Federal country-style, painted & decorated pine, the high scroll-cut splashboard & side gallery above a rectangular top over-hanging an apron w/one small drawer, on baluster-turned legs w/peg feet, dramatically grain-painted

Stands 26: Fine Federal Washstand

in ochre & brown, northern New England, first quarter 19th century, 20 ¼ x 35 ¾", 37 ¼" h. 9,775.00
(Illustration: Stands 27)

Washstand, Victorian Gothic Revival substyle, rosewood, scrolled white marble splashboard above a rectangular marble top over a beaded case w/single long frieze drawer over a pair of cabinet doors w/arched panels, on square block feet on casters, mid-19th century......577.00
(Illustration: Stands 28)

Washstand, Victorian Renaissance Revival substyle, walnut & burl walnut, a high white marble splashback w/notched corners & two small shelves above the rectangular white marble top w/molded edges over a case w/three long drawers, each w/three raised burl panels & black pear-shaped pulls, molded base, on casters, ca. 1875, 17 x 31", 29" h. 1,495.00
(Illustration: Stands 29)

Stands 27: Painted Federal Washstand

Stands 28: Gothic Revival Washstand

Stands 29: Renaissance Revival Washstand

Art Deco stand, marble, octagonal top w/fluted apron on a tapering square standard, on a stepped & fluted square base, white & green marble, impressed & incised "FRANCE," ca. 1925, 24 ⅜" w., 14 ¼" d., 29 ¼" h. 747.00

**Stands 31:
Fine Federal Stand**

Stands 30: Classical Three-Drawer Stand

Classical country-style three-drawer stand, pine, the rectangular top above three graduated drawers, recessed side panel sides, on tapering ring- and baluster-turned legs, on blunt arrow feet, Penn-sylvania, 1810-1850,

Stands 32: Shaker Stand

20" w., 23 ½" d., 29 ⅝" h. 690.00
(Illustration: Stands 30)

Federal stand, inlaid cherry, the rectangular top above an apron w/wavy birch raised panels w/mahogany crossbanded borders on tapering turned & reeded legs, New England, ca. 1815, refinished, 16 ½" w., 17" d., 28 ¼" h. 2,300.00
(Illustration: Stands 31)

Federal one-drawer stand, tiger stripe maple, the rectangular top over a frieze drawer, on slender tapering square legs, New England, ca. 1810, old refinish, 18 ½" w., 15" d., 23 ¾" h. 1,265.00

Federal one-drawer stand, curly maple, rectangular top over single drawer & splayed tapering square legs, 17 ¾" w., 17" d., 26" h. (replaced pull) 1,980.00

Federal country-style two-drawer stand, cherry & curly maple, the rectan-gular one-board top over a deep apron w/two drawers, on ring- and baluster-turned legs, 19th century, refinished, patch to top & small repair to front edge strip, 21 ¾" w., 16 ¾" d., 28 ¼" h. 770.00

Shaker work stand, red-painted cherry & birch, the rectangular top above a frieze w/one drawer, on square tapering legs, Hancock, Massachusetts, ca. 1840, 17 ½ x 24 ½", 28 ½" h. 4,025.00
(Illustration: Stands 32)

STOOLS

Classical footstools, mahogany, rectangular serpentine upholstered tops over high serpentine sides w/continuous beading, on serpentine bracket feet on casters, the tops upholstered w/blue velvet, ca. 1840, 19 ½" w., 16" d., 16" h. 1,650.00
(Illustration: Stools 1)

Stools 1: Classical Footstools

Classical piano stool, carved mahogany, the bowed tablet crestrail above a rosette & scroll-carved slat flanked by molded & scrolled stiles above a trapezoidal seat over a ring-turned swivel pedestal on a quadripartite base w/leaf-carved knees & animal paw feet, on casters, New York City, ca. 1810-20, 17 ¼" sq. seat, 33 ⅛" h. 2,990.00
(Illustration: Stools 2)

Country-style stool, painted, worn splint seat on turned cylindrical legs joined by two sets of box stretchers, worn black paint over old red, 27 ½" h. 148.00

George I footstool, walnut, the rectangular drop-in upholstered seat raised on scroll-carved cabriole legs ending in pad feet, England, early 18th century, 23" l 2,300.00
(Illustration: Stools 3)

George III stool, mahogany, the rectangular padded & upholstered seat on straight legs joined by stretchers, England, late 18th century, 19 ¾" w., 16" d., 19" h. 920.00
(Illustration: Stools 4)

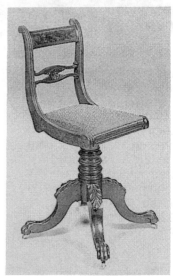

Stools 2: Classical Piano Stool

Stools 4: George III Stool

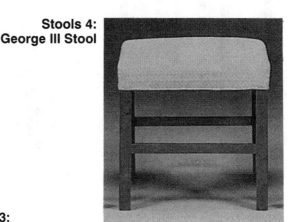

Stools 3: George I Footstool

Stools 5: George IV Stool

Stools 6: Mission Oak Footstools

George IV stool, painted & parcel-gilt, the rectangular overupholstered seat w/foliate-carved apron, raised on circular tapering legs, England, ca. 1820 ....3,163.00
(Illustration: Stools 5)

Mission-style (Arts & Crafts movement) footstool, oak, rectangular top w/original leather w/tack trim & arched apron raised on four square legs

joined by uneven stretchers, worn leather & worn recent finish, branded Gustav Stickley mark, Model No. 301, early 20th century, 16 x 20", 15 ½" h. 1,210.00
(Illustration: Stools 6, left)

Mission-style (Arts & Crafts movement) "gout" footstool, oak, rectangular top w/original brown leather, raised on four short flaring feet, skinned

medium brown finish, remnants of paster mark of Gustav Stickley, Model No. 302, 12" l., 4 ¾" h. 935.00
(Illustration: Stools 6, right)

Modern style "Z" stools, vinyl & chrome, original round red vinyl upholstery on chromed tubular steel Z-shaped frame w/footrest & loop foot, designed by Gilbert Rohde, labeled by the manufacturer, Troy

Stools 7: Chrome "Z" Stools

Stools 9: Shaker Footstool

Stools 8: Pilgrim Century Joint Stool

Sunshade Company, Troy, Ohio, ca. 1930, upholstery tears, 23 ¾" h., pr. 230.00
(Illustration: Stools 7)

Pilgrim Century joint stool, white oak & sycamore, the rectangular molded-edge top above a plain apron on turned legs joined by a box stretcher, ending in bulb feet, American or English, ca. 1700, 13 ¼ x 19 ¾", 22 ¼" h. 1,265.00
(Illustration: Stools 8)

Shaker footstool, slanted rectangular top supported on side rails w/turned feet joined by front & rear stretchers, worn dark original finish w/"Mt. Lebanon N.Y. Shaker" label on underside of top, 11 ½" w., 11 ½" d., 7" h. 522.00
(Illustration: Stools 9)

Turn of the century organ stool, oak, a round seat w/molded edge adjusting

Stools 10: Turn of the Century Organ Stool

above a base w/four canted baluster- and ring-turned legs ending in metal & glass ball-and-claw feet & joined by turned stretchers to a central post, ca. 1900-1910, 14 ½" d. 225.00
(Illustration: Stools 10)

Victorian footstool, Rococo substyle, rosewood, the carved serpentine seatrail on carved cabriole legs on casters, upholstered w/needlepoint, mid-19th century, 17" w., 17" d., 14" h. 412.00
(Illustration: Stools 11)

Windsor footstools, painted & decorated, oval top decorated w/large stylized tulip blossom & leafy stems against a black ground, on simple turned & canted legs, inscribed under the top "Willis - Eastn...Ester," early 19th century, some paint wear, pr. 9,200.00
(Illustration: Stools 12)

Stools 11: Victorian Footstool

Stools 12: Decorated Windsor Footstools

Tables

Art Deco console table, wrought iron & marble, the D-form green marble top above an apron set w/leafage, berries & stylized blossoms, the pedestal in U-form set w/a cluster of flowerheads at the base, on a stepped plinth, stamped "EDGAR BRANDT," ca. 1925, 22 ¾ x 61", 35" h. 40,250.00
(Illustration: Tables 1)

Art Deco dining table, gilt-bronze mounted mahogany & fruitwood marquetry, the rectangular inlaid top raised on carved & inlaid round legs w/urn-form feet & gilt-bronze trim, U-form stretcher, France, ca. 1930, 39 ½ x 79", 29 ½" h. 7,475.00
(Illustration: Tables 2)

Art Deco game table, *ebene de Macassar* & galuchat, the square top inlaid w/a game board in alternating squares of galuchat & banded in ivory, above an apron banded w/galuchat & set w/a smaller drawer on each side, ivory *sabot*, attributed to Dominique, France, ca. 1925, 29 ½" w., 27½" h. 8,625.00
(Illustration: Tables 3)

Tables 1: Art Deco Console Table

Tables 2: Art Deco Dining Table

Tables 3: Art Deco Game Table

Tables 5: Art Deco Vanity Table

Art Deco occasional table, wrought iron & marble, the oval green marble top raised on six tall slender scrolling fern leaves joined by a circle at the bottom, on an oval stepped green marble base, designed by Paul Kis, ca. 1930s, 24 ½ x 32 ½", 32" h.....11,500.00
(Illustration: Tables 4)

Art Deco vanity table, *ebene de Macassar* & lacquer, the rectangular top w/stepped edges set w/a rectangular mirror center panel w/small drawer below, flanked by two flip-top cosmetic wells, U-form slender tapering legs ending in ivory lacquered feet, France, ca. 1925, 18 x 33 ½", 27 ½" h. 2,875.00
(Illustration: Tables 5)

Tables 4: Art Deco Occasional Table

Art Nouveau center table,
carved mahogany &
marble, the round ochre
yellow veined marble top
set into a molded frame
carved at each leg w/a
cluster of lilac blossoms &
leafage, on square molded
legs w/swelled feet, design
attributed to René Lalique,
ca. 1900, 35 ¼" d.,
29 ½" h. 5,175.00
(Illustration: Tables 6)

Art Nouveau dining table,
mahogany, "Chicoree"
patt., the rectangular top
w/molded edges & rounded
corners overhanging a
molded apron & heavy
molded tapering legs
carved w/floral panels,
designed by Louis
Majorelle, France, ca.
1900, w/five replacement
leaves, 47 ¼ x 58",
28 ¾" h. 12,650.00

Art Nouveau side table,
fruitwood marquetry, the
square top w/outset pointed corners inlaid overall in
various woods w/magnolia
blossoms & leaves, raised
on four slender forked
supports joined by four-
lobe lower shelf also inlaid
w/magnolia blossoms,
signed in marquetry
"Gallé," France, ca. 1900,
23 ½" w., 43" h. 1,725.00
(Illustration: Tables 7)

Art Nouveau tea table,
marquetry inlaid & carved
mahogany, the shaped
rectangular top inlaid w/a
roundel w/a goose girl &
her flocks w/clusters of
leaves, within a rusticated
border, raised on a leafy
vine-wrapped twig legs
joined by a medial shelf,
Schmann, France, ca.
1900, 22 x 29", 32" h. ...4,255.00
(Illustration: Tables 8)

**Tables 7:
Art Nouveau Side Table**

Tables 6: Art Nouveau Center Table

Tables 8: Art Nouveau Tea Table

Tables 9:
Arts & Crafts Game Table

Arts & Crafts game table,
oak, the round top inlaid
w/a dark & light wood
game board, w/pull-out
sections at each side,
raised on rectangular legs
joined by an upper shelf on
four spindles above an X-
form stretcher at the base,
ca. 1910, 30" h. 460.00
(Illustration: Tables 9)

Arts & Crafts 'trestle'
table, oak, the rectangular
leather-covered top
w/large tack trim above a
shaped trestle base w/a
thick medial stretcher
w/through tenon & keys,
original chestnut top
w/new leather, Gustav
Stickley, Model No. 637,
early 20th century,
30 x 48", 29" h..............2,200.00
(Illustration: Tables 10)

Charles II occasional
table, ash & beech, the
thumb-molded rectangular
top on ball-turned legs
joined at top & bottom by
turned stretchers, England,
late 17th century, two
stretchers of later date,
25 ½" w., 16 ½" d.,
21" h. 2,185.00
(Illustration: Tables 11)

Tables 10: Arts & Crafts Trestle Table

Tables 11: Charles II Occasional Table

Chinese Export occasional table, red lacquer, the clover leaf-shaped red lacquer top over an apron w/gilt flowers & birds on a ring-turned standard on four foliate-carved, gilded & ebonized downscrolled legs, China, early 19th century, 38 ½" d., 29 ½" h. 1,980.00
(Illustration: Tables 12)

Chippendale card table, mahogany, the rectangular fold-over top w/squared outset corners opening to a baize-lined playing surface w/four scooped wells, above a conforming apron w/one short drawer, on cabriole legs carved w/shells & double pendant husks & ending in claw-and-ball feet, Newport, Rhode Island, ca. 1760, 15 ⅝ x 30 ⅜", 27 ⅜" h...48,300.00
(Illustration: Tables 13)

Chippendale card table, mahogany, the hinged rectangular fold-over top over a flattened-arch apron w/one long cock-beaded drawer, on cabriole legs ending in claw-and-ball feet, Philadelphia, ca. 1765, 17 x 34 ⅛", 29" h...................35,650.00
(Illustration: Tables 14)

Tables 12: Chinese Export Table

**Tables 13:
Newport Chippendale Card Table**

**Tables 14:
Philadelphia Chippendale Card Table**

Chippendale drop-leaf breakfast table, mahogany, the oblong top with hinged D-shaped leaves above a cyma-shaped apron on cabriole legs ending in claw-and-ball feet, restorations to top, Boston, ca. 1760, overall 33" w., 33 ½" l., 26" h..1,840.00
(Illustration: Tables 15)

Chippendale dining table, cherry, rectangular top flanked by wide drop leaves, on cabriole legs ending in claw-and-ball feet, possibly Rhode Island, ca. 1780, old refinish, minor imperfections, open 50 ¼ x 52 ½", 27 ¼" h. 6,900.00
(Illustration: Tables 16)

Chippendale drop-leaf dining table, walnut, the rectangular top flanked by drop leaves above a plain apron on cabriole legs ending in claw-and-ball feet, Philadelphia, some restorations to top, feet slightly reduced, ca. 1770, overall 41 ½" w., 36" l., 28 ¾" h..........4,025.00
(Illustration: Tables 17)

Tables 15:
Chippendale Breakfast Table

Tables 16:
Chippendale Cherry Dining Table

Tables 17:
Chippendale Walnut Dining Table

**Chippendale drop-leaf
  dining table**, mahogany,
the rectangular top
w/rectangular drop leaves
above a flattened-arch
apron on four stop-fluted
square legs, Newport,
Rhode Island, ca. 1750,
overall 47 ⅞" w., 48 ¼" d.,
27 ¾" h. 3,450.00
(Illustration: Tables 18)

**Chippendale Pembroke
  table**, walnut, the
rectangular top w/D-
shaped leaves above a
single drawer, on tapered
square molded legs joined
by cross stretchers, Pennsylvania, ca. 1800, old
finish, overall 42 ¼" w.,
32" l., 28 ¼" h. (brass &
stretchers replaced)........495.00

Chippendale game table,
walnut, rectangular fold-

Tables 18: Newport Chippendale Dining Table

**Tables 19:
Chippendale Game Table**

**Tables 20:
Chippendale Curly Maple Tea Table**

over top above an apron
w/a single long drawer
w/two butterfly brasses & a
keyhole escutcheon, on
square legs w/scroll-cut
brackets, Pennsylvania,
ca. 1780, minor
imperfections,
13 x 38", 28 ½" h. 5,750.00
(Illustration: Tables 19)

**Chippendale tilt-top tea
table**, curly maple, the
circular dished top tilting &
revolving above a birdcage
support & vase-form
standard, the lower section
of the standard fluted &
leaf-carved, on tripod base
w/cabriole legs ending in
claw-and-ball feet, repair to
one foot, Pennsylvania, ca.
1770, 35" d., 28 ½" h. ...8,050.00
(Illustration: Tables 20)

**Chippendale tilt-top tea
table**, mahogany, the
serpentine top w/molded
edges tilting above an urn-
form standard on tripod
base w/cabriole legs
ending in snake feet,
Massachusetts, ca. 1780,
32 x 32", 28 ½" h. 2,875.00
(Illustration: Tables 21)

**Chippendale tilt-top tea
table**, mahogany, the
circular top tilting above a
vase-form standard
w/spiral fluted flattened-urn
on a tripod base w/cabriole
legs ending in elongated
claw-and-ball feet, Rhode
Island, ca. 1770, 34 ¼" d.,
27 ⅜" h. 1,955.00
(Illustration: Tables 22)

Chippendale tea table,
mahogany, the round top
tilting above a birdcage
mechanism above the

**Tables 21: Massachusetts Chippendale
Tea Table**

Tables 22: Rhode Island Chippendale Tea Table

baluster-turned standard on a tripod base w/cabriole legs ending in pad feet, probably New England, ca. 1780, old refinish, minor imperfections, 34" d., 28½" h. 1,035.00
(Illustration: Tables 23)

Chippendale tilt-top tea table, mahogany, the crotch-figured single-board circular dished piecrust top tilting & revolving above a birdcage support, on a fluted & acanthus-carved compressed ball standard, the lower section of the standard carved w/a ring of beads above X-carved reserves, on acanthus- and cabochon-carved legs ending in claw-and-ball feet, Philadel-phia, ca. 1765, 34 ⅞" d., 28" h. 596,500.00
(Illustration: Tables 24)

Tables 25:
Chippendale Work Table

Tables 23:
Chippendale Tea Table

Tables 24:
Rare Philadelphia Chippendale Table

Chippendale country-style work table, walnut, the rectangular three-board top w/rounded corners above an apron fitted w/two thumb-molded drawers of unequal width, on tapering turned legs & compressed ball feet, Pennsylvania, 1780-1820, 58 ¼" w., 35 ½" d., 30" h. 1,840.00
(Illustration: Tables 25)

Chippendale Revival dining table, carved mahogany, oval divided top w/a carved border band, a deep apron w/a crank hole at one end for opening the top, on four scroll-carved cabriole legs ending in claw-and-ball feet, England, late 19th - early 20th century, 70 ½ x 70", 29" h. 880.00
(Illustration: Tables 26)

Classical drop-leaf breakfast table, mahogany, rectangular top w/two shaped leaves above a single-drawer frieze w/turned pendants, reeded urn-form standard on water-leaf-carved downturning legs w/brass animal paw feet on brass casters, probably New York, ca. 1820, overall 48 ¼" w., 36" deep, 27 ⅝" h. 7,475.00
(Illustration: Tables 27)

Classical drop-leaf breakfast table, mahogany, the rectangular top w/two D-shaped leaves above an apron w/single drawer, on a classically-carved standard w/carved & scrolled legs

**Tables 26:
Chippendale Revival Dining Table**

**Tables 27:
Classical New York Breakfast Table**

ending in paw feet, Philadelphia, in the manner of Anthony Quervelle, early 19th century, 46 ¾" w., 37" d., 28" h. ....1,650.00 (Illustration: Tables 28)

Classical card table, mahogany, the hinged fold-over rectangular top w/molded edge above a scrolled apron, on a foliate-carved obelisk-shaped standard on a stepped plinth base w/scrolled feet on casters, Boston, early 19th century, 34 ¾" w., 35 ½" d., 27 ¼" h. ....1,100.00 (Illustration: Tables 29)

Classical card table, the rectangular hinged fold-over top w/outset front & beaded edges above a conforming apron w/ormolu mounts & beaded lower edge over a lyre pedestal w/brass rods, on downswept incised legs ending in brass paw feet on casters, Boston, 1815-1820, 36 ⅜" w., 36" d., 30 ⅞" h. ....2,070.00 (Illustration: Tables 30)

Classical center table, mahogany, the serpentine white marble top w/chamfered corners above a conforming apron

Tables 28:
Classical Philadelphia Breakfast Table

Tables 30:
Lyre-base Classical Card Table

Tables 29:
Boston Classical Card Table

on downscrolled legs joined by serpentine stretchers, on bracket feet, ca. 1840-1850, 35" w., 35" d., 27 ¼" h. 1,320.00
(Illustration: Tables 31)

Classical center table, mahogany, the variegated green & white round marble top over a veneered apron w/beaded edge, on an acanthus-carved turned standard on four acanthus-carved legs ending in paw feet, 19th century, 43" d., 29" h...2,200.00
(Illustration: Tables 32)

Classical console table, mahogany, the D-shaped white marble top above a veneered apron on a ring- and acanthus-carved standard on four down-swept reeded legs ending in paw feet on brass casters, early 19th century, 46 ¼" w., 23 ¾" d., 29 ¼" h. 880.00
(Illustration: Tables 33)

Classical dressing table, tiger stripe maple & mahogany, a high scroll-cut splashboard w/knob finials above the

**Tables 31:
Classical Center Table**

**Tables 32:
Round Classical Center Table**

Tables 34: Classical Dressing Table

splashboard w/knob finials
above the rectangular top
w/notched front corners
above a long mahogany
drawer w/two maple
knobs, raised on ring-,
baluster- and knob-turned
legs w/peg feet, ca. 1825,
refinished, imperfections,
19½ x 36", 35" h. 1,840.00
(Illustration: Tables 34)

**Classical Boston pier
table,** ormolu-mounted
mahogany, the rectangular
white marble top above a
frieze w/a central floral
mount flanked by two
wreath-form mounts, on
tapering columns w/ormolu
capitals, the shaped plinth
base w/mirror plate behind,
on acanthus-carved &
ribbed feet, Boston,
Massachusetts, ca. 1820,
marble replaced, 19 x 40¼",
36¾" h. 4,025.00
(Illustration: Tables 35)

**Tables 33:
Classical Console Table**

Tables 35: Classical Boston Pier Table

Tables 36: Classical Pier Table

Classical pier table,
mahogany, the rectangular
white marble top above an
ogee-molded apron
acanthus-carved down-
scrolled supports, the
paneled & mirrored back
on incurved plinth base,
Boston, early 19th century,
19 x 43¼", 35½" h. 3,520.00
(Illustration: Tables 36)

Classical pier table,
mahogany, the rectangular
white marble top above an
ogee-molded apron
w/beveled edge on
scrolled supports w/curved
brackets, the mirrored
back above a scrolled
serpentine shelf, on
scrolled feet, ca. 1840,
41½" w., 18 ½" d.,
36 ½" h. 2,090.00
(Illustration: Tables 37)

Classical sewing table,
mahogany, a rectangular
top w/cut-corners above
a conforming case w/two
drawers w/round brass
florette pulls, raised on
lyre-form supports
w/outswept feet joined
by a baluster-turned
stretcher, the case hung
w/a rectangular cloth
work basket, New Eng-
land, ca. 1820, replaced
brasses, refinished &
restored,16 ¾ x 21 ½",
29 ½" h. 1,210.00
(Illustration: Tables 38)

Classical side table,
mahogany, rectangular
black marble top w/round-
ed corners above a
conforming ogee apron
raised on a pair of S-scroll
supports above a flaring

**Tables 37: Late
Classical Pier Table**

**Tables 38:
Classical Sewing
Table**

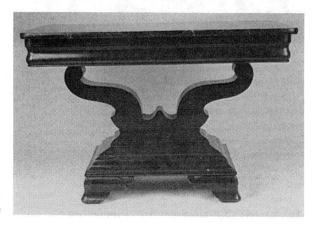

**Tables 39: Classical
Side Table**

stepped base on ogee
bracket feet, Massa-
chusetts, ca.1835, minor
veneer loss, 20 ½ x 44 ½",
29 ½" h. 2,530.00
(Illustration: Tables 39)

Classical work table,
burled maple, the
rectangular top w/rose-
wood crossbanded edge
over a case w/one short
drawer & a similar
recessed short drawer
flanked by diminutive
applied columns, on a
flaring rectangular support
above a concave rectan-
gular base w/scrolled legs
ending in animal paw feet
on casters, Boston, 1810-
1820, 24" w., 16 ½" d.,
29 ¾" h. 4,025.00
(Illustration: Tables 40)

Classical work table,
mahogany veneer, the
rectangular molded-edge
top w/rounded-corner
drop-leaves above a case
w/three bolection-molded
drawers the bottom a
sham drawer opening
to a rounded well, on
flaring molded column legs
joined by a shaped H-
stretcher, on disk feet &
casters, Boston, 1810-
1820, 19 x 38¼",
29¼" h. 3,450.00
(Illustration: Tables 41)

Classical work table,
carved mahogany &
mahogany veneer, the
square top flanked by D-
shaped end drop leaves
above an apron w/a
narrow long drawer above
a very narrow long drawer,

Tables 40: Classical Maple Work Table

**Tables 41:
Classical Mahogany Work Table**

each w/two wooden knobs above a suspended cloth work bag, raised on columnar supports joined by a thick, curved-sided medial shelf above bulbous leaf-carved feet on casters, Massachusetts, ca. 1833, old finish, some imperfections, w/family provenance, 20" sq., 29" h. 1,955.00
(Illustration: Tables 42)

Early American country-style tea table, painted, oblong top above a deeply arched apron & canted turned legs ending in button feet, old surface w/red paint, New England, 18th century, minor imperfections, 22 x 32", 26" h. 9,200.00
(Illustration: Tables 43)

Early American country-style work table, walnut, the rectangular top widely overhanging an above

Tables 44: Early Walnut Work Table

Tables 43: Early American Tea Table

Tables 42: Classical Work Table

w/one small & one long drawer w/wooden knobs, on heavy baluster-turned legs w/block & baluster-turned stretchers joined by a flat stretcher, ball feet, old refinish, probably Pennsylvania, last half 18th century, restoration, 32½ x 63", 29" h...........1,380.00
(Illustration: Tables 44)

Federal card table, inlaid mahogany, the rectangular top w/hollow front & banded apron, on five line-inlaid square tapering legs ending in crossbanded cuffs, Baltimore, ca. 1800, minor repairs to inlay, 17½ x 36", 28¼" h. 1,495.00
(Illustration: Tables 45)

Federal card table, mahogany inlaid with bird's-eye maple & rose-wood, the oblong top w/bowed front & serpentine sides above a frieze inlaid w/an oval reserve, rectangular inlaid dies flanking on line-inlaid square tapering legs ending in crossbanded cuffs, New England, ca. 1805, 17½ x 36", 30" h. 5,463.00
(Illustration: Tables 46)

Federal card table, brass-inlaid mahogany, the oblong fold-over top w/conformingly-shaped hinged leaf swiveling to reveal a well, the brass-inlaid apron below on a double-lyre support w/brass strings, the plinth base raised on brass-inlaid down-turning legs ending in brass animal paw feet,

Tables 45: Federal Card Table

Tables 46: Inlaid Federal Card Table

on brass casters, repairs to lyres, Boston, ca. 1810, 17 x 34 ⅜", 29 ½" h.................................4,025.00
(Illustration: Tables 47)

Federal card table, curly maple, the fold-over top w/bowed front & serpentine sides w/conformingly-shaped leaf, a conformingly-shaped apron w/geo-metric-inlaid edge, on square tapering legs ending in crossbanded cuffs, New England, ca. 1810, 16 ½ x 34", 29 ¼" h.................................5,462.00
(Illustration: Tables 48)

Federal card table, inlaid flame-birch & mahogany, the demi-lune fold-over top w/inlaid edge above a flame-birch apron w/veneered reserves, on square tapering legs w/crossbanded cuffs, North Shore, Massachusetts, ca. 1800, 35 ⅝" w., 33 ½" d., 29 ½" h. 6,325.00

Federal card table, the rectangular fold-over top w/rounded front corners & out-set center & reeded edge opening above a conforming apron, raised on slender tapering reeded legs w/ring-turned cuffs & cylindrical feet, Philadelphia, 1800-10, 35 ½" w., 29 ¼" h. 863.00
(Illustration: Tables 49)

Tables 47: Federal Boston Card Table

Tables 48: Federal Curly Maple Card Table

**Tables 49:
Federal Philadelphia Card Table**

Federal dining table, two-part, inlaid cherry, each D-shaped section w/a drop leaf, low arched aprons divided by reeded panels above spiral-turned legs ending in peg feet, New England, ca. 1825, old refinish, 42 x 61", 29" h. 3,450.00
(Illustration: Tables 50)

Federal dining table, three-part, mahogany, the center section w/a rectangular top flanked by wide drop leaves, raised on square beaded legs, the two D-form end sections also on square beaded legs, old finish, minor imperfections, ca. 1780-1800, 60 x 127", 28" h. 6,325.00
(Illustration: Tables 51)

Federal dining table, inlaid mahogany, comprising two D-shaped end sections & a rectangular center section w/two drop leaves, the checkered line-inlaid apron w/ebony-banded border centering rectangular inlaid dies, on line-inlaid square tapering legs ending in cross-banded cuffs, New England, ca. 1810, minor repairs, 47 ¾ x 102", 28 ½" h. 3,450.00
(Illustration: Tables 52)

Federal dressing table, cherry, the rectangular top w/rounded corners above a conforming case w/arched kneehole flanked by two short cockbeaded drawers, on ball- and baluster-turned legs,

Tables 50: Federal Cherry Dining Table

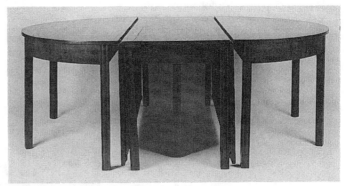

Tables 51: Federal Three-Part Dining Table

Tables 52: Federal Dining Table

probably Pennsylvania, 1830-1840, 36 ¾" w., 17" d., 26 ¾" h. 1,035.00
(Illustration: Tables 53)

Federal country-style dressing table, grain-painted to imitate curly maple, rectangular top w/beveled edge & scrolled-end splashboard over a single drawer, on turned legs, original paint w/touchup repair, 19th century, 34" w., 17 ¼" d., 29 ½" h. plus splash-board...440.00
(Illustration: Tables 54)

Federal drop-leaf table, inlaid mahogany, the rectangular top w/D-shaped leaves above a conforming demi-lune inlaid apron w/drawer, on reeded tapering legs w/flattened ball & cylindrical feet in socket casters, Boston, possibly shop of John & Thomas Seymour, 1800-1815, 39¼ x 44" d., 30" h. 6,325.00
(Illustration: Tables 55)

Tables 53: Federal Dressing Table

**Tables 54:
Federal Country-Style Dressing Table**

**Tables 55:
Federal Drop-Leaf Table**

**Federal drop-leaf side
 table,** tiger stripe maple, a
 rectangular top flanked by
 D-shaped drop leaves
 above an apron w/a
 drawer at one end, on
 square slightly tapering
 legs, New England,
 ca. 1820, old finish,
 16 x 35½", 29" 1,092.50
 (Illustration: Tables 56)

Federal game table,
 mahogany & inlaid bird's-
 eye maple, rectangular
 fold-over top w/serpentine
 sides above a conforming
 apron w/panels of maple
 inlay, turned tapering
 reeded legs w/slender
 swelled post feet, probably
 Massachusetts, ca. 1815,
 old finish, 18 x 36½",
 30¼" 2,990.00
 (Illustration: Tables 57)

Federal Pembroke table,
 cherry, the oblong top w/D-
 shaped leaves above a
 banded drawer & apron,
 on square tapering line-
 inlaid legs headed by
 paterae & ending in cross-
 banded cuffs, early 19th
 century, overall 35" w.,
 32" d., 27 ¼" h. 2,200.00

Federal Pembroke table,
 mahogany, the rectangular
 top w/bowed ends &
 serpentine-shaped leaves
 above a frieze w/drawer,
 on molded square legs
 w/pierced brackets,
 Massachusetts, ca. 1770,
 overall 35 ⅝ x 33 ¼",
 27 ½" h. 5,175.00

Federal Pembroke table,
 cherry, the oblong top

Tables 56: Federal Tiger Maple Table

**Tables 57:
Federal Mahogany & Maple Game Table**

w/serpentine-shaped leaves above a frieze w/drawer, on square tapering legs, New England, ca. 1795, overall 37 ½ x 40", 29" h. ....2,875.00 *(Illustration: Tables 58)*

Federal sewing table, inlaid mahogany & maple, the oblong top w/checkered line-inlaid edge above a single drawer, a sewing bag slide below, each corner w/three-quarter-round ring turned colonnettes, on reeded tapering legs ending in tapered feet, Massachusetts, ca. 1810, 14 ¾ x 17 ⅞", 29 ⅛" h. ....2,875.00 *(Illustration: Tables 59)*

Federal work table, carved mahogany, the rectangular hinged top opening to a fitted interior & hinged writing surface opening to a well, above a case w/two drawers flanked by stop-fluted pilasters, over reeded legs & a shelf, on vase-turned feet & socket casters, New England, 1800-1810, 21 ½" w., 15 ½" d., 28 ¾" h. ....863.00 *(Illustration: Tables 60)*

Federal country-style work table, pine & poplar, batten-braced removable three-board top widely overhanging a deep apron w/two short drawers centering a cross hatched panel, on tapering square legs, legs clipped, 19th century, 50 ½" w., 30 ½" d., 25 ½" h. 495.00

Tables 58: Federal Pembroke Table

Tables 59: Federal Sewing Table

Tables 60: Federal Work Table

Federal Revival side table, walnut & walnut veneer, the oblong top w/molded edge above an apron w/blocks above six ring- and baluster-turned reeded tapering legs joined by T-stretchers, ca. 1920s, 20 x 32", 28 ¼" h. ....150.00 *(Illustration: Tables 61)*

George I card table, mahogany & padouk, rectangular fold-over top above a deep apron, on cabriole legs w/shell & scroll-carved knees & ending in claw-and-ball feet, England, first half 18th century, 14½ x 26½", 26" h. ....6,325.00 *(Illustration: Tables 62)*

George I dressing table, oak, the rectangular molded top above a long frieze drawer & two short drawers flanking a scroll-carved kneehole on

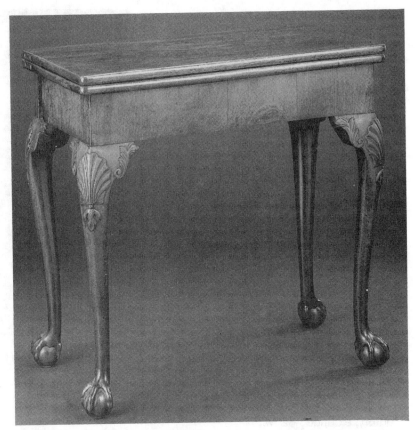

Tables 62: George I Card Table

Tables 61: Federal Revival Table

Tables 63: George I Dressing Table

cabriole legs ending in pad feet,
England, early 18th century, 32" w.,
19" d., 28 ½" h. 1,380.00
(Illustration: Tables 63)

George I dressing table, walnut, the
rectangular molded top above three
frieze drawers & arched apron, on
cabriole legs pointed pad feet, w/overall
crossbanding, England, early 18th
century, 18 x 30", 27" h. 8,050.00
(Illustration: Tables 64)

George II card table, mahogany, the
rectangular fold-over w/outset squared
corners, the conforming apron below on
frontal acanthus-carved cabriole legs
ending in claw-and-ball feet, the straight
tapering rear legs ending in pad feet,
England, mid-18th century, repairs to
rear leg & swing rail, 13 x 27",
28 ¾" h..4,312.00
(Illustration: Tables 65)

George II drop-leaf dining table,
mahogany, the rounded top & leaves on
scroll-carved cabriole legs ending in pad
feet, England, second quarter 18th
century, extended 52" w.,
47" d., 28" h. 3,450.00
(Illustration: Tables 66)

Tables 64: George I Dressing Table

Tables 65: George II Card Table

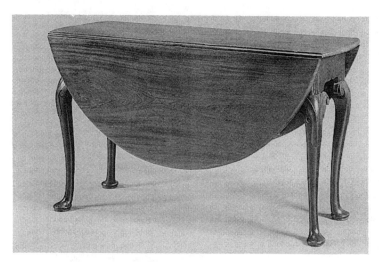

Tables 66: George II Dining Table

George II side table, walnut, the rectangular top w/grey-veined white marble above a molded-edge apron, raised on shell-carved cabriole legs ending in claw-and-ball feet, restored, England, mid-18th century, 31 x 60", 31" h. ....6,900.00 *(Illustration: Tables 67)*

George III card tables, inlaid mahogany, each w/D-shaped fold-over top opening to a baize-lined surface above a conforming apron, raised on circular tapering reeded legs, England, ca. 1795, 17 ¼ x 35 ½", 29 ¼" h., pr. ....10,350.00 *(Illustration: Tables 68, one of two)*

George III two-pedestal dining table, mahogany, the rectangular top w/rounded corners, each

Tables 67: George II Side Table

Tables 69: George III "Drum" Table

Tables 68: George III Card Table

baluster-form standard
above four reeded down-
swept tapering legs ending
in brass paw feet on
casters, England, late 18th
century, overall 54 x 90",
28" h. 24,150.00

George III "drum" table,
mahogany, the gilt-tooled
leather-inset circular top
swiveling above a frieze
w/four cockbeaded
drawers, alternating
w/false drawers, above an
urn-turned standard on
four reeded downswept
legs ending in brass paw
feet on casters, England,
ca. 1800, 31" d.,
30" h. 8,050.00
(Illustration: Tables 69)

George III Pembroke table,
satinwood-banded
mahogany, the rectangular
top & D-shaped leaves
above a frieze drawer, all
w/satinwood banding, on
ring-turned tapering legs,
England, late 18th century,
overall 41" w., 31" d.,
28" h. 4,025.00
(Illustration: Tables 70)

George III Pembroke table,
mahogany, the banded
line-inlaid rectangular top
& D-shaped drop leaves
above a frieze drawer on
an urn-form standard
w/reeded downswept legs
on casters, England, late
18th century, overall,
37 x 47¾", 28" h...........4,370.00

George III Pembroke table,
painted satinwood, the
rectangular top & D-
shaped leaves painted
w/border of flowers above

Tables 70: George III Pembroke Table

Tables 71: George III Pembroke Table

a frieze drawer opposed by a false-fronted drawer, booth similarly painted, raised on bellflower-painted square tapering legs, ending in casters, England, ca. 1780, overall 31 ½ x 37 ¼", 28½" h. 17,250.00
(Illustration: Tables 71)

George IV marble-top pier table, mahogany, the rectangular green marble top above a molded apron, raised on foliate-carved scrolling legs ending in animal paw feet, plain back legs, England, ca. 1830, 20 x 46½", 35" h. 17,250.00
(Illustration: Tables 72)

Hutch (or chair) table, scrubbed pine & paint, the scrubbed pine three-board top w/breadboard ends lifting above single-board sides joined by a seat w/top opening to storage well, on shoe feet, the base w/old red paint, New England, 18th century, 44 ¼" w., 35 ¾" d., 29" h. 4,600.00
(Illustration: Tables 73)

Hutch (or chair) table, pine, the four-board rectangular top lifting above single-board ends on shoe feet joined by a seat over one large dovetailed drawer, old refinish, 57" w., 46" d., 30" h. (top replaced).....1,100.00

Louis XV country-style side table, inlaid walnut, the thumb-molded crossbanded rectangular top above an apron w/long molded drawer & scrolled

Tables 72: George IV Marble-Top Pier Table

Tables 73: Early Hutch Table

edge, on slender tapering cabriole legs, France, late 18th century, 30" w., 20" d., 26 ¼" h. 1,760.00
(Illustration: Tables 74)

Louis Philippe center table, inlaid boullework, the serpentine-shaped top w/cartouche of Diana driving a carriage, banded by a gadrooned & foliated ormolu mount above a conforming drawer, the skirt centered w/a goddess, raised on boullework-decorated cabriole legs ending in cast *sabots*, France, first half 19th century..................1,650.00
(Illustration: Tables 75)

Mission-style (Arts & Crafts movement) dining table, oak, circular fixed top above a plain apron, on square legs joined by through-tenoned X-stretchers, decal mark of L. & J.G. Stickley, ca. 1910, 42" d., 29 ⅛" h. 1,495.00
(Illustration: Tables 76)

Tables 75: Louis Philippe Center Table

Tables 76: Stickley Mission Dining Table

Tables 74: Louis XV Side Table

Mission-style (Arts & Crafts movement) dining table, oak, round split top above a square pedestal w/four square downswept legs on casters, original medium finish, Lifetime Furniture Company, Grand Rapids, Michigan, Model No. 9057, Paine Furniture retail tag, ca. 1907, w/three leaves, 48" d., 29" h. ....1,035.00 *(Illustration: Tables 77)*

Mission-style (Arts & Crafts movement) dining table, oak, circular top w/plain apron on a non-dividing tapering square base w/four shoe feet, four leaves, original medium finish, Handcraft Furniture decal, L. & J.G. Stickley, Model No. 717, ca. 1907, 48" d., 29¾" h. ....3,450.00 *(Illustration: Tables 78)*

Mission-style (Arts & Crafts movement) dressing table, oak, a large rectangular framed mirror swiveling between tapering uprights attached to the splashboard

Tables 77: Lifetime Mission Dining Table

Tables 79: Mission Oak Dressing Table

Tables 78: Mission-style Oak Dining Table

w/butterfly joints above the rectangular top over a case w/a row of three drawers above an arched kneehole opening flanked by two drawers, on square legs, original dark strap hardware w/ring pulls, original medium brown finish, red decal mark of Gustav Stickley, Model No. 907, early 20th century, 22 x 48", overall 4' 7" h. 2,750.00
(Illustration: Tables 79)

Mission-style (Arts & Crafts movement) drop-leaf table, oak, a narrow rectangular top flanked by wide drop leaves w/clipped corners above an apron w/square gate leg supports, recent dark brown finish, unmarked Gustav Stickley, Model No. 638, 40" sq. open, 30" h.............................1,540.00
(Illustration: Tables 80)

Mission-style (Arts & Crafts movement) lamp table, oak, square top w/clipped corners on angled square legs joined by through-tenoned X-stretchers, refinished, L. & J.G. Stickley, Model No. 580, 36" sq., 29" h. 880.00
(Illustration: Tables 81)

Mission-style (Arts & Crafts movement) library table, inlaid oak,

Tables 80: Mission Oak Drop-Leaf Table

Tables 81:Mission-style Lamp Table

Tables 82: Mission Oak Library Table

rectangular top over a curved apron w/single short drawer w/ebony inlay, on square legs w/ebony inlay joined by a flat medial stretcher, restored finish to top, Limbert Furniture Company, Grand Rapids, Michigan, 41 ¼" w., 26 ¼" d., 29 ¼" h. 2,750.00
(Illustration: Tables 82)

Mission-style (Arts & Crafts movement) library table, oak, rectangular top above an apron w/three short drawers over a lower medial shelf fitting into side stretchers, on square legs, hammered iron hardware, Gustav Stickley, Model No. 619, ca. 1910, refinished, 36 x 66", 30" h. 4,312.00
(Illustration: Tables 83)

Mission-style (Arts & Crafts movement) occasional table, oak, circular top on four square legs joined by through-tenoned cross stretchers surmounted by a flat circular disk, Lifetime Furniture Company, Grand

Tables 85: Rohlfs Occasional Table

Tables 83: Mission-Style Library Table

Tables 84: Mission-Style Occasional Table

Rapids, Michigan, Model No. 930, ca. 1910, refinished, 18" d., 29¼" h. ..517.00
(Illustration: Tables 84)

Mission-style (Arts & Crafts movement) occasional table, oak, octagonal top on conforming cabinet of eight pierced panels, two hinged as doors on shaped cut-out feet, original finish & hammered copper hardware, branded "R" within a bow saw, Charles Rohlfs, Buffalo, New York, ca. 1900, 34 ½" d., 29 ⅛" h. 14,950.00
(Illustration: Tables 85)

Mission-style (Arts & Crafts movement) occasional table, oak, rectangular top overhanging top arched stretchers & two side panels w/inlaid organic designs in copper, pewter & wood, on shoe feet, designed by Harvey Ellis after Baillie Scott, fine recent dark brown finish, large red decal mark of Gustav Stickley, 20 x 26", 30 ¼" h. 31,900.00
(Illustration: Tables 86)

Mission-style (Arts & Crafts movement) tea table, oak & tile, rectangular top w/four flat rails framing twelve green Grueby Pottery tiles over an arched apron & lower through-tenoned & keyed rectangular shelf, on square legs, original medium finish, red decal mark of Gustav Stickley, ca. 1903, top w/water stains & light toning, 24" w., 20 ¼" d., 25" h. 29,900.00
(Illustration: Tables 87)

Napoleon III card table, ormolu-mounted boullework, the rectangular

**Tables 86:
Harvey Ellis Occasional Table**

Tables 87: Mission Oak Tea Table

Tables 88: Napoleon III Card Table

fold-over top w/serpentine edges above a shaped apron, the front w/boullework panels flanking a figural ormolu mount, on simple cabriole legs w/figural ormolu mounts at the tops & ormolu *sabots*, France, late 19th century, 18 x 37", 29 ½" h................................1,610.00
(Illustration: Tables 88)

Queen Anne drop-leaf dining table, maple, the rectangular molded top w/demi-lune drop leaves above an apron w/outset ovolo skirt w/shaped arch, on cabriole legs ending in pad feet, New England, ca. 1750, 37 ½" d., 38 ½" d., 28 ¼" h...2,760.00
(Illustration: Tables 89)

Queen Anne dining table, walnut, a rectangular top w/rounded ends flanked by wide D-form drop leaves, on cabriole legs ending in cushioned pad feet, brass plaque reads "Nathaniel Bradlee, 1746-1813," Massachusetts, ca. 1760, 48 x 60", 28 ½" h. 11,500.00
(Illustration: Tables 90)

Queen Anne drop-leaf dining table, carved walnut, the rectangular top w/two conforming leaves above a shaped apron, on cabriole legs ending in

Tables 89: Queen Anne Drop-leaf Dining Table

Tables 92: Queen Anne Occasional Table

Tables 90: Queen Anne Dining Table

stockinged trifid feet,
Pennsylvania, ca. 1750,
overall 54" w., 44 ¼" d.,
27 ¾" h. (patches at hinge
junctures)......................6,325.00

**Queen Anne dressing
table**, walnut, the
rectangular top w/thumb-
molded edge above a
conforming case fitted
w/three short thumb-
molded drawers over a
cockbeaded flattened-arch
apron w/acorn drop-finials,
on cabriole legs ending in
pad & disk feet, Boston,
ca. 1740, 19 x 34",
28 ¼" h........................18,400.00
(Illustration: Tables 91)

**Queen Anne occasional
table**, painted wood, the
rectangular top w/plain
apron, on tapering
cylindrical legs ending in
compressed ball feet, red
paint, New England, ca.
1740, 27 ½" w., 19 ¾" d.,
26 ½" h. 1,035.00
(Illustration: Tables 92)

Queen Anne tavern table,
original blue-green paint,
the rectangular top
w/breadboard ends over
an apron w/single long
drawer w/early turned
pull, on cabriole legs
ending in pad feet, New
England, 18th century,
minor repairs, 43" w.,
24 ¼" d., 26 ½" h. 14,950.00
(Illustration: Tables 93)

Queen Anne tavern table,
maple, the oval top above
a shaped apron on drama-
tically splayed circular
tapering legs ending in

Tables 93: Queen Anne Tavern Table

Tables 91: Queen Anne Walnut Dressing Table

pad feet, retains an old finish, New England, 1740-70, 22 ¾ x 32 ½", 25 ¾" h. 20,700.00

Queen Anne "porringer-top" tea table, old black paint, the rectangular top w/porringer-shaped corners above a flattened-arch apron on cabriole legs ending in pad feet, Connecticut, 18th century, 32 ¾" w., 23" d., 26 ½" h. 13,800.00
(Illustration: Tables 94)

Queen Anne tea table, maple & pine, oval top above a scalloped apron, raking turned tapering legs ending in button feet, New England, mid-18th century, 26 x 36¾", 26" h. 3,450.00
(Illustration: Tables 95)

Queen Anne tray-top tea table, curly maple, the figured rectangular top w/thumb-molded edge above a shaped skirt on cabriole legs ending in pad feet, New England, ca. 1760, 16½ x 26¾", 25½" h. 18,400.00
(Illustration: Tables 96)

Tables 94:
Queen Anne Tea Table

Tables 95:
Queen Anne Oval-Top Tea Table

Tables 96:
Queen Anne Tray-Top Tea Table

Regency center table, mahogany, the circular top tilting above a ring-turned & gadrooned baluster standard on four downswept molded legs, ending in brass feet w/casters, England, ca. 1800, 47 ¼" d., 28 ½" h. 6,900.00
(Illustration: Tables 97)

Regency two-pedestal extension dining table, mahogany, the divided rounded rectangular top extending to accommodate two leaves, on baluster stems & down-swept legs ending in brass feet on casters, w/two extra leaves, England, early 19th century, extended 50 x 94½", 32" h. 11,500.00
(Illustration: Tables 98)

Regency game table, burl, nearly square fold-over top opening to form a leather backgammon board above an apron w/a single drawer w/a pen well & ink drawer, raised on square tapering legs w/line-inlay, spade feet, England, early 19th century, 16 x 18", 31" h. 2,587.00
(Illustration: Tables 99)

Tables 97: Regency Center Table

**Tables 99:
Regency Game Table**

**Tables 98:
Regency Two-Pedestal Dining Table**

Regency library table, brass-inlaid rosewood, the circular top w/central sunburst medallion & scrolling foliate borders on a faceted standard w/scrolled & geometric banding supported on scrolling arms, on a concave four-sided plinth ending in brass paw feet w/casters, England, ca. 1820, restoration to veneer, 54" d., 31¾" h. 29,900.00
(Illustration: Tables 100)

Regency sofa table, mahogany, the rectangular top w/D-shaped drop leaves above two frieze drawers opposed by false drawers, on a trestle support joined by a ring-turned stretcher, raised on splayed molded legs on casters, England, first quarter 19th century, 60" w., 29¾" d., 28½" h. 7,475.00
(Illustration: Tables 101)

Regency writing table, inlaid mahogany, the rectangular leather-inset top w/three drawers opposed by false drawers, raised on trestle supports w/turned stretcher, England, first quarter 19th century, 26½ x 39", 29½" h. 4,313.00
(llustration: Tables 102)

"Sawbuck" table, pine, rectangular one-board top w/breadboard ends, raised on

Tables 100:
Regency Brass-Inlaid Library Table

Tables 102: Regency Writing Table

Tables 101: Regency Sofa Table

X-ends joined by angled brace supports & flat stretchers, old natural finish on top & old worn red stain on base & underside of top, 19th century, 30" w., 17 ¼" d., 25" h. (age cracks & minor edge damage to top)...........................1,155.00

"Sawbuck" table, stained birch, the rectangular cleated two-board top widely overhanging X-form legs joined by long rectangular medial braces, top & base w/traces of probably original red stain, New England, second half 18th century, 33 x 77 ¼", 26" h................................6,325.00
(Illustration: Tables 103)

Shaker sewing table, red-stained butternut, the rectangular top above a frieze w/three drawers w/bone pegs on the dies, on square tapering legs, New Lebanon, New York, 17 ½ x 28", 25 ½" h..........................14,950.00
(Illustration: Tables 104)

Shaker work table, cherry, the oblong top w/rounded corners above a frieze w/two drawers, the rectangular supports below joined by a turned medial stretcher, on slightly arched shoe feet, Kentucky, ca. 1860, 16 ½ x 24 ½", 29 ¼" h...2,070.00
(Illustration: Tables 105)

Tables 104: Shaker Sewing Table

Tables 105: Shaker Work Table

Tables 103: Early "Sawbuck" Table

Tavern table, cherry, rectangular top over an apron w/one long drawer, on ring- and baluster-turned legs ending in baluster-turned feet, joined by stretchers, Pennsylvania, ca. 1750, 22 ½ x 33 ⅞", 27" h. 6,900.00
(Ilustration: Tables 106)

Tavern table, country-style, rectangular top overhanging a deep molded-edge apron w/single long drawer w/original turned pull, on ring- and baluster-turned legs joined by box stretchers, on ball feet, original blue paint w/scrubbed pine top, New England, mid-18th century, 28 ½ x 41 ½", 26 ½" h. 4,312.00
(Illustration: Tables 107)

Tavern table, early American country-style, painted maple & pine, rectangular top w/bread-board ends widely over-hanging an apron w/one long drawer w/small wooden knob, turned tapering legs w/peg feet, original red paint, New England, ca. 1790, 28 ½ x 44 ½", 28" h. 6,900.00
(Illustration: Tables 108)

Tavern table, maple, birch & pine, the rectangular top above a molded apron on vase- and reel-turned legs joined by molded box stretchers, ending in ball

Tables 108: Early American Tavern Table

Tables 107: Country-Style Tavern Table

Tables 106: Early Tavern Table

Tables 109: New England Tavern Table

feet, New England, ca. 1760, 19 ¼ x 31 ½", 23 ½" h..........................4,025.00
(Ilustration: Tables 109)

Tavern table, country-style, stained birch & pine, the rectangular top w/breadboard ends above a conforming case w/a single long drawer on double baluster- and block-turned legs joined by a box stretcher, on compressed ball feet, New England, 1740-1770, 46 ¾ x 21 ¾", 25 ¼" h. 4,830.00
(Ilustration: Tables 110)

Turn of the century library table, oak, rectangular top w/rounded corners above a deep apron w/a long flush-mounted drawer, raised on heavy columnar legs joined by a wide medial stretcher & on heavy ball feet on casters, 25 ½ x 42", 30 ¾" h. 690.00
(Ilustration: Tables 111)

Victorian tilt-top breakfast table, inlaid mahogany, the rectangular top w/rounded corners tilting above a baluster standard, raised on hipped downswept legs, on casters, England, 39 ½ x 66", 29" h...........4,600.00
(Ilustration: Tables 112)

Victorian center table, Aesthetic Movement substyle, giltwood & alabaster, the galleried rectangular top above a swag-carved & paneled apron over a galleried lower shelf flanked by turned & carved columns, on square feet on casters, last quarter 19th century, 29 ¼" w., 18 ½" d., 31 ½" h. 1,495.00
(Ilustration: Tables 113)

Victorian center table, Renaissance Revival substyle, inlaid elm, the oval top w/outset rounded corners above an inlaid apron, raised on blind fret-carved circular tapering legs headed by pierced

Tables 110: Country Tavern Table

Tables 112: Victorian Inlaid Mahogany Breakfast Table

Tables 111: Turn of the Century Library Table

Tables 113: Victorian Aesthetic Table

foliate-carved brackets, on casters, England, mid-19th century, 42 x 60", 29" h. 3,450.00
(llustration: Tables 114)

Victorian center table, Renaissance Revival substyle, giltwood & onyx, oblong cartouche-form top inset w/onyx above a scroll-decorated wide apron w/florette blocks heading the turned urn-form legs w/baluster-turned feet on casters, a pierced medial stretcher joining the legs, losses, last quarter 19th century, 35 x 55", 30 ½" h. 2,415.00
(llustration: Tables 115)

Victorian console table, Rococo style, the faux grey marble serpentine top above a rocaille-carved & pierced apron surmounting a mirrored back, on four foliate-carved cabriole legs ending in animal paw feet & joined by a rocaille-carved stretcher, top later, Europe, mid-19th century, 46" w., 17 ¾" d., 35 ½" h. 2,200.00
(llustration: Tables 116)

Victorian dressing table, Aesthetic Movement substyle, faux bamboo bird's-

Tables 114: English Victorian Table

Tables 115: Renaissance Revival center table

**Tables 117:
Victorian Aesthetic Dressing table**

Tables 116: Victorian Rococo console table

eye maple, the super-structure w/an oval mirror within a bamboo frame swiveling between flared bamboo-form uprights above the rectangular top w/outset ends over a long center drawer flanked by outset drawers, raised on branch-form bamboo-turned trestle supports, ca. 1890, 23 ½ x 49 ½".......3,450.00 *(llustration: Tables 117)*

Victorian library table, Renaissance style, inlaid rosewood, the cross-banded & line-inlaid rectangular top w/canted corners & foliate-carved edge over fluted & shell-carved apron, on baluster-carved center columns, the corners w/winged griffin figures, joined by stretchers ending in medallion- and foliate-carved down-curved feet on casters, England or America, late 19th century, 56" w., 36" d., 29 ¾" h. ....4,840.00 *(llustration: Tables 118)*

Victorian occasional table, Aesthetic Movement substyle, walnut, the rectangular top w/molded edge & inset onyx panel over an incised apron & incised medial shelf flanked by carved & pierced circular sides ending in splayed tapered square legs joined by a ring-and baluster-turned H-stretcher, last quarter 19th century, 24" w., 16" d., 29 ¼" h. ....460.00 *(llustration: Tables 119)*

Tables 119: Victorian Aesthetic Occasional Table

Tables 118: Renaissance Style Library Table

Victorian occasional table, Renaissance Revival substyle, walnut, maple & marquetry, the circular top centering a marquetry musical trophy medallion surrounded by segmented line-inlaid bird's-eye maple panels & an ebonized edge over a molded apron w/scrolled pendants, on a baluster-turned standard w/incurved brackets w/tassel pendants, on a cross-frame stretcher base w/turned feet on casters, attributed to Berkey & Gay, ca. 1870, 26 ¾" d., 30 ¼" h. 3,025.00
(Ilustration: Tables 120)

Victorian side table, Aesthetic Movement substyle, cherry, the octagonal top w/molded edge & scalloped apron on bracketed turned supports enclosing a gallery of spindles above a carved, pierced panel, on carved bracket legs joined by a turned stretcher, late 19th century, 24" w., 16" d., 34" h. 935.00
(Ilustration: Tables 121)

Victorian side table, mahogany, the rectangular top w/molded edge flanked by two leaves above a plain apron w/two bamboo-turned gate legs & four bamboo-turned legs ending in out-turned feet, joined by a similarly turned H-stretcher, England, mid-19th century, 29" w., 25 ¼" d., 27 ½" h. 770.00
(Ilustration: Tables 122)

Tables 120: Renaissance Revival Occasional Table

Tables 121: Victorian Aesthetic Table

Tables 122: Victorian Bamboo-turned Table

Victorian side table, Eastlake substyle, maple, a rectangular top w/molded edge above a narrow sawtooth-cut apron, on four incurved flat legs joined by a wide cross stretcher w/a central post w/knob finials, ca. 1890, 19 x 29", 28 ¾" h..........240.00
(Ilustration: Tables 123)

Victorian side table, Renaissance Revival substyle, walnut, a rectangular white marble top w/notched corners above a conforming apron w/raised burl panels & center roundels, raised on flat & flaring upswept supports tapering to a four-part base w/four flat scroll-cut legs joined by turned stretchers & a center post, on white porcelain casters, ca. 1870-80, 20 x 29 ½", 29" h. 995.00
(Ilustration: Tables 124)

Victorian side table, Rococo substyle, walnut, a white marble 'turtle' top above a conforming serpentine apron w/turned corner drops, raised on four baluster- and ring-turned supports above four molded downswept legs centered w/a turned small compote, on white porcelain casters, ca. 1850-60, 24 ¾ x 33 ½", 30" h. 1,195.00
(Ilustration: Tables 125)

Victorian tilt-top table, papier-maché, the floral decorated shaped oval top tilting above a baluster-shaped standard

Tables 123: Victorian Eastlake Side Table

Tables 126: Victorian Papier-Maché Table

Tables 124: Renaissance Revival Marble Top Table

Tables 125: Victorian Turtle-Top Table

on a shaped circular base w/scrolled feet, England, ca. 1860 .... 412.00
(Ilustration: Tables 126)

Victorian work table, Rococo substyle, mother-of-pearl inlaid papier-maché, the domed round top panel surmounting an octagonal inlaid top w/molded edge over a conforming case inlaid w/Gothic-style scenes of ruins, the lift-top opening to a damask interior, on a fluted & gadrooned vase-form standard, on scalloped tripod base w/gilt foliate-scrolled motifs, on scrolled feet on casters, England, ca. 1840, 20 ½" w., 31 ½" h. 1,650.00
(Ilustration: Tables 127)

Wallace Nutting-signed Hepplewhite-Style dining table, inlaid mahogany, three-part, the center section w/a rectangular top flanked by wide drop-leaves above a line-inlaid apron, two D-form end sections w/line-inlaid aprons, all on square tapering legs, Model No. 670, early 20th c. 4,125.00
(Ilustration: Tables 128)

Wicker occasional tables, the round oak top above large scrolls in the apron & S-curved lattice-woven legs joined by S-scrolls to a central drop, leg scrolls flanking a medial wood shelf below, late 19th century, 21" d., 27 ¾" h., pr. 2,415.00
(Ilustration: Tables 129, one of two)

Tables 127: Victorian Papier-Maché Work Table

Tables 129: Round Wicker Table

Tables 128: Wallace Nutting Dining Table

Wicker occasional table, wicker & oak, the rectangular oak top w/woven wicker apron supported on woven lyre-shaped sides above a bottom oak shelf w/a partial bobbin gallery, on splayed legs, early 20th century, 28 ½" w., 23" d., 29 ½" h. 1,380.00
(llustration: Tables 130)

William & Mary drop leaf "tuck-away" table, maple, the rectangular top w/rounded ends & two demi-lune drop leaves on block- and baluster-turned legs on arched feet, New England, 18th century, old refinish, overall 30" w., 28 ½" d., 26 ¾" h. 6,900.00
(llustration: Tables 131)

William & Mary "gate-leg" dining table, curly maple, the oblong top w/two D-shaped leaves above an apron w/single drawer on ring- and baluster-turned legs joined by turned stretchers, on ball feet, New England, ca. 1750, one foot replaced, overall 51 ½" w., 43" d., 28 ½" h. 13,800.00
(llustration: Tables 132)

Tables 130: Wicker Rectangular Table

Tables 132:
William & Mary "Gate-Leg" Table

Tables 131:
William & Mary Tuck-away Table

**William & Mary "gate-leg"
table,** maple, the hinged
oval top above a molded
apron fitted w/drawer over
baluster- and ring-turned
legs joined by similarly
turned stretchers, on
carved Spanish feet,
Massachusetts, ca. 1720,
ends of leaves pieced,
drawer replaced, patch in
rear apron, some feet
pieced, 61¼" w., 54¼" d.,
29" h. 17,250.00
(Illustration: Tables 133)

**William & Mary tavern
table**, maple & pine, the
rectangular top widely
overhanging a single frieze
drawer on baluster-turned
legs joined by stretchers

Tables 134: William & Mary Tavern Table

Tables 133: William & Mary "Gate-Leg" Table

on vestigial remainders of
ball feet, New England,
18th century, old refinish,
42 ¼" w., 23 ¼" d.,
26 ½" h. 1,610.00
(Ilustration: Tables 134)

**William & Mary tavern
table,** walnut, a
rectangular top w/angled
corners above a scalloped
apron, raised on ring- and
baluster-turned canted
legs joined by knob- and
baluster-turned stretchers,
on knob feet, possibly
Boston, early 18th century,
old finish, some imper-
fections, 19 x 31 ½",
24 ¼" h..........................8,050.00
(Ilustration: Tables 135)

**William & Mary Trestle-
base drop-leaf table,**
maple & pine, a narrow
rectangular top w/rounded
ends flanked by D-form
drop leaves above a trestle
base w/heavy baluster-
and ring-turned supports &
matching turned swing-out
supports, New England,
early 18th c., old refinish,
restoration, 31 ¾" x 38",
25½" h. 6,325.00
(Ilustration: Tables 136)

Tables 135: William & Mary Tavern Table

Tables 136: William & Mary Trestle-base Table

WARDROBES & ARMOIRES

Armoire, Art Deco, rosewood & parchment, a rectangular top above a pair of tall parchment doors opening to an arrangement of a center shelf & five drawers, in the manner of Jean Pascaud, France, ca. 1940, 20 x 59", 5' 1 ½" h. 9,200.00
(Illustration: Wardrobes 1)

Armoire, Classical, mahogany, a rectangular top w/a reeded edge on the deeply coved cornice above a wide inset center arch flanked by small Gothic arches above a pair of tall double-paneled doors w/scroll-carved trim,

two pairs of classically carved & turned columns at the sides resting atop tall Gothic arch blocks above the plinth base raised on double-dolphin front feet & bulbous back feet, Philadelphia, early 19th century, 25 x 72", 8' h..............12,100.00
(Illustration: Wardrobes 2)

Armoire, American French Provincial, inlaid mahogany, a rectangular top w/a round-cornered coved cornice above an almond-shaped inlaid panel of chicory flowers above a pair of tall cupboard doors each inlaid w/a pair of large rectangular panels

centered by oval inlays of classical urns & flanking a narrow central inlay panel of a fanned shell, scroll-cut apron w/short cabriole front legs, probably New Orleans, late 18th - early 19th century, 20 x 45", 6' 9" h. 10,450.00
(Illustration: Wardrobes 3)

Armoire, French Provincial, carved fruitwood, the molded cornice over scalloped paneled doors centered by florets over floral urn-carved scalloped skirt, paneled sides, on short cabriole legs, France, 19th century,

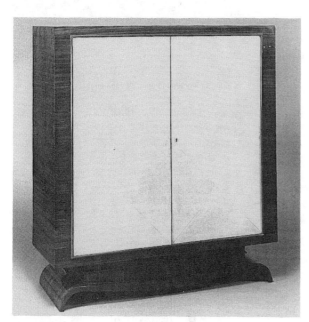

Wardrobes 1: Art Deco Armoire

**Wardrobes 2:
Large Classical Armoire**

**Wardrobes 4:
Fruitwood
French Provincial
Armoire**

**Wardrobes 3:
New Orleans
Armoire**

54" w., 24" d., 8' 1" h. ..3,520.00
(Illustration: Wardrobes 4)

Kas (American version of
the Netherlands *Kast* or
wardrobe), maple & poplar,
demountable, the rectan-
gular top w/a molded
cornice above a frieze
band over a molding
above a pair of tall raised-
panel doors w/pintel
hinges above a mid-
molding & dovetailed base
on short bracket feet,
raised panel sides, old
refinish, attributed to
New Bremen, Ohio,
19th century, one end of
molding replaced, 71" w.,
24 ¼" d., 5' 6" h. 3,080.00
(Illustration: Wardrobes 5)

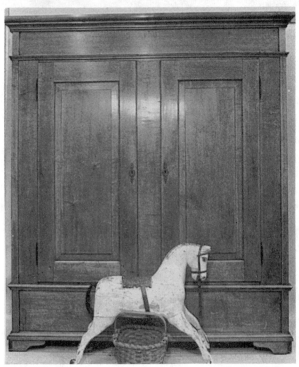

**Wardrobes 5:
Ohio Maple Kas**

Wardrobes 6: Chippendale Cherry Kas

Wardrobes 7: Chippendale Walnut Schrank

Kas, Chippendale, cherry, the rectangular top w/an architectural pediment molded above a case w/a pair of double-fielded raised panel doors flanked by fluted pilasters & opening to an interior fitted w/shelves flanked by fluted pilasters all above a mid-molding & a pair of short deep drawers, on large ball feet, restoration to pediment, New Jersey, 1760-90, 20 x 60", 6' 3" h. 4,025.00
(Illustration: Wardrobes 6)

Schrank (massive Germanic wardrobe), Chippendale, walnut, the rectangular molded cornice above a pair of four-panel cupboard doors centered & flanked by double ogee moldings opening to three shelves, an applied mid-molding above three short thumb-molded drawers & carved base molding, the sides double-paneled, Lancaster County, Pennsylvania, ca. 1770, 83" w., 28 ½" d., 6' 9" h. 19,550.00
(Illustration: Wardrobes 7)

Schrank, Chippendale, cherry, the overhanging cornice w/dentil molding above a frieze w/painted inscription, "17--," over a multi-paneled case & cupboard doors opening to a compartment, a mid-molding above three thumb-molded short drawers & molded base on turned flattened-ball feet, Pennsylvania, 18th century, 60" w., 22 ¾" d., 6' 8 ¼" h. 6,325.00

Wardrobe, Mission-style (Arts & Crafts movement), oak, a rectangular top w/molded edge above a pair of tall cupboard doors w/multiple panels & copper V-pulls opening to a full-length mirror, a pull-out

Wardrobes 8: Turn of the Century Wardrobe

Wardrobes 9: Renaissance Revival Wardrobe

Wardrobes 10: Victorian Rococo Wardrobe

clothes rack & sliding sock shelf over two small & four long graduated drawers, on a molded base w/tapering legs, original medium brown finish, branded mark & paster of Gustav Stickley, early 20th century, 21 ½ x 40 ½", 5' 4" h.....4,950.00

Wardrobe, turn of the century, oak, the arched crest w/a heavy rounded C-scroll rail curving down into the top of the case & ending w/leafy scrolls flanking the long door w/a long mirror w/a gently curved top trimmed w/a carved arch & corner scrolls, long double-panels down the sides, the slightly outset base w/a serpentine top over a long

serpentine drawer w/two bail pulls on flat paw-form front feet on casters, ca. 1890-1910, 18 x 44 ½", 7' 4" h. 2,495.00
(Illustration: Wardrobes 8)

Wardrobe, Victorian, Renaissance Revival substyle, carved walnut, the molded arched pediment w/central urn & two shaped corner finials above a leaf- and scroll-carved frieze over two arched-panel doors, the bottom section w/two carved short drawers w/oval banding on a plain base w/rounded corners & square disk feet, ca. 1860................1,760.00
(Illustration: Wardrobes 9)

Wardrobe, Victorian Rococo substyle, carved mahogany, the shaped & arched crest w/rounded corners & crown-form finials above a conforming egg-and-dart-carved frieze band above a carved cartouche framed by leafy scrolls over a large cupboard door w/edge molded & centered by a large rectangular mirror w/delicate scroll borders, the lower section w/a single long drawer w/scroll trim on a deep molded base w/an egg-and-dart band & scroll-cut apron, on squatty disc front feet long & block back, attributed to Prudent Mallard, New Orleans, Louisiana, ca. 1850 ....11,000.00
(Illustration: Wardrobes 10)

WHATNOTS & ETAGERES

Etagere, Federal, mahogany, ring- and baluster-turned uprights w/acorn finials & X-form dividers centering three graduated shelves, the medial shelf below fitted with a drawer, on ring- and baluster-turned legs, on casters, New England, ca. 1820, one finial replaced, 24 ¾" w., 13 ½" d., 4' 7 ¼" h. 4,313.00
(Illustration: Whatnots 1)

Etagere, Federal, mahogany, two rectangular open shelves w/slender columnar supports & ball finials at the top, above a paneled cupboard door, on short baluster-turned legs on casters, New York, ca. 1805, refinished, minor imperfections, 17 ¼ x 20", 5' 1" h. 5,175.00
(Illustration: Whatnots 2)

Etagere, Victorian, Rococo substyle, mahogany, the pierced carved gallery above two rectangular open shelves w/scroll-carved supports, above a lower section w/single drawer over two open shelves supported by reeded vase-form posts, mid-19th century, 37" w., 15 ½" d., 5' 7" h. 990.00
(Illustration: Whatnots 3)

Whatnots 1: Federal Etagere

Whatnots 3: Victorian Mahogany Etagere

Whatnots 2: Federal Etagere with Cupboard

Whatnot, country-style, painted wood, five graduated shelves on baluster-turned spindles w/acorn finials on vase-form turned legs on ball feet, old black paint, minor damage, 19th century, 26" w., 11½" d., 46" h. 192.00
(Illustration: Whatnots 4)

Whatnot, Victorian Rococo substyle, walnut, corner-style w/five graduated open shelves w/molded curved front edges, scroll-cut back braces, each shelf raised on ring- and baluster-turned supports w/turned finials, turned legs w/knob feet, ca. 1860, 23" w., 5' h.................................440.00
(Illustration: Whatnots 5)

Whatnots 4:
Country Painted Whatnot

Whatnots 5:
Victorian Corner Whatnot

SELECT BIBLIOGRAPHY

Bivins, John, Jr. *The Furniture of Coastal North Carolina, 1700-1820.* Winston-Salem, N.C.: Museum of Early Southern Decorative Arts, 1988.

Bjerkoe, Ethel Hall. *The Cabinetmakers of America.* New York: Doubleday and Co., 1957.

Bowman, John S. *American Furniture.* New York: Exeter Books, 1985.

Butler, Joseph T. *Field Guide to American Antique Furniture.* New York: Facts on File Publications, 1985.

Carpenter, Ralph E., Jr. *The Arts and Crafts of Newport, Rhode Island, 1640-1820.* Newport: Preservation Society of Newport County, 1954.

Cathers, David M. *Furniture of the American Arts & Crafts Movement.* New York: New American Library, 1981.

Cescinsky, Herbert. *English Furniture from Gothic to Sheraton.* New York: Dover, 1968, rpt.

Comstock, Helen. *American Furniture, Seventeenth, Eighteenth, and Nineteenth Century Styles.* New York: The Viking Press, 1962.

Cooper, Wendy A. *Classical Taste in America, 1800-1840.* New York: Abbeville Press, 1993.

Downs, Joseph. *American Furniture, Queen Anne and Chippendale Periods in the Henry Francis du Pont Winterthur Museum.* New York: Macmillan Co., 1952.

Dubrow, Eileen and Richard. *American Furniture of the 19th Century, 1840-1880.* Exton, PA.: Schiffer Publishing, Ltd., 1983.

Dubrow, Eileen and Richard. *Furniture Made in America, 1875-1905.* Exton, PA.: Schiffer Publishing, Ltd., 1982.

Duncan, Alastair. *Art Nouveau Furniture.* New York: Clarkson N. Potter, Inc., 1982.

Fairbanks, Jonathan L. and Elizabeth Bidwell Bates. *American Furniture, 1620 to the Present.* New York: Richard Marek Publishers, 1981.

Fales, Dean A., Jr. *American Painted Furniture, 1660-1880.* New York: Crown Publishers, 1986.

Fitzgerald, Oscar. *Three Centuries of American Furniture.* Englewood Cliffs, N.J.: Prentice-Hall, 1982.

Forman, Benno M. *American Seating Furniture, 1630-1730.* New York: W.W. Norton & Co., 1988.

Fredgant, Don. *American Manufactured Furniture.* Atglen, PA: Schiffer Publishing, Ltd., 1988.

Gilborn, Craig. *Adirondack Furniture and the Rustic Tradition.* New York: Harry N. Abrams, 1987.

Gusler, Wallace B. *Furniture of Williamsburg and Eastern Virginia, 1710-1790.* Richmond, VA: Virginia Museum, 1979

Heckscher, Morrison H. *American Furniture in the Metropolitan Museum of Art, II, Late Colonial Period: The Queen Anne and Chippendale Styles.* New York: The Metropolitan Museum of Art and Random House, 1986.

Jobe, Brock, and Myrna Kaye. *New England Furniture: The Colonial Era.* Boston: Houghton Mifflin Co., 1984.

Kane, Patricia E. *300 Years of American Seating Furniture.* Boston: New York Graphic Society, 1976.

Kaplan, Wendy. *The Art That Is Life.* Boston: Little, Brown & Company, 1987.

Kaye, Myrna. *Fake, Fraud or Genuine? Identifying Authentic American Antique Furniture.* Boston: Little, Brown & Company, 1987.

Kettell, Russell Hawes. *The Pine Furniture of Early New England.* New York: Dover, 1949, rpt.

Kirk, John T. *American Furniture and The British Tradition to 1830.* New York: Alfred A. Knopf, 1982.

Kirk, John T. *The Impecunious Collector's Guide to American Antiques.* New York: Alfred A. Knopf, 1982.

Knell, David. *English Country Furniture: The National & Regional Vernacular, 1500-1900.* London: Barrie & Jenkins, 1992.

Kovel, Ralph and Terry Kovel. *American Country Furniture, 1780-1875.* New York: Crown Publishers, 1965.

Lockwood, Luke Vincent. *Colonial Furniture in America,* 2 vols. New York: Castle Books, 1951, rpt.

Madigan, Mary Jean. *Nineteenth Century Furniture.* New York: Art & Antiques, 1982.

Marsh, Moreton. *The Easy Expert in American Antiques.* Philadelphia: J.B. Lippincott, 1978.

McNerney, Kathryn. *Pine Furniture - Our American Heritage.* Paducah, KY: Collector Books, 1989.

Miller, Edgar G., Jr. *American Antique Furniture, A Book for Amateurs,* 2 vols. New York: Dover, 1966, rpt.

Montgomery, Charles F. *American Furniture, The Federal Period in the Henry Francis du Pont Winterthur Museum.* New York: The Viking Press, 1966.

Morningstar, Connie. *American Furniture Classics.* Des Moines, IA: Wallace-Homestead Book Co., 1976.

Morningstar, Connie. *Early Utah Furniture.* Logan, UT: Utah State University Press, 1976.

Neat Pieces: The Plain-Style Furniture of 19th Century Georgia. Atlanta: Atlanta Historical Society, 1983.

Nutting, Wallace. *Furniture Treasury.* vols. I, II. New York: Macmillan, 1928.

Nutting, Wallace. *Furniture Treasury.* vol. III. New York: Macmillan, 1933.

Sack, Albert. *The New Fine Points of Furniture.* New York: Crown Publishing, 1993.

Santore, Charles. *The Windsor Style in America.* Philadelphia: Running Press, 1981.

Santore, Charles. *The Windsor Style in America,* Vol. II. Philadelphia: Running Press, 1987.

Schiffer, Herbert F. *The Mirror Book, English, American & European.* Exton, PA: Schiffer Publishing, 1983.

Stillinger, Elizabeth. *The Antiquers.* New York: Alfred A. Knopf, 1980.

Symonds, R.W. and B.B. Whineray. *Victorian Furniture.* London: Studio Editions, 1987.

Ward, Gerald R. *American Case Furniture in the Mabel Brady Garvan and Other Collections at Yale University.* New Haven, CT: Yale University Art Gallery, 1988.

Warner, Velma Susanne. *Golden Oak Furniture.* Atglen, PA: Schiffer Publishing, Ltd., 1992.

APPENDIX I
AUCTION SERVICES

The following is a select listing of larger regional auction houses which often feature antique furniture in their sales. There are, of course, many fine local auction services which also feature furniture from time to time.

East Coast:

Christies's
502 Park Ave.
New York, NY 10022
Phone: (212) 546-1000

Douglas Auctioneers
Route 5
South Deerfield, MA 01373
Phone: (413) 665-3530

William Doyle Galleries
175 E. 87th St.
New York, NY 10128
Phone: (212) 427-2730

Willis Henry Auctions
22 Main St.
Marshfield, MA 02059
Phone: (617) 834-7774

Dave Rago
9 So. Main St.
Lambertville, NJ 08530
Phone: (609) 397-9374

Skinner Inc.
357 Main St.
Bolton, MA 01740
Phone: (508) 779-6241

Sotheby's
1334 York Ave.
New York, NY 10021
Phone: (212) 606-7000

Withington, Inc.
R.D. 2, Box 440
Hillsboro, NH 03244
Phone: (603) 464-3232

Midwest:

DuMochelles Galleries
409 East Jefferson Ave.
Detroit, MI 48226
Phone: (313) 963-6255

Dunning's Auction Service
755 Church Rd.
Elgin, IL 60123-9302
Phone: (708) 741-3483

Garth's Auctions
P.O. Box 369
Delaware, OH 43015
Phone: (614) 362-4771

Hanzel Galleries
1120 So. Michigan Ave.
Chicago, IL 60605
Phone: (312) 922-6234

Gene Harris Antique Auction Center
P.O. Box 476
Marshalltown, IA 50158
Phone: (515) 752-0600

Leslie Hindman Auctioneers
215 West Ohio St.
Chicago, IL 60610
Phone: (312) 670-0010

Don Treadway Gallery
P.O. Box 8924
Cincinnati, OH 45208
Phone: (513) 321-6742

Wolf's Auctioneers & Appraisers
1239 West 6th JSt.
Cleveland, OH 44113
Phone: (216) 575-9653

Far West:

Butterfield & Butterfield
7601 Sunset Blvd.
Los Angeles, CA 90046
Phone: (213) 850-7500

Pettrigrew Auction Company
1645 So. Tejon St.
Colorado Springs, CO 80906
Phone: (719) 633-7963

South:

Morton M. Goldberg Auction Galleries
547 Baronne St.
New Orleans, LA 70113
Phone: (504) 592-2300

Neal Auction Company
4038 Magazine St.
New Orleans, LA 70115
Phone: (504) 899-5329

New Orleans Auction Galleries
801 Magazine St.
New Orleans, LA 70130
Phone: (504) 566-1849

AMERICAN

Style: Pilgrim Century
Dating: 1620-1700
Major Wood(s): Oak
General Characteristics:

Case pieces:	rectilinear low-relief carved panels
	blocky & bulbous turnings
	splint-spindle trim
Seating pieces:	shallow carved panels
	spindle turnings

Style: William & Mary
Dating: 1685-1720
Major Wood(s): Maple & walnut
General Characteristics:

Case pieces:	paint decoration
	chests on ball feet
	chests on frame, chests with two-part construction
	trumpet-turned legs
	slant-front desks
Seating pieces:	molded, carved crestrails
	banister backs
	cane, rush (leather) seats
	baluster, ball & block turnings
	ball & Spanish feet

Style: Queen Anne
Dating: 1720-50
Major Wood(s): Walnut
General Characteristics:

Case pieces:	mathematical/proportions of elements
	use of the cyma or S-curve
	broken-arch pediments
	arched panels, shell carving, star inlay
	blocked fronts
	cabriole legs pad feet
Seating pieces:	molded yoke-shaped crestrails
	solid vase-shaped splats
	rush or upholstered seats
	cabriole legs
	baluster, ring, ball & block-turned stretchers pad and slipper feet

Style: Chippendale
Dating: 1750-85
Major Wood(s): Mahogany & walnut
General Characteristics:

Case pieces:	relief-carved broken-arch pediments
	foliate, scroll, shell, fretwork carving
	straight, bow, serpentine fronts
	carved cabriole legs
	claw & ball, bracket or ogee feet
Seating pieces:	carved, shaped crestrails with out-turned ears
	pierced, shaped splats
	ladder (ribbon) backs
	upholstered seats
	scrolled arms
	carved cabriole legs or straight (Marlboro) legs
	claw & ball feet

Style: Federal (Hepplewhite)
Dating: 1785-1800
Major Wood(s): Mahogany & light inlays
General Characteristics:

Case pieces:	more delicate rectilineal forms
	inlay with eagle and classical motifs
	bow, serpentine or tambour fronts
	reeded quarter columns at sides
	flared bracket feet
Seating pieces:	shield backs
	upholstered seats
	tapered square legs

Style: Federal (Sheraton)
Dating: 1800-20
Major Wood(s): Mahogany & mahogany veneer & maple
General Characteristics:

Case pieces:	architectural pediments
	acanthus carving
	outset (cookie or ovolu) corners & reeded columns
	paneled sides
	tapered, turned, reeded or spiral turned legs
	bow or tambour fronts
	mirrors on dressing tables
Seating pieces:	rectangular or square backs
	slender carved bannisters
	tapered, turned or reeded legs

Style: Classical (American Empire)
Dating: 1815-50
Major Wood(s): Mahogany & mahogany veneer & rosewood
General Characteristics:

Case pieces:	increasingly heavy proportions
	pillar & scroll construction
	lyre, eagle, Greco-Roman & Egyptian motifs
	marble tops
	projecting top drawer
	large ball feet, tapered fluted feet or hairy paw feet
	brass, ormolu decoration
Seating pieces:	high-relief carving
	curved backs
	out-scrolled arms
	ring turnings
	sabre legs, curule (scrolled-S) legs
	brass-capped feet, casters

Style: Victorian -- Early Victorian
Dating: 1840-50
Major Wood(s): Mahogany veneer, black walnut & rosewood
General Characteristics:

Case pieces:	Pieces tend to carry over the Classical style with the beginnings of the Rococo substyle, especially in seating pieces.

Style: Victorian -- Gothic Revival
Dating: 1840-90
Major Wood(s): Black walnut, mahogany & rosewood
General Characteristics:

Case pieces:	architectural motifs
	triangular arched pediments
	arched panels
	marble tops
	paneled or molded drawer fronts
	cluster columns
	bracket feet, block feet or plinth bases
Seating pieces:	tall backs
	pierced arabesque backs with trefoils or quatrefoils
	spool turning
	drop pendants

Style: Victorian -- Rococo (Louis XV)
Dating: 1845-70
Major Wood(s): Black walnut, mahogany & rosewood
General Characteristics:

Case pieces:	arched carved pediments
	high-relief carving, S- & C-scrolls, floral, fruit motifs, busts & cartouches
	mirror panels
	carved slender cabriole legs
	scroll feet
	bedroom suites (bed, dresser, commode)
Seating pieces:	high-relief carved crestrails
	balloon-shaped backs
	urn-shaped splats
	upholstery (tufting)
	demi-cabriole legs
	laminated, pierced and carved construction (Belter)
	parlor suites (sets of chairs, love seats, sofas)

Style: Victorian -- Renaissance Revival
Dating: 1860-85
Major Wood(s): Black walnut, burl veneer, painted & grained pine
General Characteristics:

Case pieces:	rectilinear arched pediments
	arched panels, burl veneer
	applied moldings
	bracket feet, block feet, plinth bases
	medium and high-relief carving, floral & fruit, cartouches, masks & animal heads
	cyma-curve brackets
	Wooton patent desks
Seating pieces:	oval or rectangular backs with floral or figural cresting
	upholstery outlined w/brass tacks
	padded armrests
	tapered turned front legs, flared square rear legs

Style: Victorian -- Louis XVI
Dating: 1865-75
Major Wood(s): Black walnut & ebonized maple
General Characteristics:

Case pieces:	gilt decoration, marquetry, inlay
	egg & dart carving
	tapered turned legs, fluted

Seating pieces: molded, slightly arched crestrails
keystone-shaped backs
circular seats
fluted tapered legs

Style: Victorian -- Eastlake
Dating: 1870-95
Major Wood(s): Black walnut, burl veneer, cherry & oak
General Characteristics:

Case pieces: flat cornices
stile and rail construction
burl veneer panels
low-relief geometric and floral machine-
   carving
incised horizontal lines

Seating pieces: rectilinear
spindles
tapered, turned legs, trumpet-shaped legs

Style: Victorian -- Jacobean & Turkish Revival
Dating: 1870-90
Major Wood(s): Black walnut & maple
General Characteristics:

Case pieces: A revival of some heavy 17th century
forms, most commonly in dining room
pieces.

Seating pieces: Turkish Revival style features:
   oversized, low forms
   overstuffed upholstery
   padded arms
   short baluster, vase-turned legs
   ottomans, circular sofas
Jacobean Revival style features:
   heavy bold carving
   spool and spiral turnings

Style: Victorian -- Aesthetic Movement
Dating: 1880-1900
Major Wood(s): Painted hardwoods, black walnut,
        ebonized finishes
General Characteristics:

Case pieces: rectilinear forms
bamboo turnings, spaced ball turnings
incised stylized geometric & floral
   designs, sometimes highlighted with
   gilt

Seating pieces: bamboo turnings
rectangular backs
patented folding chairs

Style: Art Nouveau
Dating: 1895-1918
Major Wood(s): Ebonized hardwoods, fruitwoods
General Characteristics:

 Case pieces: curvilinear shapes
         floral marquetry
         carved whiplash curves
 Seating pieces: elongated forms
         relief-carved floral decoration
         spindle backs, pierced floral backs
         cabriole legs

Style: Turn-of-the-Century
Dating: 1895-1910
Major Wood(s): Golden (quarter-sawn) oak, mahogany
         hardwood stained to resemble
         mahogany
General Characteristics:

 Case pieces: rectilinear and bulky forms
         applied scroll carvings
         Empire Revival designs with scroll-cut
          pilasters and paw feet
 Seating pieces: square feet, or oversized claw & ball feet
         Empire Revival & Colonial Revival forms
          with a mixture of design details

Style: Mission (Arts & Crafts movement)
Dating: 1900-15
Major Wood(s): Oak
General Characteristics:

 Case pieces: rectilinear
         through-tenon construction
         copper decoration, hand-hammered
          hardware
         square legs
 Seating pieces: rectangular splats
         medial & side stretchers
         exposed pegs
         corbel supports

Style: Art Deco
Dating: 1925-40
Major Wood(s): Bleached woods, exotic woods, steel &
         chrome
General Characteristics:

 Case pieces: heavy geometric forms
 Seating pieces: streamlined, attenuated geometric forms
          overstuffed upholstery

ENGLISH

Style: Jacobean
Dating: Mid-17th century
Major Wood(s): Oak, walnut
General Characteristics:
  Case pieces: low-relief carving, geometrics & florals
                     panel, rail & stile construction
                     applied split balusters
  Seating pieces: rectangular backs
                     carved & pierced crests
                     spiral turnings
                     ball feet

Style: William & Mary
Dating: 1689-1702
Major Wood(s): Walnut, burl walnut veneer
General Characteristics:
  Case pieces: marquetry, veneering
                     shaped aprons
                     6-8 trumpet-form legs, curved flat
                        stretchers
  Seating pieces: carved, pierced crests
                     tall caned backs & seats
                     trumpet-form legs, Spanish feet

Style: Queen Anne
Dating: 1702-14
Major Wood(s): Walnut, mahogany, veneers
General Characteristics:
  Case pieces: cyma curves
                     broken arch pediments & finials
                     bracket feet
  Seating pieces: carved crestrails
                     high, rounded backs
                     solid vase-shaped splats
                     cabriole legs
                     pad feet

Style: George I
Dating: 1714-27
Major Wood(s): Walnut, mahogany, veneer & yewwood
General Characteristics:
  Case pieces: broken arch pediments
                     gilt decoration, japanning
                     bracket feet
  Seating pieces: curvilinear forms
                     yoke-shaped crests

shaped solid splats
shell carving
upholstered seats
carved cabriole legs
claw & ball feet, pad feet

Style: George II
Dating: 1727-60
Major Wood(s): Mahogany
General Characteristics:

Case pieces:	broken arch pediments
	relief-carved foliate, scroll & shell carving
	carved cabriole legs
	claw & ball feet, bracket feet, ogee bracket feet
Seating pieces:	carved, shaped crestrails, out-turned ears
	pierced shaped splats
	ladder (ribbon) backs
	upholstered seats
	scrolled arms
	carved cabriole legs or straight (Marlboro) legs
	claw & ball feet

Style: George III
Dating: 1760-1820
Major Wood(s): Mahogany, veneer, satinwood
General Characteristics:

Case pieces:	rectilineal forms
	parcel gilt decoration
	inlaid ovals, circles, banding or marquetry
	carved columns, urns
	tambour fronts or bow fronts
	plinth bases
Seating pieces:	shield backs
	upholstered seats
	tapered square legs, square legs

Style: Regency
Dating: 1811-20
Major Wood(s): Mahogany, mahogany veneer, satinwood & rosewood
General Characteristics:

Case pieces:	Greco-Roman & Egyptian motifs
	inlay, ormolu mounts
	marble tops
	round columns, pilasters
	mirrored backs
	scroll feet

240

Seating pieces: straight backs, latticework
                   caned seats
                   sabre legs, tapered turned legs, flared
                       turned legs
                   parcel gilt, ebonizing

Style: George IV
Dating: 1820-30
Major Wood(s): Mahogany, mahogany veneer & rosewood
General Characteristics:
                   Continuation of Regency designs

Style: William IV
Dating: 1830-37
Major Wood(s): Mahogany, mahogany veneer
General Characteristics:
  Case pieces: rectilinaer
                   brass mounts, grillwork
                   carved moldings
                   plinth bases
  Seating pieces: rectangular backs
                   carved straight crestrails
                   acanthus, animal carving
                   carved cabriole legs
                   paw feet

Style: Victorian
Dating: 1837-1901
Major Wood(s): Black walnut, mahogany, veneers &
                   rosewood
General Characteristics:
  Case pieces: applied floral carving
                   surmounting mirrors, drawers, candle
                       shelves
                   marble tops
  Seating pieces: high-relief carved crestrails
                   floral & fruit carving
                   balloon backs, oval backs
                   upholstered seats, backs
                   spool, spiral turnings
                   cabriole legs, fluted tapered legs
                   scrolled feet

Style: Edwardian
Dating: 1901-10
Major Wood(s): Mahogany, mahogany veneer & satinwood
General Characteristics:
                   Neo-Classical motifs & revivals of earlier
                       18th century & early 19th century styles